Child Sense

*

*

*

Child Sense

From Birth to Age 5,
How to Use the 5 Senses to Make
Sleeping, Eating, Dressing, and
Other Everyday Activities Easier
While Strengthening Your Bond
with Your Child

PRISCILLA J. DUNSTAN

Foreword by Linda Acredolo, Ph.D., and Susan Goodwyn, Ph.D.

Bantam Books   New York

Published in the United States by Bantam Books,
an imprint of The Random House Publishing Group,
a division of Random House, Inc., New York.

BANTAM BOOKS and the rooster colophon are registered
trademarks of Random House, Inc.

LIBRARY OF CONGRESS CATALOGING-IN-PUBLICATION DATA

Dunstan, Priscilla.
Child sense : from birth to age 5, how to use the 5 senses to make
sleeping, eating, dressing, and other everyday activites easier while
strengthening your bond with your child / Priscilla J. Dunstan ;
foreword by Linda Acredolo and Susan Goodwyn.
p.   cm.
ISBN 978-0-553-80667-0
eBook ISBN 978-0-553-90709-4
1. Sensory stimulation.   2. Senses and sensations in infants.
3. Senses and sensations in children.   4. Parenting.   I. Title
BF723.S35 D86 2009
155.4'121—dc22   2009021031

Printed in the United States of America on acid-free paper

www.bantamdell.com

2 4 6 8 9 7 5 3 1

FIRST EDITION

Book design by Chris Welch

Dedicated to the special men in my life:

Tom, for being my reason for life
(I am so very proud of the person you are)

Max, for giving me life

Philip, for giving Tom and me back our life

Mark, for having shared in my life

Foreword

Linda Acredolo, Ph.D., and Susan Goodwyn, Ph.D.

Coauthors, *Baby Signs: How to Talk with Your Baby Before Your Baby Can Talk*

As psychologists who have devoted much of the last twenty-five years of our lives to research that is focused on improving communication between parent and child, we are delighted to endorse the work being done by Priscilla Dunstan. Although Priscilla takes a very different approach to communication, her basic mission is the same as ours: to help parents and children communicate effectively so that the relationship between them flourishes. In our case, we encourage parents to help their preverbal babies "talk" by using simple signs. In Priscilla's case, she is helping parents better understand the messages their children are conveying, not necessarily in signs or words, but in their overall approach to the demands of everyday life. And like our own work, much of hers was originally inspired by her own life as a mom.

Her work began over a decade ago with her discovery, as the new mother of a very fussy baby, that her son made a number of distinct sounds that clearly signaled specific states such as hunger, sleepiness, and gas pain. When she began to notice that babies everywhere seemed to be making those same sounds to signal the same needs, she had the beginnings of what became her universal baby language classification system. That discovery led her to establish a research center in Sydney, Australia, which became the foundation for both the clinical and the research work she did with hundreds of families over the next decade.

Building on that initial discovery, Priscilla has always been motivated, in her life and her work, by the goal of bridging the communication gap between parent and child. *Child Sense* describes the results of the next stage of her research: her discovery of a sense-typing classification system that gives parents a key to understanding how their child experiences, interprets, and understands the world. While there are many classification systems that give insight into personality differences, Priscilla's stroke of insight was to realize that the most basic means of organizing the signals we get from the world around us is through our senses, and that each of us, from infancy on, has one primary sense orientation: touch, sight, sound, or taste/smell. Her simple, easy-to-use checklists in Chapters 2 and 3 will enable you to identify first your child's dominant sense, and then your own and your partner's. We know you will enjoy, as we did, working through these checklists because the descriptions she provides really ring true. It's fascinating to discover how much of your child's behavior (and perhaps your own!) is captured in these descriptions. There's a real "eureka" moment when it all starts to come together into a coherent portrait.

As you read through the pages that follow, you will quickly be able to understand at an intuitive level how the sense-type classification system helps you understand the previously mysterious behaviors of your child. Many of the behaviors that you may have interpreted as stubbornness, bad temper, or the unpredictability and irrationality of childhood are in fact very easily understood with the help of Priscilla's system. Once you understand that what your child is doing reflects an innate part of her orientation to the world, the knowledge will transform your approach to parenting.

When your two-year-old refuses to use a fork and insists on diving into her food with her hands, the insight that, as a tactile child, she depends on the sensations of touch to learn about the world can help you understand her motivation and deal with her more patiently. If your visually oriented three-year-old insists on arranging the dolls and toys and stuffed animals in a certain way and has a tantrum if you get them out of order when tidying up her room, you may be able to see the world through her eyes and understand how important that sense of order is to her feelings of safety and well-being. If your four-year-old with a taste/smell orientation gets his feelings hurt easily and seems to you to need some toughening up, you may be able to help him more effectively once you understand that children in this sense category are by nature hypersensitive, not just to a range of sense phenomena, but also to emotions—both their own and those of other people.

Priscilla's approach to parenting is not passive, however. She doesn't simply advise you to accept behaviors that are undesirable; she helps you transform them by using your awareness of your child's sense orientation. If your auditory baby has trouble sleeping even though you've thoroughly soundproofed his nursery, you may be surprised to discover that your child is one of those auditory babies who need a certain level of background noise to be able to settle. A little bit of experimentation—with soft music, or a white-noise machine—may help you come up with the solution that works for him.

And later, that same auditory child who seems to you to have an unusual amount of trouble making transitions may move through his day much more easily if you develop a repertoire of songs, such as the "putting on your shoes" song and the "going to potty" song and the "night-night bedtime song." The pages of this book are filled with tips and techniques for managing the everyday problems that every parent faces.

Child Sense is all about helping you customize your parenting to the unique needs of your child. As a first-time parent you may be overwhelmed by the seemingly inexplicable behavior of an extremely fussy child, while your best friend looks the very picture of maternal contentment with hers. Or perhaps your first child was one of those angels who slept and nursed with a minimum of trouble, but you are now dumbfounded by the fact that your second child is the opposite. Is it you or your baby who is at fault here? Neither, of course: it's just that every child is different, and even within the four sense categories there are many differences. What Priscilla's approach to parenting does is to enable you to use your intimate knowledge of your child to come up with sense-based strategies that make life simpler and happier for everybody.

There's nothing more rewarding in life than the bond between parent and child. *Child Sense* will help you deepen and strengthen that bond, establishing the foundation for a mutually rewarding and loving relationship.

Contents

A Better Bond

Recently a woman who has been a client of mine said to me, "For the first time in my child's life, I can see the beauty in him." As she spoke these words there were tears of relief and joy in her eyes and a look of wonder and tremendous pride on her face. This mother of three was speaking about her five-year-old son, whose behavior had always been so hard for her to manage that every moment since his birth had felt like a struggle. She has two older children, stepchildren from her husband's first marriage, whom she seemed to get along with just fine. But her youngest, who is her own biological child, was someone she simply could not relate to. What had suddenly made her see him—his beauty—for the first time?

She had learned a unique, empowering approach to communicating with her child that helped her be much more effective in how she talked to him, guided him, played with him, calmed him, and responded to his needs. As a result, this little boy's behavior changed quite dramatically. The tantrums and meltdowns that were making life so difficult for everyone in the family have all but disappeared, and he has become a much happier, more confident, more cooperative child. Needless to say, this has made her a much happier, more confident mother.

The not-so-mysterious key to how she was able to make this wonderful change is the story I wish to tell you in this book. It all comes down to a new approach to parenting, which I was able to teach her. As you'll discover, using this new approach to manage your child's behavior and guide your child through some of the developmental tasks of the first five years of life will both boost your child's self-confidence and feelings of security and enhance the relationship between you.

Seeing Your Child's Behavior
Through a Different Lens

Have you ever felt at your wits' end just trying to get your kids through the day? Do you find yourself frequently so frustrated and unsure of yourself that you cave, giving in to their endless array of demands—whether they are babies, toddlers, or pre-schoolers? Are you unnerved by your lack of patience with your kids and by their misbehavior and refusal to do what you ask? Are you so worn out after twelve hours spent trying to wake them, feed them, and get them to and from all their myriad activities that by the time you've put them to bed you barely have an ounce of energy left for yourself or your partner? When parenting isn't going well, the daily grind can be so discouraging and disruptive that it can make you doubt your ability to guide your children through life and give them the skills they need to thrive.

What I have discovered through my own experience as a mother, as well as more than eight years of practical one-on-one work helping thousands of families in the clinic that I founded in Sydney, Australia, is that most of the everyday kinds of conflicts that plague so many parents stem simply from a communication gap—a gap that goes to the heart of how every person in the world takes in and responds to the physical environment in which we live.

To put it very simply, each of us, from birth on, has one dominant sense mode—seeing, hearing, touching, or tasting and smelling (which are combined within one classification in this book). This dominant sense mode affects everything in our lives: how we take in information and process it, learn, interact with others, experience and respond to our own needs, communicate those needs to those around us, and so forth. My observations of the many families with whom I've worked have taught me that usually when a child is acting out or misbehaving, the underlying reason is that he does not really understand what is expected of him and, conversely, is unable to express what he needs in a way that the parent can comprehend or recognize. It's this communication gap that creates most of the problem behaviors in daily life.

So how can you bridge the communication gap? If you can learn to identify your children's dominant sense modes—to decide whether your children are predominantly tactile, visual, auditory, or taste/smell—then you will have a much firmer foundation for good communication. You will be able to tailor your parenting style to the individual needs of each of your children and create dramatically better relationships with them. And this is something I can help you do.

You may wonder who I am and what kind of work I have done with families. I am not a psychologist and I am not a doctor. I was born, grew up, and until recently lived in New South Wales, Australia, where for many years I had a career in music that began when I was a young child. Recently I've moved to the United States with my son, Tom, and we now live in Los Angeles. I first came to the field of parenting and children in the same way that all of you have: as a parent. And just like many of you, I felt overwhelmed and inadequate during the early days of my life with my new baby. But over time, I discovered that a gift I had previously put to use mainly during my musical career—specifically, an unusual and acute sense of hearing, which enables me to hear and remember very subtle nuances of sound—came to my rescue. As you will read in the first chapter, this odd trait of mine led me to discover a solution to the problem of my infant son's endless crying and eventually to a system for understanding the cries not just of my own son but of all babies.

At my clinic in Sydney as well as here in Los Angeles, I show parents and their children how to deal with the everyday issues that all families face. A desperate mother will say to me, "My friend came to you and she figured out how to turn her tyrant three-year-old into an angel. Can you do that for me too?" Another mom will plead, "Please, please help me. My baby needs to be held all the time; I'm exhausted and frustrated. I feel trapped." Another mother will confess, "My two-year-old won't sleep alone. I've tried controlled crying; I've tried locking her in her room; I've tried staying with her until she falls asleep. Nothing works. I don't want her to sleep with me, but I'm about to give in. Can you please help me? I don't know what to do." These are not the kinds of problems that most parents would take to their pediatricians, and they certainly wouldn't reach out to a psychologist, because the issues just seem too mundane for a specialist's attention. They may also hesitate to bring up these issues with friends or their own parents, for fear of seeming incompetent. So parents and children remain stuck in a negative cycle of bad behavior and unmet demands that makes everyone feel miserable. These daily dramas are precisely the kinds of dilemmas that I can help with, using what I have learned about the impact of the sensory modes on behavior and communication.

Often parents who come to see me for an initial consultation leave in tears—not because I've upset them but because they feel so much relief at finally being heard. For years their problems and concerns, no matter how troubling, have seemed so ordinary that they've never even spoken about them. But when they get to me, perhaps because I can relate to them as a parent, they spill all their fears and worries.

I typically begin my work with a family by spending about an hour and a half with each child in order to observe and then categorize him or her by sense. Over the weeks that follow, I will spend nearly four times that amount of time with the parents, refining my observations about the child's sense mode if necessary and teaching the parents how to adjust their parenting style accordingly. Really, what my work is about is helping parents *parent*.

Once a mother becomes aware of her child's sense orientation, she can understand how her child is navigating various age-related developmental tasks and how his dominant sensory mode may be impacting his behavior. For instance, a two-year-old child I worked with was having trouble separating from his mother at day care drop-off, throwing himself on the floor and holding on to his mother's ankles as if for dear life when she tried to leave. His mother had tried to quell his tantrums with encouraging words about how much fun he would have with the other kids, with time-outs, with a "You're a big kid, now toughen up" approach, with bribery, and with punishment. None of these strategies seemed to alleviate the trouble the boy (and his mother) was having. However, once I helped the woman identify her son's dominant sense as tactile, she was able to use that knowledge to make certain adjustments to their daily routine that would give him the confidence to separate each day from her. Understanding how much he needed the reassurance of her touch, she made a point of taking a few extra minutes every morning before they left the house to give him a little dose of cuddle time. Once she took him to day care, she got down to his eye level and gave him a big squeeze or hug to reassure him, then explained that as soon as he got home from day care they were going to have more cuddle time. As you will soon see, being touched and held is everything to a tactile child. So when this mother showed her son that she understood what he needed, she gave him the feeling of security that helped him overcome his fear of being left. The sense of safety and security she created with these very simple changes in how she approached the problem is just as important as food or even sleep: It gives children the energy they need to grow emotionally, mentally, and physically.

Another parent shared this about her experience: "When I discovered my child was auditory, I tried to understand the world from his point of view, and I realized how incredibly sensitive he is to tone of voice and loud noises. I began to notice that if I talked to him using a harsh or rushed voice, he would either tune me out or have a crying fit. I realize now that he was not being naughty or disobedient. In his own way, he'd been trying to let me know that he didn't understand what I was saying half the time. When I taught myself to speak to him in a gentler, quieter tone of voice, his behavior gradually began to change. He actually started listening to me and paying attention to directions."

One father, a single parent, came to me to discuss his nearly four-year-old daughter, who was so disruptive when they did errands such as grocery shopping that he had begun to consider she might have some kind of serious behavioral problem. He explained to me, "I can't take her anywhere—she always wants, wants, wants. She grabs at and wants to touch everything, especially candy at the checkout line. I try to get her to understand that candy, for instance, is bad for her teeth and it's not good to eat too much sugar. But it doesn't matter what I say. It's like she has no control over what she is doing! If I say no, she just ends up in hysterics." When I asked him to be more specific about the kinds of things that his daughter seemed to want so badly, he was quick to respond: "Anything that is 'pretty,' as she says! Which means anything in a bright, shiny wrapper." To me, this was a clear indication that his daughter was visual. I figured that she didn't really want the candy but instead was attracted to the glittery packaging. (By way of further explanation, you should know that in Australia candy is ubiquitous and most often comes packaged in sparkly, multicolored foil wrappers.) I suggested to this frustrated and concerned father that if it really was the packaging that was attracting her, as I suspected, then he might be able to appeal to another trait typical of his daughter's visual sense mode—a desire for order—to curb her seemingly out-of-control behavior. The plan we worked out was for the father to make a game of their shopping experience, inviting his daughter to see if she could put back in its place anything she might have grabbed. Soon after, the father reported back to me that the strategy worked beautifully— and not only when shopping. His daughter now enjoyed putting away her toys and tidying up her room.

Another parent said, "I used to worry constantly that my child's hypersensitivity to everything—bright lights, loud sounds, the tastes of various foods—meant that she wasn't normal. But once

I understood her through the lens of her sense type, which is taste/smell, I not only breathed a huge sigh of relief but also began to figure out ways to cope with her reactiveness. It took time for me to identify all the things she was sensitive to, but I realized it didn't mean that I was spoiling her by trying to modify things in her environment so she'd be more comfortable. I just accepted that she is who she is. Now I feel such a sense of achievement at being able to communicate more effectively with my daughter. Finally, I feel like I'm doing a good job as a parent. And even more important, I can see that my daughter is gaining so much confidence in herself. Day by day, I watch her become more sturdy on her feet."

Knowing and understanding the nature of your child's sense type allows you to stop fighting against who she is, as the mother above did, and instead begin responding creatively and constructively to her unique way of approaching the world. When you do this—and often the changes you have to make are really minor ones—you can literally transform your home life.

The words of gratitude I've received from the hundreds of parents who have been part of my study (which I will describe in the first chapter), as well as the hundreds more with whom I have worked worldwide, mean a great deal to me, because as a parent myself, I know how crucial it is to feel confident in my understanding of my child. In fact, this understanding is the key to creating a trustworthy, positive bond between parent and child. I value this bond in all that I do. My own desire to have a strong connection to my child—knowing and believing that that connection, especially during the first five years of his life, will be the single most powerful influence on his development—is what has fueled and informed all of my work and research with children and families.

Customizing Your Approach to Your Child

Let me ask you a few questions:

1. Have you ever started to weep from exhaustion and frustration when dealing with a baby who will not let you put her down, no matter how long you've been holding her throughout the day?
2. Have you ever wondered why your new baby wakes up at the slightest noise in the house, when your first child could sleep through dinner at a crowded restaurant?
3. Have you ever wondered why your baby can't settle down in her stroller unless she is facing you? Or have you in fact never realized that that is the key to calming her?
4. Have you ever felt at your wits' end trying to figure out why one of your three children is such an extremely picky eater, never willing to eat leftovers, when the rest of your brood enjoys whatever you prepare for dinner?
5. Have you ever witnessed your three-year-old wreaking havoc by throwing all of his toys into the center of the room and then stomping on them? Does he seem to vacillate between acting as if he is completely indifferent to you and crying out for a hug or a cuddle, curling up in your arms as if he was still an infant?
6. Have you ever wondered why your four-year-old needs to have all her shoes lined up in a certain way, wear her hair in one particular style, and arrange her stuffed animals on her bed in a specific way that no one is allowed to touch or alter?

7. Have you ever questioned why your child seems to mimic your every mood—when you're tense, she's tense; when you're sad, she's sad?

8. Have you ever wondered why your oldest child demands perfect silence while doing his homework but your youngest child enjoys listening to music while doing her homework?

Buried in each of these questions is a clue about what the children's dominant sense mode is and how it affects their way of being in the world. (Answering yes to questions 1 and 5 suggests your child is tactile; yes to questions 2 and 8, auditory; yes to 3 and 6, visual; yes to 4 and 7, taste/smell.) A much fuller checklist in Chapter 2 will enable you to identify your child's sense accurately; you will also learn how to identify your own and your partner's dominant sense, both of which can play a significant role in this communication conundrum. When you learn to recognize, cue into, and then respond appropriately to these specific modalities, you will quickly be able to put to practical use your new understanding of how your child experiences her world and why she behaves the way she does.

Most of the parents I encounter, both in Australia and in the United States, often have moments of desperation. They've lost their confidence in their ability to parent and are afraid that they are no longer in control—of themselves or their children. As a result, they constantly feel as if their families are in mere survival mode, barely able to get through the day.

I see these situations all the time, and I am confident that I can offer a good repertoire of tips and techniques for solving many common problems relating to daily issues such as eating, sleeping, toilet training, tantrums, and so on. But the most important thing I have to offer is something much more fundamental: I know that you know your child best, and that beyond helping you to teach your baby to sleep through the night, turn your child into a good eater, or prevent your child from kicking and biting the other kids in day care, what I can share with you is a whole new way to interpret your child's behavior and respond to it. This new approach is based on the five senses that we all possess but rarely tap into in a conscious, proactive way.

When you come to appreciate the fact that your child's dominant sense is his first point of reference, exercising a profound influence on the way he experiences the world around him and tries to communicate with the people in his environment, then you can reshape your interactions with him to make it easier for him to understand and respond to you. To a visual child, who is always concerned about how things look, you might say, "Can you see how messy your room is? Do you want to make it look nice and clean for when Daddy comes home?" To a tactile child, who is physical and practical and responds best to clear, direct suggestions, you might say, "I have a mission for you: Clean up your room as fast as you can!" To an auditory child, who is very responsive to music, you might say, "Do you want to put on your favorite CD while you clean your room?" And to a taste/smell child, who tends to be very emotionally connected to her parents and eager to please, you might say, "I was so proud of you last week when you put away all your toys; doesn't it feel good to do that? Let's do it again!"

By reinforcing the positive when communicating what you want and articulating the message or goal in a way that your child can relate to, you set up the child to win. With this approach, you will learn how to approach each problem, issue, or challenge by asking yourself, "What can I do so that my child succeeds in this moment, at this task?" For when your child succeeds at going to bed without crying or eating dinner without whining or going to day care without having a meltdown, you have succeeded too. It's a win-win for you and your child.

Practical Solutions to Everyday Problems

Perhaps your relationship with your child (or your partner's relationship with your child) is currently marred by friction and misunderstanding. After identifying your child's dominant sense, you will learn how to tap into it in order to clear the way for better communication and easier management of behavior and daily activities. This will involve understanding how your own and your partner's dominant sense modes also affect your relationship with your child. You will gain insight into how your child experiences and communicates his emotional needs, how he learns best, what activities engage him, why he interacts with others the way he does, and what kinds of play most appeal to him, both on his own and with his peers. And you will learn many simple, practical strategies to ease him through the events and routines of the day—from eating to dressing, going on outings, and going to sleep. But the biggest thing you will learn is how to cue into the meaning of your child's behaviors, which so often seem inexplicable and sometimes just plain contrary and infuriating. With this understanding, rooted in your child's dominant sense, coming up with the solutions to everyday issues and challenges will actually happen fairly intuitively.

This process may take time and can involve a fair amount of trial and error. Sometimes you'll find that the solutions described by either me or the parents with whom I've worked don't have the same effect in your family. But I promise that these suggestions will spark in you a solution that *does* work, because once you understand your child's sense orientation, you'll have the knowledge you need to create solutions that speak directly to the needs of the child you know best in the world—your own. And from that place of empowerment, you will be able to parent your child with energy, patience, and wisdom.

So this book will not offer you hard-and-fast rules of behavior or prescriptive advice. Instead, it will offer you insight about the impact of the senses on daily life so that with yourself, your partner, your child, and other family members in mind, you can figure out how to communicate with your child in more effective ways. What do I mean by effective? You choose language and a style of communication that speaks directly to her sensory mode; you help her manage her own behaviors so that she develops a sense of confidence and self-assurance; you give her the guidance she needs to express her own emotional needs effectively, master the tasks of learning, and relate positively to the world and people around her—all with a feeling of pride and accomplishment. And when you do this for your child during her earliest years, you give her a strong foundation of self-knowledge that will last her a lifetime.

What to Expect in This Book

In Part One of this book, you'll learn the basics. In the first chapter, I'll tell you about my background and how my research formed the basis of this book. In Chapter 2, I provide checklists you can use to learn how to identify your child's dominant sense. In Chapter 3, you will use a different set of checklists to help you identify your own and your partner's.

In Part Two there are four chapters, each of them focused on one of the four sense modes, with descriptions of how that mode affects the navigation of developmental tasks within the three age groups covered in this book: birth to one year, one to three years, and three to five years. For each of the different sense mode classifications I will give you suggestions for how to manage your child's feeding, sleeping, and dressing routines, as well as how to adapt your toilet-training techniques. For children in each age group, I also show how the different sense modes impact their emotional needs, the manner in which they process information and learn, and the way in which they begin to play and interact with their peers and others. At the end of each of these four chapters, I address the challenge of mismatch—when a parent and child differ in their dominant sense—and how parents can troubleshoot these differences in a constructive way. (I do assume that all children are relatively healthy and not suffering from any overt behavioral or emotional disorder. Of course, if a child has a real behavioral disorder or psychological condition, I always refer parents to a physician or specialist.)

Keep in mind that you may not be able to accurately identify your child's sense right away. Be patient with yourself. If you still feel uncertain after going through the various checklists in Chapter 2, you may want to jump ahead to the chapter in Part Two that corresponds to the sense group you think your child might belong to. Once you read through that chapter, you'll probably have a pretty good idea whether or not it applies to your child and, if necessary, you can go back to the checklists to start the identification process over.

In the final chapter, I take a closer look at special challenges such as moves, going to school, birth of a sibling, divorce, and loss from death or abandonment—those dramatic moments or times in a child's life that may cause the child to regress or act out. This is when knowledge of a child's dominant sense can be a real lifesaver for parents.

PART ONE

You and Your Child

ONE

Discovering the Key to the Sense Types

During the months of pregnancy, many of us fantasized about the bond we would soon have with our child. We imagined cooing to each other, holding each other close in a bubble of mutual wonder, fascination, and intimacy. Even before our baby is born, we are able to bring to life a deep love for that child. Yet after the child does finally arrive and is in our arms for the first time, this lovely imaginary bubble often bursts all too soon. We find ourselves faced with the seemingly incomprehensible cries and needs of a baby we have difficulty soothing, and sometimes with something even more disturbing: a feeling of complete incompetence about our ability to take care of this new life we have brought into the world.

I know this feeling of uncertainty intimately. Before I became a mother, I imagined that blissful state with my soon-to-be-born son. At the time, my partner and I had moved out into the countryside on a piece of land with hills, horses, and a great expanse of sky. We had dreamed about having an idyllic life close to nature, where we would raise our child free of the stresses of the city or

suburbia. But life after Tom's arrival was quite different from what
I'd imagined. My country refuge began to seem like a trap. With
Tom's father both working a lot and traveling overseas regularly, I
found myself quite isolated and alone. My baby cried incessantly,
and instead of feeling blissful, I went through months of muddled
bewilderment, frustration, and self-doubt. I tried to soothe Tom
by rocking him, nursing him, and taking him for walks. He would
cry some more, and I would give him a warm bath or sing to him.
Once I even tried doing some simple yoga movements while
holding him, hoping that the rhythms of my motion and my
breathing would calm him. Nothing I did seemed to work, and I
was growing more and more upset—almost frightened.

Unbeknownst to me, Tom was in a constant and intense state of
physical agitation due to colic, which was the reason behind the
long periods of nonstop crying and his inability to respond to
soothing. Compounding my misery over my inconsolable baby
was my own suffering from horrible migraines, which often left
me visually impaired. There were times during this stressful period when I literally could not see my baby. Day by day, my confidence in my ability to take care of my child dwindled, leaving me
unsure of what to do and truly worried about whether I was up to
the enormous job of motherhood. However, it was thanks to my
migraines that I stumbled across a partial solution to Tom's distress. When I had the migraines there were times when I couldn't
eat anything, with the unexpected result that Tom's issues with gas
and intestinal discomfort actually lessened. This led me in a
roundabout way to the discovery that what I ate had a big effect
on my baby. When I began looking at my eating habits I realized
that dairy products were the staples of my diet, and that the cheese
and yogurt I liked so much were making Tom sick. It turned out
that Tom was suffering from colic and reflux, greatly aggravated

by his allergic reaction to the lactose in my breast milk from any kind of dairy I had ingested.

But my diet was just part of the problem. When I stopped eating dairy, Tom's reflux did decrease dramatically, but he was still very fussy, unable to stay asleep for long, and unresponsive to any of the calming tactics I tried during his long bouts of crying. The next stage in my journey to discovering how to help my child began with a strength that I never dreamed would come to my rescue as a parent: my ability to listen.

My acute sense of hearing is in part due to my very early exposure to music. My mother started my musical training before I was even born, by playing classical music while I was still in her womb. Then, as soon as I was physically able, she introduced me to the violin, using the Suzuki method. Since I couldn't read music at the age of three and four, my mother would play something for me and I would play it back from memory. Because of this ability, I was labeled as having an eidetic memory, which means that my sense of hearing is so precise that I can remember any sound or piece of music with great accuracy after hearing it only one time. Related to this ability to memorize music is an even stronger ability to recognize patterns. My skill and ease with music and pattern recognition led to my early career as a professional violinist and later as an opera singer. (Indeed, music is just that: a pattern created by the arrangement of musical notes.) My ability to pick up on sound patterns was also what eventually led to my discovery of a universal baby language.

Blinded by migraines and worried about my ability to be able to respond to Tom's needs when I could barely see him, I began to listen to his cries with such acuteness that I eventually discerned that certain sounds were repeated time and again. Gradually I realized that each of these sounds had a precise meaning that expressed a different need. The first distinct sound I recognized within a cry was "neh," the sound associated with hunger; it actually made my breasts leak. Through trial and error, I identified a second cry, which sounded like "eairh," and seemed to indicate lower gas pain. A third cry, "owh," meant he was sleepy. I eventually isolated five distinct sounds, each of which expressed a different physical sensation and need: hunger, sleepiness, discomfort, gas, and a need to be burped. Once I understood the meaning behind his different cries, I happily fed him, burped him, held him, and helped him to sleep, essentially meeting all of his most urgent needs. Often I was even able to anticipate what Tom needed, thereby avoiding the crying altogether.

To make a long story short, over time I began to realize that babies everywhere made the same sounds that Tom made to signal the same needs. I'd be in a park and see a young mother looking miserable as she tried futilely to stop her child from crying. Based on my experience with Tom, I'd venture a guess about what the baby wanted. Lo and behold, the baby would calm down, and the mother would look at me as if I was a miracle worker. And it didn't matter what the ethnic group of the mother and baby was. The cries always seemed to be the same, across all cultures. I felt I was on to something that could help all mothers. As it turned out, I seemed to have stumbled upon the Rosetta Stone of baby language.

The Language of Babies

Having discovered what I believed to be a universal baby language, common to babies all over the world, I wanted to share it. As the daughter of a scientifically rigorous child psychologist, I knew that if I wanted to make the case for the existence of this language so that I could bring it into the public eye and help other struggling mothers, I would need to produce a body of evidence that met exacting research standards. So under the guidance of my father, Max Dunstan, a renowned Australian psychologist who until his retirement was the director of the Educational Testing Center at the University of New South Wales and a specialist in testing and educational protocol, I began what turned out to be an eleven-year period of research. During this time I opened an office in Sydney and began working one-on-one with families (mostly mothers and their babies), collecting data for my emerging research project. (Later on, I would expand this office into a full-fledged clinical research center.) The research involved more than a thousand babies and their parents, from seven different countries and of thirty different ethnic backgrounds, and it fell into five separate phases: an observation phase, during which I observed hundreds of babies, both in real time and on tape—in doctors' offices, hospitals, my own and others' baby clinics, playgrounds, and even shopping malls—and analyzed their cries; a classification phase, in which, with the help of my father, I created a research protocol that enabled me to record, describe, and classify the five distinct cries; an intervention phase, in which I interacted with parents in order to troubleshoot and advise them on how to use this information about infant cries; a clinical trial phase, in which, with the help of professors and physicians who worked at Brown University's world-renowned Infant Behavior, Cry and Sleep Clinic (IBCSC), also called the Colic Clinic, we further refined the parameters and measurements of my research in a clinical setting; and finally, a private research phase, in which we hired an independent research company to verify our findings.

The results were gratifying. We found that

- 90 percent of all mothers thought that the ability to understand and recognize the five distinct sounds babies made when crying was very beneficial
- 100 percent of first-time mothers reported it highly valuable
- 70 percent reported their baby settled faster
- 50 percent of mothers experienced more unbroken sleep*
- 70 percent reported feeling more confident as a mother, experiencing greater self-esteem, a reduction in stress, and a feeling of being more relaxed and in control
- 50 percent of mothers felt a deeper bond with their baby*
- 50 percent experienced better feeding*
- 2 out of 3 fathers reported reduced levels of stress and more positive marital relationships as an immediate result of greater paternal involvement

*Specific to the United States and Australia
Source: Dunstan Baby.

My research into infant baby sounds also ended up bringing me worldwide attention, culminating in an appearance on *The Oprah Winfrey Show*. And though I was quite surprised by the breadth of this international exposure, I was thrilled because it helped me to achieve my goal of reaching as many mothers as possible. I knew that when parents learned to discern their baby's cries, they would immediately transform their ability to respond to their children in wonderful, satisfying ways, enhancing their bond with their child.

What does this all have to do with the book you now hold in your hands? The research I conducted independently in Australia and that which I did with colleagues at Brown University's Colic

Clinic, as well as my ongoing one-on-one work with families in what soon expanded into a research center in Sydney, not only offered an amazingly simple yet very effective way for parents and other caregivers to understand and meet their babies' needs but also led to a profound and potentially even more important discovery, which is the subject of this book.

At Home and in the Research Center

As had happened before, my son, Tom, played an important role in inspiring me to this further discovery about how children communicate. Once I began to meet his physical needs in a consistent, direct way, Tom's colic began to subside. I found that most of the time I was able to calm and comfort him. He became a much happier baby, and I became a much happier (and relieved) mother. But as time went on and Tom grew toward toddlerhood, I began to sense another challenge to our ability to communicate with each other. No longer a fussy, agitated baby whose needs, once I had learned to decipher them, turned out to be relatively simple and straightforward, he was now a wild, rambunctious little boy. I found myself constantly guessing about what was behind his actions and behaviors. As all parents know, once our children move beyond one year of age, they show themselves to be quite the complicated creatures.

At first I thought that some of his new behaviors—throwing all his toys in the middle of the room, running and jumping on the furniture no matter how many times I told him not to, and nearly tackling me with his boisterous affection—were simply the rowdiness of a boy with mounting levels of testosterone flowing through his veins. But Tom sometimes became very physical with me too—alternately pushing me away or refusing to let me go, which I found quite puzzling. I can recall one incident very clearly when we went to visit my father. Tom and I were on our own by this point, and Tom was so excited to see and spend time with his grandfather that he actually pushed me out of the way. This aggressive, physical manner was quite startling, and the more of it I saw in the months that followed, the more I began to feel as if Tom was actually the dominant one in our relationship—and he was all of two! His intense physicality seemed such a driving force in his personality, and was so different from my own temperament, that it was hard for me to handle, and again I felt as though I didn't know what to do. I began to ask myself questions: Should I discipline him by taking away his toys? Give him a time-out? Try to explain to him why these behaviors were not okay? I tried all those approaches, and I also tried to settle him down with soft music and to distract him by putting him in front of a DVD or reading him a story. But nothing seemed to work once he got himself wound up to a certain point.

Although I'd used my knowledge of baby language quite effectively to understand his needs as an infant, both his needs and his way of expressing them were becoming more complicated as he moved further into childhood. I was feeling so tired—so physically and emotionally drained by these demands—that I began to worry that, while our relationship was not exactly antagonistic, something was coming between us, weakening our bond. Being the daughter of a psychologist and well schooled in what the experts had to say about attachment theory, I feared that anything that undermined our connection to each other would be a threat to his well-being. After all, hadn't I learned that his bond with me was what would enable him to feel safe and secure in the world? Wasn't I supposed to be the main source of his ability to form positive, healthy attachments? Wasn't it up to me to provide him with the emotional and psychological building blocks that would form the foundation of a strong sense of self and give him the ability to thrive and grow emotionally, cognitively, and socially? And wasn't our bond important not just in the first few months of life but throughout his childhood?

But my understanding of the importance of establishing a close bond with Tom didn't seem to be making it any easier to understand or communicate with him. When he was a baby, it took a lot of trial and error before I understood Tom's cries and figured out the best way to respond. Then everything in our lives calmed down, especially me. Never doubt that necessity is the mother of invention! But now that he was older and was expressing his needs in such a multitude of ways, I was again confused and uncertain. What did he want, and how could I make him happy without my feeling that he was the one in charge? As his mother, wasn't I supposed to know how to handle him?

While I was trying to find ways to understand my toddler son better, my research and my clinical work with babies expanded. I established a larger, more encompassing office, which enabled me to conduct more extensive research while continuing to meet with children and their families in a clinical setting. As part of my ongoing research into the universal baby language, I began filming the babies, trying to get clear recordings of the exact sounds they made as they cried, and ended up creating a working inventory of hundreds of videotapes. The filming took place in numerous places—some at families' homes, some at my research center, and some in a music studio that had an array of audiovisual equipment and three individual soundproofed rooms. On the most intense filming days at the music studio, as many as forty babies would be brought in by their parents—usually their mothers, but sometimes the fathers—to be filmed individually, during sessions that could last up to an hour and a half. If a baby was brought into a soundproofed room and deposited on the floor with the parent nearby but not on camera, the baby would sometimes immediately produce a few really good cries (expressing one or more of the five needs for which I had identified the sounds), in which case the session would take only fifteen to twenty minutes. At other times, however, the sessions would go on considerably longer because of the amount of time it took me and my crew to capture a good, or usable, cry on film.

As you might imagine, the daily environment on such filming days was quite chaotic: I'd run from one soundproofed room to the next, filming one baby after another. The goal was to capture the "fussing" part of the infants' vocalizations, what I call the pre-cry stage, which is when they make the sounds that are such clear indications of the different, specific needs. If the need isn't met—if, for example, the child is hungry and doesn't get fed within a short period of time of his making the pre-cry sound for hunger—then the distress escalates and he just begins wailing. Aside from the fact that this would be distressing to both me and the parents, this was a problem because it interfered with my getting what I wanted on tape.

In order to create the best footage in the least amount of time, I needed to find very efficient ways to elicit the pre-cries while avoiding undue distress, and this required me to be very sensitive to what kind of circumstances calmed and distracted the babies, what agitated them, and what, ultimately, allowed them to be just relaxed enough to utter the pre-cry. As I began to cue into how the babies seemed to react to being taken away from their moms and put in a room by themselves, it gradually dawned on me that the babies were falling into three different groups, each of which had certain distinct behavioral patterns that distinguished it from the other groups. I began making mental notes to myself about these patterns, and the more babies I worked with, the clearer these patterns became to me. What really solidified these observations, and eventually led to my understanding that the behaviors I was watching were related to the sensory modes, was my nightly review of the films we had done each day. The cumulative effect of viewing so many of those films over time resulted in my identifying three recognizable groups, which I labeled—in my own mind—visual, tactile, and auditory.

The so-called visual babies were those who quickly became hysterical as soon as their mother or father was out of sight but then became quiet and calm as soon as the camera lens and lights were focused on them, clearly distracted and even entertained by the visual stimulation. These babies produced their best pre-cries when their parents were close enough for the child to see them (while remaining off camera).

The tactile babies were those who became upset as soon as their mothers put them down. Though I didn't want the moms to be visible on camera we could adjust the camera angles so that the moms couldn't be seen. We then discovered that if the moms touched these kids in some way, rubbing their tummies or even just holding on to a toe or a foot, that comforted them enough to produce the recognizable pre-cry sounds that I wanted.

The third group, which I called auditory, was made up of babies who were generally easygoing unless they heard the cries of other babies, which would trigger their own hysterics. One of the things I eventually realized was that when these babies were in the waiting room prior to filming, they would get so upset at the sound of other babies crying that it was hard to calm them down when it came time to film them. Once I had enough experience to be able to identify these babies pretty quickly, I would have them wait with their parents in one of the soundproofed rooms instead of the regular waiting room. During the filming, if they remained in earshot of their mother's voice, the babies would remain calm and I could usually elicit the needed cries quite easily.

My realization that the way in which the three groups of babies needed their mothers—in their sight, within earshot, or in physical contact with them—was really the beginning of the research that led to this book. But the truth is that at the time I made these observations, I had no idea whether they were going to be useful in any way other than helping me with the work I was doing on the videotapes.

Although the behavioral differences of the three groups of children were indeed interesting, they were outside the realm of what I was researching and so I didn't give them much thought. However, some of the parents I was working with at the time began talking to me about their concerns regarding their older children, so I was already being drawn into thinking about parenting issues that went beyond my baby language studies. The problems they described were nothing out of the ordinary and of the kind that always arise with small children—sleeping and eating difficulties, tantrums, defiant behavior, separation anxiety, and so on. In fact, many of them were the same issues I was dealing with in my own home. However, as all parents know, these problems are always of great importance because they can make the difference between having a good day and having a terrible one. So while I was still very much in the midst of my baby language research, I began asking parents questions related to the behavioral differences, seeing if they impacted other areas of children's behavior.

For instance, during a home visit to a baby I had labeled auditory, who was now crawling and fast becoming a toddler, I'd ask the mother to characterize her child's tantrums, and soon it became clear to me that the parents of other so-called auditory children described their children's tantrums in similar ways. The more mothers I interviewed, the more I began to think that each of my three groups—visual, tactile, and auditory—actually presented a different style of tantrum. Tactile children threw themselves on the ground and thrashed about in a very physical way. Visual children got very dramatic, with copious tears and vivid facial expressions. Auditory children simply let out high-pitched squeals. I was beginning to think that I had stumbled on something—I just didn't quite know what it was.

The Different Senses Emerge

At first, the characteristics of the children I observed seemed to fall into the three major sensory categories I've mentioned—those relating to touch, hearing, and sight. Children whose dominant sense mode was tactile were the most familiar to me, as my son, Tom, embodied the quintessential romping boy, who explores the world through his hands, having to touch, squeeze, and throttle everything in sight. The sheer physicality of the child whose dominant sense is tactile is quite dramatic. Mothers of tactile babies often complain about how exhausting it is to have to hold their children in their arms all the time and how bitterly their babies cry when put down. As toddlers, these tactile-oriented children often hug their parents and other children too hard and can be very physically aggressive—throwing things at people, shoving and pushing other children on the playground—as well as being quite bold about exploring their physical world and their own physical boundaries. All the while, they continue to need a lot of physical affection. And what messes these kids can make with their busy little hands. As preschoolers, tactile children often have trouble going to sleep because they are too wound up from their day and have difficulty with self-calming. They continue to demand to be held and cuddled at this stage, sometimes only moments after they've pushed you away.

The next sense that I discerned was auditory. Children whose dominant sense is auditory are especially attuned to sounds and voices, and to their qualities—soft, loud, angry, soothing, and so on. Babies who are predominantly auditory rely on being in earshot of their mothers. They need soothing music or songs to calm down, and they are easily startled or upset by loud, abrasive, or unfamiliar noises. Auditory toddlers tend to overreact to noisy environments, showing a preference for quieter rooms. As they get older and learn to talk, they can be very chatty. If they don't get their own way, they are likely to throw tantrums that involve lots of screaming. As preschoolers, they can often entertain themselves by singing or talking to themselves, even when no one else is around. But when they do need attention, they will register their complaints about not being listened to loudly and clearly. They tend to show very particular tastes in music, which coincide rather closely with their moods. If they are happy, they will relish bouncy music, but if they are grouchy or upset, this same music might actually set them off.

The third dominant sensory mode that I observed was the visual. Babies whose dominant mode is visual typically need their mothers to be in their line of sight at all times, as their primary experience of the world around them comes through their eyes. This has many implications for parenting style. For example, a child whose first way of interacting with the world is visual will not understand a mother who smiles as she says, "Now sweetie, don't go near the fire." The child will be so focused on her mother's loving smile that she will more than likely miss the cue about the fire. At the toddler stage visual children will get very excited when they see other children running around a playground or when they watch the moving images on a television screen. And because of that sensitivity to visual stimuli, you may have to turn off the TV or wheel their strollers around so that they can't see the playground in order to calm them down. For the same reason, these kids usually need to be put in a dim or dark room to go to sleep. Older children who are visual may have strong preferences about what they wear and perhaps how their rooms look. You'll be amazed by how much these things matter to them and how upset they can get if forced to wear colors they don't like or carry a backpack that doesn't have their favorite cartoon character on it.

A Fourth Group

As I continued trying to understand more about the significance of these three classifications of children and their respective characteristics, there was one group of kids that didn't seem to belong to any of the categories I had identified. I kept moving these kids from one group to another because sometimes they seemed visual, while at other times they seemed to be tactile or auditory. I called them the "green" group, and I could never decide where they really belonged. However, when I began to look at them more closely, I noticed that these children were consistent in certain ways: They all exhibited a rather head-in-the-clouds, dreamy way of behaving and often seemed lost in their own worlds. They also seemed to be very physically as well as emotionally sensitive. They reacted strongly to intense stimuli of any kind, and their feelings were easily hurt. To me, these qualities indicated a heightened mind-body connection of the kind one often sees in people of a very intuitive nature. For that reason, I began calling them the "intuitive" group instead of the "green" group. Beyond that, I didn't really know how to define their category or how to work it into the classification system I had devised, since it didn't seem to be sense-related like the other three. Then two events occurred that finally illuminated the nature of this fourth group of children.

First, one day I got an intense sinus pain in my head that seemed to make all my senses—especially my vision, hearing, and sense of touch—so intensified that I mentally withdrew, blocking out my awareness of the external world. It was as if I had created a bubble around me as a form of protection against the onslaught of sensory input. After the sinus pain subsided and my hypersensitivity to sensory stimuli lessened, I began to wonder what it would be like for people to have this sort of acute sensitivity all the time and how it might affect their personalities. I guessed that people whose senses were always so acute or heightened might similarly withdraw into themselves as a protective mechanism. It then occurred to me that perhaps that's what was happening with this last group of children—the so-called intuitive ones. I immediately began reviewing my notes from the past few years. Sure enough, I felt I was seeing a direct connection between the dreamy, imaginative nature of these children and their rather extraordinary sensory sensitivity. Their tendency to immerse themselves in a private, inner world was perhaps a direct result of the need to retreat from the external world when it became too intense for them to handle.

The second event that helped bring this category into clearer focus occurred during one of my weekly meetings with my father, during which I would update him on how my research was going. When I explained to him that I had classified three groups of babies and children by sense mode—tactile, auditory, and visual—but that I couldn't figure out how to categorize this fourth group, he said simply, "Well, what about the other two senses?" Had I overlooked something that was staring me in the face?

Guided by my father's question, I looked specifically at this group's sense of taste and smell and found that these children did indeed show a dramatic sensitivity to the foods they ate (or often refused to eat!) and to any odors, no matter how subtle, in the air. These were the kids their parents described as "extremely picky" about their food and likely to react badly to any change in their usual meals. If they were used to one brand of hot dogs and Mom bought another because the store was out of the usual one, beware the tantrum at lunchtime.

But what was the connection between their heightened sensitivity to taste and smell and their emotional sensitivity, which was quite noticeable? Knowing that taste and smell are the most primal of our senses and that they are rooted in the limbic system of the brain, I suddenly made the connection: the limbic system is also the seat of our emotions. Now many of the observations I had made about these children began to make more sense to me. I understood why they were both so inward and so sensitive to external stimuli, why they often withdrew into themselves and played happily on their own while also having such strong emotional connections to the people they loved.

So this group too could be described by a sense mode—which I named "taste/smell" since those two senses are so closely linked and the children in this group seemed sensitive to both. Taste/smell children are very particular about food and will show distinct preferences, even as babies. In their early years they tend to want foods that are bland in color, taste, and texture. They are very sensitive to emotions, their own and those of others. As babies they can sense if their mother is upset, and they will become upset too. If another baby is crying, they will often burst into tears. And if another child is laughing, taste/smell children may also begin to laugh. In their toddler years, this awareness of other people's feelings develops into an early ability to empathize. And by the time taste/smell children enter preschool or kindergarten at age four or five, they begin to show explicit signs of being highly intuitive, yet another expression of their facility at picking up on and understanding emotional cues.

Bringing It Home

My new awareness of these sensory classifications began to impact my understanding of Tom. I could see that Tom was expressing his needs—all of them—through his body. This physicality was also his way of expressing emotion. When Tom would come racing into the room, banging pots and pans and hurling himself into me with all his might, I tended to shrink from all that noise and physical aggression. It was important for me to realize that all of the energy that was pouring out of him was really an eruption of joy and love. Even if it was different from my way of expressing feelings, I was going to have to start taking him on his own terms. Although it is very easy to label older tactile children as insensitive, it's more accurate to say that, being so logical and practical, they respond to people in a rather black-and-white manner, not having much awareness of feelings that are at all subtle and not being very adept at understanding mixed feelings.

I also realized that my way of being in the world was just very different from Tom's. Given my acute sensitivity to sound, I take my cues from spoken words, music, tone of voice, and other aural input, and I'm very sensitive to noise. When things get too loud for me, my tendency is always to withdraw and shut down, which upset Tom a lot and helped explain why I was having so much trouble with my little wild one. My style of communication, which is verbal, wasn't helping matters either, and I didn't understand why he was so unresponsive. When I asked him sweetly to quiet down, pick up his toys, or clean up his mess, which was how I would want to be spoken to, he would look at me blankly. He wasn't being defiant or stubborn; I just wasn't getting through to him.

This insight had a profound impact on me. I realized that the problems I was having with Tom had to do with our different ways of communicating love, expressing our needs, and learning about the world. Tom is tactile and he uses his hands, his feet, his shoulders, his back. In fact, he uses every inch of his body, and tends to make a lot of noise while doing it, not noticing its effect on those around him, while I shrink from too much noise and—out of my desire for everyone around me to feel happy and understood—generally speak in a soft, gentle tone of voice, which Tom obviously wasn't hearing.

Because of what I was observing in my own daily life, I soon decided to make the sensory modes the focus of a new research project—as a way to understand both my family situation (my relationship with Tom) and that of what I was sure were millions of other parents experiencing comparable difficulties in communicating with their children.

A Second Research Project

Wanting to make sure that my observations in my clinic were substantiated through a rigorous scientific process, I again turned to my father, who helped me establish a new research protocol, adapting the one I had created with Brown University's Colic Clinic for my infant cry study. I decided to limit the scope of my research to children between the ages of one month and five years, breaking the children into three separate age groups: up to one year, one to three years, and three to five years. Using the collective sampling method, which precludes any kind of screening process in order to get the largest cross section of the population, I began to systematically observe, record, and analyze the behavior of children as it pertained to the four sensory modes I had recognized.

The pool of study subjects expanded to include almost two hundred children from about 150 families, across a broad spectrum of race, ethnicity, nationality, social and economic background, and family makeup (only child, multiple children, children who were in two-parent households or in one-parent households, children who lived part-time with one parent and part-time with the other, and children who lived in an extended family that included grandparents and/or aunts and uncles). I observed children not just in Australia but also in New Zealand, Thailand, and the United States. In addition to the 150 families, as part of a separate study I also did research on a group that included deaf children and children with sight problems, because I wanted to see how the dominant sense mode expressed itself in children with sensory deficits.

In order to study the children (and their families) at close range, I divided them into groups of ten and had them come into my clinic with their parents. There I observed the children in a play area I had set up, dividing it into four sections, each of which was filled with toys and activities that were designed to appeal, respectively, to each of the four sensory modes. The tactile area was filled with stuffed animals, building blocks, and lots of cars, trucks, and trains; the visual area contained crayons, colored markers, and lots of paper for drawing, as well as a big trunk filled with colorful dress-up clothes; the auditory area had musical instruments as well as stuffed animals and toy computers that talk back when buttons are pressed; the taste/smell area held small animal figures, dolls, dress-up clothes, and other toys that are conducive to all kinds of fantasy role playing and other activities that may involve enacting little dramas among imaginary characters.

When the children arrived at my clinic, they quickly dispersed and migrated toward the section of the room that appealed to their dominant sense. This choice provided a quick and easy way of doing an initial classification of a child's dominant sense: the area the child chose to play in generally corresponded with his or her dominant sense. Of course, children did wander from play station to play station, but they usually gravitated first to the area associated with their dominant sense, and if they tried other areas, they tended to return to where they started.

While the children played during this first visit, I did an initial intake interview with the parents, asking them questions about their child's behavior. In follow-up visits, I then spent about an hour and a half with each of the children, one-on-one, observing them and, if they were old enough, asking them specific questions so that I could further refine my first hunches about their dominant sense. After this observation phase, I gave parents or caregivers a pamphlet describing what I believed to be their child's dominant sense and the telltale behavioral traits that would enable them to confirm that this was indeed their child's classification.*

I also asked parents to keep a diary, recording for two weeks the behavior of their children and the way in which they interacted with them. I asked them to simply write down what they found disruptive, annoying, or difficult about their children, and how they wanted these behaviors to change. The behaviors they described usually had to do with waking, feeding, bathing, dressing, sleeping, playtime, and other daily routines. They also recorded how their child expressed emotional needs, learned new information, and played and interacted with friends, siblings, and family.

The diary was important for two reasons. First, parents' descriptions of what was happening with the child at home were always more revealing than what I could observe in my research center, because parents know their child much better than any outsider can. Also, the diary helped me to understand how the parents viewed their child's behavior. In other words, certain behaviors are problematic not in themselves but rather because they cause difficulties in a particular family. What bothers me may be very differ-

---

*Like most studies, mine included a control group to further substantiate my findings. The control group consisted of children whose parents were given an inaccurate sense-type label for their child. One out of every five children was put in the control group.

ent from what bothers you and, conversely I may be completely comfortable with behavior that drives you crazy.

After two weeks, the parents returned with their diaries and their children for the intervention phase of the study. Again, the children sought out their respective play areas while I spoke with their parents. This session enabled me to troubleshoot stubborn problems, allowed parents to ask questions, and gave us the opportunity, if necessary, to reclassify a miscategorized child. I found that in some cases parents resisted my classifications because they were so eager to believe that their child was like them or so convinced that their child fell into a given category that they just couldn't accept any other conclusion. For example, in one family I had determined that their three-year-old was taste/smell, but this was not what the father wanted to hear. Being tactile, he was sure that little Scott had to be tactile too. But after two weeks of recording Scott's behaviors and being frustrated by the child's inability to conform to the criteria of the tactile category, he was taking his anger out on Scott. Both of them looked absolutely miserable when they returned to the clinic. It took some doing to convince the father that Scott's taste/smell classification did not mean that he was in any way inferior or effeminate and that there was nothing defective about this sweet little boy. We worked out several new activities that they both enjoyed and could do together, such as playing tag—with the added element that the tagger was a pirate and the person tagged was a captive, because that appeal to the imagination made the game a lot more fun for Scott. By creating a common ground where they could meet—the father was doing something physical, which appealed to his tactile inclinations, and the boy got to exercise his vivid imagination—we made it possible for father and son to get along much better.

The intervention phase of my research process, which could

last between one and four months, depending on the needs of the parents, required them to continue using the diaries to record what happened when they began to introduce changes in how they responded to and helped direct their kids. In addition to my continued analysis of the diaries, I also conducted interviews about how the children's behaviors were changing, and in some cases I did follow-up home or school visits to help parents put some of my suggestions into action or to gather more information about a family's particular dynamic.

In the next and final phase of my research process, I put together all of the data and analyzed them, comparing the children within their respective dominant sensory mode as well as contrasting the modes themselves.

I've now conducted about three concentrated years of research into the four sensory modes, which overlapped with and built on more than eleven years of research into baby cries. Over this time, I have researched and/or worked with thousands of children and their families and have heard from many parents who tell me that they have seen "remarkable improvements in day-to-day life," that "everyone feels happier," and that "things just run much more smoothly." As one mom said to me, "Everything is now a pleasure. I am so much more relaxed as a mother. This has absolutely shifted my dynamic with my children."

What I've learned in my work using the sensory modes has transformed my relationship with my own son, and I've seen the same thing happen with my research subjects. Knowing whether your child is auditory, tactile, visual, or governed by the subtle taste/smell sense will enable you to relate more easily to your child, because you will be using language and actions that will be more readily understandable.

The bond between parent and child starts first with this ability to communicate with each other. Without clear communication, it becomes very difficult for a child to enjoy the inner sense of well-being that comes with feeling understood; without clear communication, it becomes very difficult for the mother to have the sense of confidence that comes with feeling that she is connecting with her child in a positive way. And without this two-way street, the parent-child bond that is so important to a child's sense of self will be vulnerable.

That, at heart, is what this book is all about—giving you the tools to create a deeper, stronger bond between you and your child. For when you are better able to respond to your child's needs, help him learn about the world in the way that is most accessible to him and makes most sense to him, and help him develop a stronger sense of self-confidence as he maneuvers his way through the world, then you give him what he needs to reach his fullest potential and grow into a happy, healthy, and wise person.

TWO

Identifying Your Child's Sense Mode

I n this chapter, you are going to learn how to identify your child's dominant sense mode. The information I will be sharing with you is based both on the observations I have made through my research and on my one-on-one work with children and their parents, first in Sydney and now in Los Angeles. During any given week at my clinic and research center in Sydney, where I met with families who had sought me out for help in managing the day-to-day behavioral problems they faced with their children, I saw between twenty-five and fifty different kids, ranging in age from one or two months to five years old, right before they enter first grade. One mom showed up in my office a mere four days after giving birth! Most of my clients come to me via word of mouth or have been referred to me by their pediatricians or psychologists.

Since moving to Los Angeles and establishing an office in the United States, I have continued to work one-on-one with families, including staying in touch with and advising my Australian families from afar. All of this is to say that I've witnessed again and again, in families around the world, how a knowledge of your child's sense orientation can transform daily life, liberating you from many of the problems that you may have assumed were inevitable. They're not!

I know from experience that once you determine the dominant sense of your child, you will reach a much more accurate understanding of why your child acts the way he does. You will also have much keener insight into how your child's developmental tasks are being impacted by his dominant sense type. I will offer you insight on why and how your child may be struggling with separation anxiety or what's behind his tantrums. Through examples from my research and practice, I will shed light on how children's dominant sense affects them as babies when they learn to self-soothe and as toddlers when they begin to engage with their peers, moving from parallel play to more interactive play. You will learn specific tips on how to help quiet your child or how to encourage her to sleep in her own bed through the night.

But more important, I am going to offer you ways to better understand your child—and yourself—so that you can come up with your own solutions, sometimes immediately, sometimes through a bit of trial and error. I always remind my clients that it's parents who know their children best. So my advice can only be a starting point. It's important to keep in mind that coming up with the solutions that fit you and your child is a process and can take time, patience, and a bit of flexibility.

Before you get to the checklist that will enable you to figure out your child's dominant sense, I want to share with you a bit more about how I use information about the four sensory modes in my work with families, so that you will see just how useful this knowledge will be to you.

Why It's Important to Know
Your Child's Sense

Every one of us comes into the world with one sensory mode that is dominant, and that mode will continue to be dominant for the rest of our life. In other words, if we start out as visual, we remain visual, even if we eventually develop strength or aptitude in our other senses.

The more families I worked with, the more I understood how pervasive the influence of the dominant sensory mode is on a child's way of thinking, feeling, and reacting to situations. As soon as you are able to identify your child's dominant sense, you will see evidence of it everywhere—in how she wakes up in the morning, how she acts when she's tired, how she behaves when she's hungry, how she expresses and handles negative emotions, how she transitions to school or a play date, what learning strategies are most effective with her, and so on. Being aware of your child's dominant sense mode will transform your interactions with her. With your child's dominant sense mode as a point of reference, you will be able to offer her the kind of guidance that will give her the opportunity to succeed in all ways, on her own terms.

Let me share a couple of stories from one of the mothers I worked with in Los Angeles. Liz is a fortysomething mom of two daughters. Her seven-year-old daughter Marie is taste/smell and her four-year-old daughter Jess is auditory. Liz told me:

> Over the last two days, Jess has been home sick with some kind of slight stomach upset, but on the second day she begged to come out with me to do an errand. At first I just told her, "You're sick, you can't come—you might throw

up in the car." She kept pleading with me, and I would have given in but I was worried that she wasn't out of the woods yet and an outing would make her worse. So then I thought about what she had said to me when she made a case for staying home in the first place, which was that when she doesn't feel well all the noises in her day care hurt her head. So I said, "If you come out, all the traffic sounds and the honking horns that you hear in the car will make noises that are crunchy and loud. Remember how all those noises hurt your ears when you don't feel good?" And that was the end of the conversation. Jess just said, "Okay, Mom, I'll stay home." I couldn't believe how easy it was, but it made me realize how sensitive she is when she is under the weather. She really did need to be at home.

I used the same understanding of sense dominance when I tried to convince my older daughter, Marie, to eat a peanut butter and jelly sandwich for breakfast instead of the Pop-Tart she wanted. Being a typical taste/smell child, she has a very limited palate. Already on the edge of defiance, Marie said, "Well, if you don't let me have a Pop-Tart, then I am not going to eat anything." I could have made it a hard-and-fast rule that she couldn't have the Pop-Tart—and granted, there are times when we have to do that—but I wanted her to *want* to have the peanut butter and jelly, which I knew she liked anyway. So I said, with as little affect as possible, "Marie, this is what I am worried about: If you eat that sugary Pop-Tart, it will give you a lot of energy right away, but in two hours all that energy will fade away and you'll be telling your teacher you don't feel well. You'll be grumpy and unable to focus on your work, and you'll just want to put your head on the desk and go to sleep. That's what happened when you had too much cake at the birthday party last week, remember? Then your teacher will be disappointed in you and your friend Ella won't have anyone to play with at recess and she'll miss you."

Knowing that she's taste/smell, I was trying to appeal to her sensitivity to how others feel about her, especially her teacher, whom she really adores, and her best friend. And it worked. She agreed to have the peanut butter and jelly. To make her feel good about giving in, I thanked her and told her that over the weekend we'd go to the store and try to find a new cereal or other breakfast foods she liked so she'd have more to choose from in the morning. She was excited about getting to pick out her own food, and I felt she had learned an important lesson: that she is in charge of taking care of her own body, which I know will help her in the long run become a healthy eater.

As Liz did with her two daughters, parents can use their understanding of their child's dominant sense to guide their children to make better choices, whether these choices have to do with eating, going to sleep in their own beds, dressing more appropriately for the weather, or anything else that involves assuming more responsibility for themselves.

As you will see in the upcoming chapters, your child's sensory type impacts not just his day-to-day routines as he grows from infancy to his preschool years but also how he expresses his needs and manages his feelings. Furthermore, his dominant sense affects how he begins to learn about the world and how he plays and interacts with his peers. Again it's a win-win: Knowing your children's sensory orientation will help you be more clearheaded and effective as you guide your children through the many challenges of their early years, which in turn helps them feel more confident and self-assured as they make their way through the world.

One last word before you look over the checklists that will enable you to determine your child's dominant sense mode group: These groupings have nothing to do with innate intelligence or ability. There is no hierarchy of groups; no group is superior or inferior to any other group. Each group—tactile, auditory, visual, and taste/smell—has its geniuses and low performers, creative types, successes and failures, artists, entrepreneurs, doctors, lawyers, teachers, and truck drivers. It's important that you remember this so that you can be as honest and objective as possible as you go through the sense mode identification process.

Identifying Your Child's Sense

The first thing you should do is to read through all four of the group checklists to become familiar with the traits typical of each of the four sense categories (touch, hearing, sight, taste/smell). No matter what age your child is, read about how those characteristics manifest through all three of the age ranges (babies, from birth to age one; toddlers, ages one to three; and preschoolers, ages three to five). For example, if your child is now five, go through the baby and toddler stages as well as the preschool checklists, remembering how he was in his earlier years.

It's natural to want to figure out your child's dominant sense mode immediately, but you may get frustrated when you find yourself checking off characteristics in more than one category, making you feel that your child doesn't fall into any one group. So keep in mind that this is a process. Instead of trying to make a final determination about your child right away, give yourself time to read through each sense chapter, and then go back and revisit the checklists. If you take the time to go through the process gradually, you will soon find that definite patterns begin to emerge, and that the majority of your check marks eventually fall within one category.

Group One

Baby, from Birth to Age One
- Needs to be held all the time, and cries if you put her down
- Is particular about who holds her
- Won't fall asleep unless caregiver is holding or cuddling her
- Needs movement, such as rocking or swinging or being walked around in a stroller or infant carrier, to calm down
- When feeding, needs to self-comfort by touching a soft fabric, object, or—preferably—mother or father
- Isn't comfortable enough to play by herself unless in close physical proximity to caregiver
- Wants to touch, hold, or put in her mouth all objects in the vicinity, including her own and others' body parts
- Is not content just to look at objects or people but has to reach out and make physical contact
- During waking hours is very active
- Is calmed by being swaddled when going to sleep but needs to have at least one limb left free

Toddler, Ages One to Three
- Has to push, pull, touch, bite, or hold everything within reach

- Takes all his toys from the shelf or toy box but has a short attention span and plays with each one of them for only a brief period
- Pulls/pushes caregiver to come and play
- Shows emotions in a very physical manner by either hugging or pushing
- Loves to have friends visit but then gets overexcited and pushes or grabs at them
- Has difficulty sleeping alone
- Has tantrums that are very physical—stamps his feet, runs away, lies on the floor flailing his arms and legs
- Makes drawings that are fast and furious one-color scribbles that are intended to depict people engaged in various activities, such as Dad mowing the lawn, Mom cooking, big sister chasing the dog
- Prefers hands to cutlery when eating
- Smears food everywhere, including on face, hands, and body

Preschooler, Ages Three to Five

- Radiates mess
- Prefers "helping" over playing with toys
- Needs to be held and touched before going to sleep; still very cuddly and affectionate
- Finds it difficult to sit still and hard to resist touching, banging, and moving things around him
- Prefers finger foods
- Likes being able to move around while eating
- Loves physical games and anyone who plays them
- Makes drawings that still tend to be one-color, fast and furious scribbles of action-based scenes, but pays more attention

to trying to make them look like what they are intended to depict
- When bored or overstimulated, tends to become aggressive by either throwing things, pushing playmates, or trying to physically dominate the situation
- Is very social and likes to play in groups

If five or more traits within the appropriate age range describe your child, then your child's dominant sense is probably tactile. Tactile children experience the world physically. They need some sort of physical stimulation to acquire memory. It could be an outside stimulus such as being touched, or it could be self-created, such as crawling. If happy, they skip; if sad, they need a cuddle; if angry or excited, they push or shove. Tactile children tend to learn to walk and crawl earlier than children in the other sense groupings. Their fine motor skills also tend to be slightly ahead of their peers'. Tactile children need a lot of physical contact and support. Cuddling and physical touch are necessary for them to feel safe. They will often wish to sleep with their parents, as they don't like to be alone. And they tend to learn by doing.

Group Two

Baby, from Birth to Age One
- Startles at the slightest noise
- Wakes easily in response to a new sound
- Easily distracted from eating if fed in a noisy place
- Is happy to play by herself so long as she can hear her primary caregiver nearby

- Is relaxed about being held by strangers as long as she can hear her primary caregiver nearby
- Loves music and will listen intently
- Coos and sings when happy
- Tends to move in and out of routines with ease
- Eats well
- Tends to squeal and vocalize more than most kids, especially while being fed

Toddler, Ages One to Three
- Has tantrums that are very vocal—screaming, squealing, howling
- Seeks Mom's attention when she's on the telephone
- Can get overwhelmed or distracted in a noisy environment
- Notices sounds that those around her don't immediately hear
- Tends to wake at any unusual sound
- Sings, hums, and talks early
- Loves story time, particularly anything that rhymes
- Cries when voices are raised, even if not directed at her
- Enjoys repetition of sounds and words in recognizable patterns, like those in songs and simple rhymes
- Tends to make noise during feeding—banging, singing, chatting—and now eats better in a familiar, noise-filled environment

Preschooler, Ages Three to Five
- Prone to whining and complaining
- Enjoys singing to herself and having long conversations with her toys

- Draws in a circular, patterned motion that is rhythmic
- Loves having storybooks read to her, but tends to listen rather than look
- Has strong preferences in music and will have favorite songs
- Sensitive to tone of voice and may be vocal on the subject (i.e., "Mommy, I don't like it when you use your angry voice")
- Can be self-reliant and prefers to play alone, as long as she feels grounded by familiar sounds
- Doesn't like very noisy areas, especially rooms that echo or are unfamiliar
- Alternates between being very tidy at some times and wallowing in mess and clutter at others
- Needs a very regular nighttime routine for settling but still wakes very easily at any unusual sound

If more than five of the traits in the age-appropriate list describe your child, then his or her dominant sense is probably auditory. For auditory children sound is their first point of call for information about everything that makes up their environment—people, places, objects, and so on. They notice the tone of people's voices, like or dislike certain places because of the noise level, love experimenting with sound, and respond well to music. All feelings are either vocalized or, at older ages, verbalized: if they are angry, they shout; if sad, they cry loudly; and if happy, they laugh uproariously. The sequence of events is important to auditory children, who are always looking for order and patterns; they like to know the step-by-step progression of any activity and want to be told the schedule for the day. They are mathematical and logic-minded.

Group Three

Baby, from Birth to Age One

- Loves to watch Mom and Dad and see what's going on in the family
- Cries when she can't see her caregiver
- Shows a strong preference for people who are familiar or who have facial characteristics similar to her caregivers'
- Recognizes people or places by the facial features that set them apart (a beauty mark, small scar, bushy eyebrows, and so on), the clothing they wear, or details that you may never even have noticed (the broken shutter on the outside of a house, the little brass lamp on the end table, the red swings at a playground she's seen only once before, and so on)
- Eats better when she can see someone else eating, too
- Relies on sameness and day-to-day familiarity in her environment to fall asleep (e.g., the lighting needs to be at the same level whenever she is put down, the door open or closed just so, and her toys always put away in the same places) or else she will be distracted and may have trouble sleeping
- Enjoys playing alone as long as Mom is within sight
- Finds it hard to calm unless visual stimulation is minimized— for example, by your putting a cloth over her stroller or carriage before nap time
- Likes bright colors and may show a strong preference for toys, cups, and clothes in those colors
- Prefers to lie facing her mother or caregiver in her baby carriage, and when put in the stroller wants to face her caregiver whenever possible

Toddler, Ages One to Three

- Begins to show a preference for a favorite color
- Points at things and has to have Mom look before he moves on to a new task
- Likes to be within visual range of caregivers
- Tends to wander off when something catches his eye but will get upset if he loses sight of his mother
- Notices even subtle details about the physical characteristics of the world around him
- Groups objects according to size, shape, color, or other categories, which you may or may not be able to identify
- Plays with one toy at a time
- Easily distracted by visual stimuli and finds it difficult to fall asleep unless the level of stimulation is reduced
- Likes to observe before entering a strange environment
- Starts to show preferences in clothing

Preschooler, Ages Three to Five

- Has a favorite color
- Is fussy about how his food looks
- Doesn't like mess and keeps his room or play area tidy
- Lines up similar-looking toys, grouping them according to size, shape, and color, or according to some other criterion of his own devising
- Plays with one toy at a time and tends to put the toys away when finished
- Has definite views of what is appropriate for boys and girls to wear
- Has strong preferences in dress, and may become upset if not allowed to choose what he's wearing
- Prefers brightly colored toys

- Loves to look at books with lots of colorful pictures and can do so independently (even if he cannot yet read)
- Has strong pattern recognition skills

If five or more of the traits on the age-appropriate list describe your child, then his or her dominant sense is visual. Visual children relate to the world primarily through what they see. They learn by watching how you do things and imitating you. They tend to learn to read more easily than children with other dominant senses, and they respond well to flash cards. They are easily distracted by visual input from TVs, computers, crowds, clutter, and chaotic environments, as well as by any changes from what they are accustomed to. What they see is the message they get. If they see a face that looks angry, they get scared; a happy-looking face makes them happy, and so on. They tend to like order and enjoy organizing their toys by color, shape, size, or perhaps some other criterion of their own choosing that may be invisible to you.

Group Four

Baby, from Birth to Age One
- Prefers quiet, calm environments
- Is particular about maintaining regular routines around eating, sleeping, and bathing
- Fussy about any changes in the taste of food, including changes in the taste of breast milk because of foods the mother eats or the taste of a new brand of formula
- Will only eat (or nurse) in a calm environment
- Will not fall asleep unless things are just so

- Has a single favorite toy or object
- Seems deeply affected by caregiver's mood, much more than other infants are
- Tends to mirror parents' feelings about others
- Shows great preference for family members over friends
- Will cry when other babies cry or when Mom or Dad makes a sad face

Toddler, Ages One to Three

- Has very strong taste preferences and can be fussy about foods
- Can be viewed as oversensitive and is easily upset
- Cries if another child is crying
- Has a "best friend," either real (person or pet) or pretend (such as a doll or stuffed animal), or completely imaginary
- Tries to "fix" feelings in others (e.g., will hug Mom when she seems sad or make Dad a pretend cup of coffee if he seems tired)
- Appreciates gifts given to her by people she cares about, and will form an attachment to the gift as a result
- Plays caretaking games with dolls or stuffed animals
- Will dress like those she admires—whether it's a big sister or Dora the Explorer
- Can be clingy or shy in new situations
- Finds it hard to be away from those she loves

Preschooler, Ages Three to Five

- Draws or scribbles faces, especially those that she says depict family members, emphasizing the expression on the faces to communicate emotions
- Loves to dress up and role-play

- Loves stories about families, friends, and relationships
- Is intrigued with animals and likens them to people, looking after them and giving them personalities and human traits
- Is aware of others' feelings and tries to make sure everyone is okay
- Is resistant to change and adjusts slowly to a new routine or environment
- Dresses the same way that her friends do or in a style that makes her feel close to someone or part of a group
- Loves stuffed toys and dolls and will have a special "cannot lose" toy
- Is a fussy eater, is particular about brands, dislikes leftovers, won't mix flavors or tastes, and cannot focus on eating when upset or overly excited
- Can be hypersensitive to criticism, becoming very upset if scolded or punished, and throwing tantrums if she feels her feelings have been dismissed

If five or more of the age-appropriate traits listed above describe your child, then his or her dominant sense is probably taste/smell. These children seem to pick up information in an apparently unconscious way, as though through intuition, but part of what they are picking up on—for example, smell—is sense-based. Everyone emanates a scent, and these children often have strong responses to people's smells, which can influence their feelings about people—even though these smells may be so subtle that you and I might not notice them. These children instinctively divide people into good and bad, nice and nasty, and they can be quite intractable once they have made up their mind. There will be people they like and those they don't and not much in between.

.   .   .

Once you feel that you have gotten an accurate idea of your child's dominant sense mode, you can learn how to identify your own sense and that of your partner. Just as learning about your child's sense will help anchor your understanding of him, identifying your own sense will inform your understanding of how you yourself operate in the world. You'll be more aware of what makes you react positively or negatively, and this can help you figure out some of the triggers that may be causing conflict between you and your child (or, for that matter, between you and your partner). If, for example, it turns out that you are a visual person with a strong need for order and your child is tactile, with a tendency to generate a certain amount of physical mess and chaos wherever he is, being aware of these tendencies can lead you to develop some strategies that will work for both of you, such as creating a space in which your child is free to express himself but making the rest of the house out-of-bounds for his mess.

Identifying the sense groups into which you, your partner, and your child fall, and then understanding how powerful an influence these sensory orientations have on how all of you interact with one another, has the potential to truly transform your relationships.

THREE

Identifying Your Own Sense Mode

An unspoken but hugely important premise in my sense-oriented approach to working with families is that it empowers the parent. A corollary to that premise is that an empowered parent is a better parent. When we feel confident and at ease with ourselves, we can be much more patient, nurturing, and clear with our children. And if we are more at ease, then we can give more, nurture more, and love more.

We are inundated by information on how to raise our children and often obsessed with our children's success. The end result is that we often *overparent*. Of course we need to set up boundaries and guide our kids, but in this hypervigilant parenting climate it's hard to keep a balance. The techniques that emerge from an understanding of the four dominant senses and of how sense dominance affects not just your child but you will help smooth your interactions, allowing you to step back and give him the opportunity to be whoever he is, while still feeling confident that you are keeping him safe and giving him the guidance and boundaries he needs. You will also understand yourself better: You will begin to see how your sense orientation affects your own behavior and be able to monitor how it may be the source of certain kinds of problems in relation to your child.

Keep in mind that my approach to parenting is designed to create a win-win world for both you and your child. I believe all children need the guidance and boundaries that only a parent can give them, along with plenty of opportunities to grow into their own unique selves. Our job as parents—a task that we have only about fifteen years to accomplish, because after that behaviors become hardwired and much more difficult to influence—is to set up our children for success. During these years we need to enable them to become loving, trusting, self-confident people with all the qualities they need to develop their own potential to the fullest. I believe that good parenting comes less from discipline and more from positive and negative reinforcements of behavior. In other words, I don't set out to change a child's temperament or sensory style as much as to work with it, using positive and negative reinforcement to help the child slowly but surely understand that his actions have consequences and that he is responsible for how he behaves. You will see this philosophy at work again and again in the four chapters devoted to each of the four different sense modes (Chapters 4–7), which describe how you can come up with your own strategies for helping your child navigate both everyday situations and the developmental milestones that are part of every child's life.

Identifying Your Own Sense Mode

As you get more familiar with the traits and characteristics of each of the senses, your own underlying sensory orientation and how it influences how you do things in your life will become more clear. This clarity is a very important part of using this sensory information. The more objective you can be about the way you react to situations, your style of communicating, and how you approach the world in general, the calmer you will be able to remain when dealing with your child.

For example, if your dominant sense mode is tactile and your daughter is auditory, you might keep in mind that your tendency to show your impatience by speaking in a brusque manner might very well set off your auditory child, who is probably very sensitive to your tone of voice. By using a softer, gentler tone, you can direct your child more successfully. This sense-targeted approach to the problems that arise in daily life can be applied to a myriad of situations. You will find it easier to resist being pulled into the drama of your two-year-old's tantrum; you will be less likely to get upset when your three-year-old refuses to eat leftovers; you will be more tolerant of the noise and mess that seem to radiate from your four-year-old; and you will know how to stay calm, cool, and collected as you reassure your child that he will be safe and happy at preschool after you leave.

As you go through the following questionnaire, choose the descriptions that best reflect your behaviors and responses. Just as you might have experienced when you were determining your child's sense, you may at first be confused because you'll find yourself checking off traits in more than one sense category. As I recommended when you were going through the children's checklists, keep in mind that figuring out your own sense is a process that may take some time. It's actually quite natural at the beginning of this process to feel that you aren't able to fit neatly into one of the categories. Perhaps you aren't yet familiar enough with the categories, or perhaps you are so eager to discover an easy match between you and your child that your answers are being skewed and don't accurately reflect your natural inclinations. Many of my clients tell me that it's easier for them to figure out their partner's and their child's sense than their own. Not to worry. If you're feeling frustrated, you may want to skip to the next four chapters, where I describe how different sense orientations operate in daily life, and then return to the questionnaire. Sooner or later, everyone is able to figure out where they belong in these sense groupings and to put that knowledge to good use. You will too!

ADULT QUESTIONNAIRE

In going through the following questions, even if you find yourself being able to choose more than one response to each enumerated item, select the one that *most often* applies to you.

1. Your home is:
    a. Comfortable and kind of messy
    b. Very tidy, with rugs on the floor, curtains at the windows, and probably some great audio equipment
    c. Free of mess and clutter and decorated with great attention to style, harmony, and an overall design aesthetic
    d. Filled with personal mementos, photographs of people you love, and sentimental keepsakes

2. When you dress, you choose clothing:
    a. Because it's comfortable—walking or running shoes that are easy on the feet and let you walk for hours on end if you want to, clothes that let you breathe and are

designed for ease of movement, coats that you can get in and out of without a lot of effort

b. With very simple lines, in elegant, almost geometric styles

c. That shows your distinctive fashion sense and the careful attention you pay to color coordination and to accessories ranging from socks to belts, jewelry, and scarves

d. That reflects your emotional state that day, so your clothes fit your mood

3. You show affection for those you love or care about by:

a. Always saying hello and goodbye with a kiss or a hug, a pat on the shoulder or a warm handshake, and by actively trying to do things for them that make their lives more pleasant

b. Speaking lovingly, having long conversations on the phone

c. Expressing your feelings in letters or e-mails, in little notes that you stick in lunch boxes, or in carefully chosen greeting cards that you send even when there's not an occasion, and by establishing lots of warm eye contact when you're together

d. Depends on the person—you adapt your style to suit what you feel the person and the situation require

4. As a student you learned best:

a. Experientially, interactively, by using your hands

b. By listening to your teacher or a tape or a recording of a lecture

c. Through reading, writing, and memorization

    d. Through narrative or anecdotal explanations that brought ideas, time periods, and concepts alive for you

5. When you eat, you enjoy:
    a. Talking, laughing, and engaging with other people; but when mealtimes are not social events, you're inclined to just eat on the run without paying much attention to what you're eating or how it tastes
    b. A quiet atmosphere, in which you can talk one-on-one with people at the table and nobody talks over each other, with music soft enough not to interfere with conversation
    c. Being at a table that has been set with careful attention to the aesthetics of the dishes, glasses, silverware and napkins, and being served food that looks appealing, because a pleasant ambiance is always important to you
    d. Having a close, intimate dinner that lasts for a long time so that you can share this special ritual with someone you care about, especially if that person also loves food the way you do and is willing to experiment with new cuisines and new ingredients

6. When you socialize in the evening, you prefer:
    a. Boisterous, fun parties, going out dancing
    b. Musical events (as long as they're not too loud)
    c. Hip, happening places, such as the new cool bars and clubs, where you can dress up and see and be seen
    d. Close, one-on-one interaction—intimate conversation, dinner at the homes of friends

7. Your idea of relaxing is:
    a. Cuddling up with a loved one and watching a movie
    b. Lying around chatting with a good friend
    c. Reading a magazine or novel, preferably in a clean and tidy space
    d. Anything as long as it involves friends or family

8. Your optimal work environment is:
    a. An office where you can have a lot of camaraderie and interaction
    b. An office space which allows you to shut the door and control the noise and the socializing if they get to be overwhelming
    c. An organized, clutter-free work space
    d. An office space that feels warm, friendly, welcoming

9. Your idea of a perfect vacation is:
    a. A trip that involves a lot of activity, whether it's walking all over a city, or hiking, mountain climbing, bicycling—anything that is very physical and also preferably very social
    b. A city trip in which you go to a concert, enjoy the liveliness of city streets, and chat with the people you encounter
    c. A trip that involves foreign travel, so you can visit the museums, take scenic drives, and immerse yourself in the sights of a new and different place
    d. Any trip or vacation that allows you to be with your family in a setting where you can talk and catch up and just be together, or that gives you intimate time with your partner

10. How would you describe the way you manage time?
    a. You're not that organized but you like to get things done
    b. You prioritize, and you have a schedule you try to keep to
    c. You are very organized and like to plan out your day, week, month, and year, keeping a record or diary of your schedule
    d. You don't usually plan that much in advance, preferring to be flexible enough to accommodate yourself to other people's schedules, which means that you may find it hard to find time for your own needs

11. If you were to buy a new car, the most important aspect of your decision would be:
    a. Utility—you tend to choose cars for their ample size, large amount of storage space, passenger capacity, an easy-to-read dashboard, and the powerfulness of the car's engine
    b. Its engineering—you prefer cars that are designed for their agility and quietness on the road, superior sound system, and overall placement of the car's seats, mirrors, and drink holders
    c. Its aesthetic design—your car needs to look good, with appealing design both inside and outside, an attractive color, and overall look, even if it means less practicality or comfort
    d. No strong preference—you might follow the suggestion or preference of your partner, or someone else you admire; you tend to have a difficult time making up your mind

12. You can tell if your partner or friend is upset by:
   a. His body language
   b. His tone of voice
   c. The look on his face
   d. Just a feeling that something is not right with him

13. What type of children's behavior annoys you the most?
   a. The way they jump all over you
   b. The noise they make, squealing, crying, shouting, interrupting
   c. The mess they create
   d. Bad manners, even when you know they don't mean to be rude

14. The way you feel most comfortable showing your love and affection to your kids is by:
   a. Cuddling, touching, and doing things with the kids
   b. Involving them in activities, giving them opportunities to learn and master skills
   c. Making them meals, cleaning up after them, and making sure their physical needs are met
   d. Letting them lead you with their desires, trying to respond to all their demands and wishes

What Your Responses Mean

If you answered mostly with *a*'s, then your dominant sense mode is probably Tactile. The tactile adult is practical, goal-driven, and action-oriented. She tends to be very active in a physical way. She might be adventurous and/or athletic and tends to be happiest when in motion. When tactile people can't move around as much as they like, they get fidgety because it's unnatural for them to be still for any length of time. So they might twirl their hair, tap their feet, or drum their fingers on a table, often without even being aware that they're doing so (sometimes noticing only when someone else in the room complains). The tactile person isn't bothered by mess or clutter and doesn't mind if the piles start building up in her house, and even if in a flurry of activity she swoops in and does some housecleaning, chances are that within a few hours she'll have generated some more mess. She is the person who walks through the front door and kicks off her shoes, leaving them right in the line of traffic, then drapes her coat over the nearest chair. Rather than sit down and relax after a day's work, she might need to start cooking, going through bills, or gardening, because what works best to relax her is more activity. As a parent, the tactile adult can be both easygoing and impatient. On one hand, she is understanding of a child's noise, mess, or general roughhousing, but on the other hand, the tactile parent might be a bit impatient and brusque in her manner of interacting with her children.

If you answered mostly with *b*'s, then your dominant sense mode is probably Auditory. The auditory adult is very analytical and logical. She can be quite chatty when she is relaxed but tends to be quiet when distracted or stressed out. She might rely on music to relax her. (One parent I know walks around her house with her iPod in her ears, tuning out the noise of the kids and household.) The auditory parent can be quite patient, as she will approach problem solving with her kids in a methodical manner. For this reason, her kids will rely on her to help them do their homework, solve a problem, or make a decision. However, auditory adults are not that sensitive to the feelings of others, as they rely more on their intellect than their emotional experience as a way of interacting with others, so their children may not find it helpful to confide in them. They can also be a bit judgmental without really meaning to be. But since they have high expectations of themselves, they unwittingly apply these same standards to their children.

If you answered mostly with *c*'s, then your dominant sense mode is probably Visual. Visual adults are very orderly and organized—with their time, in their homes, and in their careers. To relax, they will often tidy up their house, put things away, do laundry, and so on. They are very clear on how things should be done and often try to influence other people's actions, behaviors, and schedules (especially when the people involved are their partners and their children). They like their homes to be clean and neat; they often spend considerable energy decorating their personal space and choosing clothes or outfits for themselves and their children (and sometimes their partners too). They are conscious of always wanting to look their best, and they want their children to look good as well. Visual adults are routine-oriented and resistant to any changes to their plans; they therefore find it hard to be spontaneous, whether with their children, friends, or partners.

If you answered mostly with *d*'s, then your dominant sense mode is probably Taste/Smell. The taste/smell adult is still a very sensitive soul who relies on her intuition to read people. Very attuned to how others are feeling, she can pick up and reflect back the feelings or moods of those around her, especially those she cares about. Her house is comfortable, reflecting everyone else's preferences. As a parent, she will tend to let her children's needs trump her own. She may have to make a conscious effort to set aside the time and space she needs so that she doesn't become completely drained by the demands of her children, who may take advantage of their overcaring parent. But this is also the parent to whom a child can confide anything, knowing that her parent will never judge her.

As you become more familiar with your child's dominant sense in the chapters ahead, more than likely you will also become more in tune with your own dominant sense. Keep in mind too that we all have a secondary sense, which is usually a reflection of a parent's dominant sense. Sometimes this sense orientation may seem like our dominant sense when in fact it's something we developed as a way to get along with our own parent or caregiver. For instance, if you are tactile but were raised by a visual mother, you might find yourself being just as tidy as your mom was— *because* your mom was and expected you to be too. As in this example, these learned behaviors can sometimes mask our dominant sense. Though these behaviors are usually habits that we picked up in response to the person who raised us, they might also reflect the habits of our partner, especially a partner we've been with for a long time.

The Mismatch Challenge

If you differ in sense mode from your child, this is what I call a mismatch. I first learned about this concept through the researchers at Brown, who applied it to mothers' varying perceptions of and reactions to their babies' crying. Some mothers were not as bothered as other mothers by their babies' incessant crying. Those mothers who were highly agitated by their babies' rather normal crying were explained to me as being "mismatched" with their child. I've adapted this use of "mismatch" to refer to those instances when a parent and a child have different sense modes, resulting in some kind of gap in communication or overall behavioral style.

Certain mismatches are more bothersome than others. As mentioned earlier, if you are visual, and your child is tactile, you're likely to get upset by his tendency to create a mess. If you are taste/smell and your child is tactile, his mess will not bother you nearly as much. However, if you are taste/smell and your child is auditory, I wouldn't be surprised if your child seems cold to you and often hurts your feelings with his seemingly insensitive use of words or ability to tune you out. When you keep in mind that you and your child probably have different dominant senses and therefore different orientations in the world, you will take things less personally and be able to parent without so much emotional baggage.

Here's an example: Let's say that you are visual and your two-year-old child is tactile, and mealtimes have always been a low point in your day. Tonight you've carefully prepared a meal of pasta and vegetables and arranged it in a colorful, appetizing way on your son's favorite plate, placing beside it a new Elmo fork on a matching napkin. As soon as he takes a look at his meal, he puts his fingers through the food, spreading it across his plate and onto the table. You're frustrated because he hasn't used his fork and he's made a mess that looks disgusting, while he's delighted because he's made a mess that feels great.

Can you pause for a moment and not react to the mess that your tactile toddler has created and instead keep in mind that playing with his food is very much in his nature, a crucial part of how he experiences the world? Can you also consider managing both meal preparation and eating in a slightly different way? If I told you that your child would probably eat better and be less distracted if you gave him finger foods and allowed him to eat more with his hands, might you be convinced to give him that freedom rather than trying to encourage the use of a fork before he is ready?

Here's another example: If your two-year-old is auditory and you are tactile, you may notice that you are easily irritated by your child's constant chatter while in the car. You prefer to drive in relative silence, and your child's frequent questions and need for conversation can bother you, distracting you from what you think of as time to get yourself mentally ready for the day ahead. You also may notice that at times your quick and/or blunt response to your child's questions causes her to burst into tears. As a tactile person, you are eminently practical and can be a bit blunt in your declarations. Of course, you don't mean any harm, but your auditory child, who is sensitive to your tone of voice, doesn't know that—she needs to hear your care and tenderness through your voice.

By keeping in mind your child's dominant sense mode, you can be more understanding of the motivation behind your child's behavior, and once you understand, you might choose to make a simple adjustment that addresses the underlying problem rather than chastising him or trying to change him. There are often constructive compromises that can work for both of you. I have seen again and again that even small changes can make a dramatic difference. Daily life becomes smoother and less fraught, with many fewer tantrums and fights. But this requires a certain openness and willingness on your part to try to do things a bit differently. So as you read through the next set of chapters, in which the four dominant senses are described and brought to life in more detail, try to also keep in mind your own sense. At the end of each sense chapter is a section devoted to mismatches for that dominant sense. Use this information to help you troubleshoot your own dynamic with your child or help you understand your partner (who may have a different sense from both you and your child) and his relationship with your child.

PART TWO

The Four Senses

FOUR

The Tactile Child

hildren who are tactile "live in their bodies" in the fullest sense of the phrase. They romp, throw, dive, and climb. They wiggle and flop and flail. In a tactile child, happiness brings about joyful bouncing, boredom induces an epic slouch, and anger elicits a kicking, arm-wheeling tantrum. If you want to know how a tactile child is feeling, his body language will tell you in no uncertain terms.

We all know one of these vivacious, breathtakingly active children—and perhaps you have one of your own. This is the child who bursts into a room and wraps himself around your leg for a hug and a squeeze before peeling away in search of his next conquest, be it another grown-up's limb to climb, a fellow child to wrestle, or the family dog to cuddle within an inch of its life. This is the child who tears apart your couch and empties your linen closet to build a pillow-and-blanket fort in the middle of your living room, then begs you to crawl inside with her. This is the child who, when he sees you preparing his favorite meal, will actually wriggle with excitement or break into a comic dance. If, on the other hand, you've made something "icky" for dinner, you'd better duck, because a handful of creamed spinach may soon be hurtling in your direction.

Tactile children are rough-and-tumble kids, brimming with energy and verve. Boisterous and bold, these children seem to be in constant motion. They don't typically like to sit still for long, since there's always a new game or activity to throw themselves into with abandon. The sheer amount of physical energy tactile children unleash upon the world around them can sometimes be overwhelming and a little bewildering to parents. All this activity, however, is not simply an unfocused release of energy, nor is it aimless play. Far from it. From infancy onward, the tactile child makes sense of his world through physical contact and exploration. That whirling dervish spinning in circles around your house is reaching out to the world, teaching himself about his environment, and trying to communicate his feelings and his needs.

Tactile children are very practical and treat their own feelings—and those of others—with a no-nonsense directness. Sometimes they can be unaware of the inappropriateness of saying certain things out loud. In other words, they have few secrets and are so honest that they don't know how to dissemble, simply blurting out whatever is on their minds. This trait can be quite charming—unless, of course, what's on their minds is anger or frustration, or you hear them echoing your own negative feelings, repeating something unpleasant you've just said about your next-door neighbor at the very moment the neighbor walks through the door. Since these are not introspective or sensitive kids, they have little concern for how their words are received and will not notice that they've just insulted someone.

Building the self-esteem of the tactile child is quite a straightforward affair: All you have to do is give her a project to work on or a mission to accomplish (making sure, of course, that it is something she is capable of achieving). These kids absolutely love helping. Incredibly messy as they may be, trailing cookie crumbs, clothes, and toys in their wake, they'll also be the children who will be delighted to pitch in to clean up. For tactile children, cleaning time can often be part of playtime, as I've taught many a frustrated parent.

This was actually the motivating factor one mom used to toilet-train her son. Ian wanted to clean the toilet with the scrub brush he found in the bathroom, and his mom, Erica, said, "If you use it, then you can clean it." Ian just loved that project! If you set aside the hygiene aspect of the toilet, you can see that for a child it could just seem like a water play station. (Of course, if you let your child use it that way, then you need to have cleaned and disinfected it beforehand.)

As you read more about how tactile children express themselves, you will gain insight into what makes these children tick so that you can help them manage and master all their everyday activities, from eating to sleeping, dressing, playing, learning, and socializing. Being tactile is not just about using their hands. Tactile children explore with their whole bodies, and this includes mouths and tongues as well as hands. Biting, sucking, licking, sticking stuff in their ears, and putting elbows in all sorts of places is par for the course with these kids. For example, if Mom buys an exercise ball, the kid will kick it, throw it, lie on it, and try to do a headstand on it—anything his little imagination conjures up that involves some kind of physical exploration of the ball and its potential for motion and fun. One child with whom I worked went through a stage of touching everything with his eyelashes. We called these fairy kisses. Once we labeled it, he felt permission to express himself this way.

Tactile Baby Basics, from Birth to Age One

How the Tactile Baby Expresses Emotional Needs

Caring, reassuring, gentle touch is crucial for all babies. Indeed, loving physical contact is the first, most elemental form of communication between parent and child. Think back to those first days with your newborn and the quiet, special time you spent cradling him in your arms. You and he began your bonding journey together in this way. When you held your baby close to you, you transmitted a flood of positive messages to him, which communicated your love and let him know he was safe and cared for. Though this physical communication is important for all children, for the tactile child, it marks the beginning of a lifetime of navigating the world through touch.

Because babies who are tactile more than likely will want to be carried all the time and may also be quite particular about who carries them, this probably means you: Your tactile baby will tend to prefer you to anyone else, even a friendly babysitter or a gentle grandparent. Because they rely so much on physical contact to ground, calm, and orient themselves in their surroundings, the familiar touch is the best and most reassuring touch to a baby who is tactile. While a visual baby might feel safe, soothed, and content if he can see Mom nearby, and an auditory child will be reassured by the sound of Mom's voice within earshot, not so the tactile child. Mothers of these children will know what I'm talking about when I say that our tactile babies simply can't get enough of being held. Breaking the physical connection is difficult for these children, which is why they usually scream to high heaven when we put them down. This period of near-constant carrying can take its toll on parents (as I remember from the early days of my own parenting experience).

So many moms of tactile babies come to me with the complaint that they are exhausted from having to hold them for such long periods of time. And this doesn't end after the early days of infancy. "I can't believe how much my child needs to be in my arms," said Amy, whose nine-month-old son, Mark, is a classic tactile child. Amy arrived at my doorstep feeling stressed out and anxious over how best to handle her son, who seemed only to want to burrow in her lap or wrap himself across her chest and shoulders. She worried that he was too clingy and that he wasn't developing on schedule. She also worried that his aversion to being held by others was a sign of a reticent personality in the making.

In addition to her worries for Mark, she was under a lot of strain herself, not only physically but mentally. The physical toll of holding and carrying her son so much of the time left her feeling tired, achy, and lacking in energy; it also made her irritable and impatient with her baby. "It was one thing when he was an infant," Amy sighed. "I had no problem carrying him around in his sling, and I felt fine. But he's getting bigger and heavier, and I'm in pain a lot. Sometimes I just need a break, and I honestly don't know how to get one."

She felt trapped between two extremes, and neither seemed right to her: either tote her ever-growing boy around in her arms all day long, or try to retrain him by not picking him up when he cried for her and contend with both his cries and her own guilt.

First I sought to relieve Amy's worries about Mark's development. Her baby's need for physical contact was not a developmental deficiency; rather, he was reaching out for reassurance through touch in the way that any tactile baby would do. At nine months, Mark was old enough to recognize his mother and to feel a deep attachment to her, but not old enough to understand that his connection to her would persist even when they weren't in physical contact. More so than his peers with different dominant senses, Mark was expressing his attachment to his mother and need for emotional grounding through his constant need for physical contact. (You will read more about how Amy addressed these issues with Mark in the pages ahead.)

How the Tactile Baby Discovers the World

Babies will spend the first months of their lives in a process of discovery that is very much rooted in their bodies. For tactile babies, this process of discovery is especially important and profound. As their motor skills develop and they start to discover what their bodies can do, they begin to exercise their dominant sense, which will guide them and ground them as they grow.

For tactile children, their bodies, especially their hands, are their means to engage with the world. All babies grab things, of course, often grasping not just objects but people. However, more so than other children, tactile babies reach out to and grab at anything within their reach. They seem to possess a basic need to touch, pry, and wrangle an object as an instinctive way of trying to understand it. Fair warning: These babies routinely send fingers straight into the eyes of those who bring their faces close for a kiss, a coo, or a nuzzle.

From their earliest experiments with language, babies will rely on their dominant sense to help them grasp both the mechanics and the meaning of language. Some children take more easily to language than others because, I believe, some sensory preferences lend themselves to language development more naturally than others. An auditory baby may squeal and babble at you, and a visual baby may be content to lie still and watch you as you talk to him. But tactile children are most comfortable and secure using body language to express themselves, so often these kids are late to talk. Instead of learning a few words by age one and beginning to form sentences by age two, they may alarm you by their failure to utter more than a few words, but then amaze you by suddenly starting to talk a blue streak once they reach their second birthday or shortly thereafter. With these children, it is best to use every opportunity to connect language to tangible objects. Encourage your baby to reach out—to touch her toys, a bowl of fruit on the kitchen table, leaves hanging on trees in your backyard—as you talk to her and she babbles back at you.

Again, children understand language before they are able to speak it. At about the time your child is speaking his first words—typically around his first birthday—he'll also be able to understand basic commands and requests. This transition marks a major milestone in your child's development and in your relationship. By appealing to your child's dominant sense whenever possible, you can communicate more clearly with him and help him learn to take direction from you. For example, when you tell your tactile child to pick up his spoon, hand him the spoon as you speak the words; don't just place the spoon in front of him, thinking he'll get your message. In general he will always be able to understand you more easily if you can find a way to communicate your message through some kind of physical means. Tactile children also need to be spoken to in the most concrete language, so they hear a simple, straightforward message that is expressed loudly and clearly. Some parents have reported to me that when they keep a "poker face," showing little emotion or affect (no smiles or frowns, no raised eyebrows), they are even more effective at communicating with their tactile children.

How the Tactile Baby Begins to Play and Interact

As they move from being newborns into more advanced baby-hood (around five or six months of age), tactile babies will especially love games that are played with their hands and even their feet. Textured toys, such as soft blocks and balls, will stimulate your tactile baby's curiosity and capture her attention. Even before she is old enough to hold a toy on her own, she will respond to the texture of the material if you place a nubby toy in her grasp or rub a soft cloth block gently on her tummy.

As they grow and develop more independence, tactile children tend to be quite social. But early on these cuddle machines want nothing more than to be held by you. In the case of Amy and her son, Mark, we tried to figure out how to solve two problems at once: get some relief for her aching back and exhaustion and find some ways to encourage Mark to be less clingy and more sociable. At nine months, Mark was sitting upright, sometimes with support and sometimes on his own. We decided that rather than having Mark sit directly in her lap during playtime, Amy would try stretching out on the floor with the baby in front of her. I suggested she bring cushions down to the floor, both for the baby to crawl on and for her to stretch out on. This way, she would be comfortable and supported, and Mark could feel her next to him and be able to have physical contact with her if he needed to. But he could also venture away from her to explore and play, knowing that he could get back to her whenever he wanted.

Amy discovered that making use of floor time with her baby brought about a couple of big and very welcome changes. First, she was surprised to see her baby happily crawling over cushions and playing on his own. "He'll start out pretty much on top of me, but then something will catch his attention and he'll go off on his own a bit. He definitely needs to check in with me physically a lot, but he's also playing a little bit more independently too, which really encourages me."

Second, Amy felt some relief from the pressure she'd placed on herself to solve the problem she thought existed between her and her son. As I so often see happen, Amy's willingness to look at the situation from her son's point of view, combined with a few small adjustments, brought about great rewards for both parent and child. "It makes a big difference for me to know that he's not rejecting the outside world by staying close to me," Amy said. "It's just his way of grounding himself so he can explore."

Amy's clingy baby is likely to grow into a sociable little boy, I reassured her, one who attracts many friends at day care or preschool and thrives in group activities, such as team sports. Tactile children are not solitary by nature, and once they grow out of their need to be in constant contact with their primary caregiver, they will always gravitate toward a crowd. Amy can look forward to the day when her son begins to branch out from his exclusive attachment to her, usually at around two or three years old. The key is to give him the emotional reassurance he needs by responding positively and supportively to his longing for physical contact. Then he'll eventually be able to go out into the world and tumble around the playground with his peers, enjoying himself in his very physical and action-oriented way.

The Everyday Life of the Tactile Baby

Sleeping

Tactile babies, like most babies at one time or another, do not always go to bed quietly or readily. Being separated from Mom and Dad makes the crib a pretty unappealing place to a tactile child. A tactile baby may fall asleep in Mom's arms only to wake again, with great protests, when placed in his crib. Staying with your tactile child for a while at bedtime or nap time, placing your palm on his tummy or allowing him to grasp your finger, can help relax him so that he falls asleep more easily. Tactile babies are also greatly helped by being swaddled, as long as they have a leg or arm free. If you don't swaddle, when you place your baby under a blanket or other coverlet, make sure not to tuck it in too tightly, so that he's able to move or kick, which he likes. Remember, these children need to move around a lot even when asleep.

I know many parents of tactile children who opt to have their baby sleep in the bed with them. This provides the kind of physical closeness that tactile babies relish, and can be a positive solution for parents and child alike. If you are not comfortable with co-sleeping, however, you can put a small crib or mattress on the floor near your own bed. If that still is not right for you and your family, you might try to work more cuddle time into your bedtime routine so your child can get his fill of the physical closeness he needs to feel safe enough to drop off to sleep. Some parents have found that a rocking motion also helps to settle the baby.

Since they are so active, tactile babies will tend to fall deeply asleep and stay asleep once they finally drop off. There is no in-between. One minute your child may be eating or playing happily, and the next minute you will turn around and see him slumped over in his high chair, sound asleep. This means that if your baby is tired, he will go to sleep very quickly. But if he's not tired, don't even bother trying to get him to sleep. It won't happen. One thing you can do to encourage sleep, however, is to allow your tactile baby a brief period of activity at night or nap time to give him a chance to express his last bit of energy to wind down and calm himself before dropping off. If something does wake him from a deep sleep, he may then need another settling period to help him fall back to sleep.

Feeding

Feeding time for babies who are tactile is prime time for the close physical contact that they crave so deeply. The whole time you're holding and feeding your baby, you are sending him a host of loving messages via your touch, messages that reinforce his sense of security and well-being in your care. While breast-feeding or bottle-feeding, tactile babies will nestle close and may need to grasp your hand or touch you elsewhere. This additional contact soothes the tactile baby, reassures him that he is safe, and allows him to concentrate on feeding.

At around six months, you'll likely be starting to introduce solid foods to your baby's diet and to feed him in a high chair. Hang on, dear moms and dads, because your tactile baby is likely to have a lot of strong feelings about food and what to do with it—namely, digging into it with those ever-active hands in order not just to eat but to play. Spoons will be left untouched in favor of rooting around with fingers in all manner of meals, from cereal to pudding. As much as they will respond to the taste and especially the texture of foods in their mouths, tactile babies will want to feel their food before tasting. This can make mealtimes messy, of course, but keep in mind what is driving this behavior: From your tactile baby's perspective, this contact with his food is an important, even necessary part of the experience of eating.

One mom I worked with was trying to teach her six-month-old baby to eat from a spoon, but he seemed resistant. As the mother explained to me, "The spoon was just another thing for him to play with; he didn't seem to connect the idea of eating and the spoon." I made the simple suggestion that she place interesting toys in front of him on his high chair tray while she fed him. She explained that she had already tried distracting her son with toys. When I asked her to describe the toys, she said they were mostly picture books. I suggested that she try more tactile toys, such as small animals with nubby textures or illustrated books with varying textured surfaces for him to touch.

About two weeks later, the mom called me to report: "I started to engage him more with toys, which keeps his hands full while I am feeding him. Now he seems to find breakfast time fun. What a change! Feeding time used to be a nightmare."

Again, don't be surprised if your tactile baby resists using a fork or spoon, even when he nears his first birthday. If that is the case, there is nothing wrong with letting him forgo utensils in favor of using his fingers for a while longer. He'll let you know when he's ready to try to eat with a spoon or fork. Until then, try to relax, knowing that it is very common for tactile children to be late in mastering cutlery, even though their fine motor skills are often well developed.

When they do get around to putting some food in their mouths instead of just playing with it on their plates, tactile children will respond strongly to the texture of food, much more so than to taste. The consistency of food matters a great deal to tactile kids. In general, tactile children tend to prefer foods that are firm rather than runny, thick and creamy rather than thin. If your tactile baby is anything like mine was, he will want his peas and carrots smooth rather than chunky and will only eat applesauce that is pureed rather than full of apple bits. But be prepared to tune in to his individual preferences, whatever they are, because they could be the exact opposite of my child's likes and dislikes. Every child is different.

In terms of getting your tactile baby used to and comfortable with sitting still in his high chair, I suggest not placing him in the chair until you are ready to feed him, and then keeping the feeding time short and sweet. Any extra time spent in the confinement of the chair may exacerbate his desire to wriggle free, making the task of feeding more challenging than it needs to be.

Dressing and Diapering

When it comes to dressing a tactile baby, the texture of the fabrics your child wears and the fit of the clothes will matter a great deal to him. However, since he's not able to tell you his preferences, it's up to you to try to figure them out, experimenting until you understand what pleases him and what makes him fidget or fret. One likely cause for irritation is any kind of clothing that limits his movement or constricts the body. Thus clothes with elastic cuffs may annoy your tactile baby, who very much wants and needs freedom to flap those hands and feet. If you see him squirming and looking uncomfortable, you'll know why. Mittens or booties that are too snug will have the same effect. In general, tactile babies do not like close-fitting clothes, preferring clothes that are roomy and gentle on the skin. In fact, tactile children tend to prefer their clothes a size bigger than they actually need. They will want any labels or tags cut out, so nothing scratches their skin, and won't like wool or any other fabric that is itchy. They prefer lightweight cottons and fleeces. Your child may also be sensitive to the detergent you use to do the laundry, in which case you may need to switch to a brand that contains no perfume, dyes, or fabric softener, and you may also need to rinse his clothes twice.

Diapering a tactile baby can be a bit of a challenge because tactile babies wriggle a lot. I often suggest that, rather than fight the wriggling, parents change their baby on the floor, where he can't roll off a high surface and fall. You might also want to give your baby something interesting to hold on to and play with while diapering is going on. Keep a bucket of little toys nearby so you can have a ready supply of diversions.

Outings

However much they like to be held in Mom's arms, tactile babies also like to explore, and consequently they tend to resist anything that constricts their movement. This can make traveling with tactile babies a challenging task because they often hate riding in a stroller, which from their point of view has two strikes against it: the physical separation from Mom or Dad and the limits it puts on their physical freedom. These babies will often try to escape their strollers and will scream if you keep them confined—whether in a stroller, a high chair, a playpen, or a car seat—for too long. Short stroller trips might be more manageable for these babies, and often parents of these children opt to minimize the time spent in strollers and instead use carriers such as slings or baby backpacks, which provide that all-important physical contact and can make daily outings more peaceful for everyone.

Obviously car seats have the same disadvantages as strollers as far as the tactile child is concerned. Wrangling a tactile baby into a car seat can be quite a challenge as she wriggles and squirms, objecting to being separated from you. In this case, a little planning can help: Tactile babies are best placed so that a parent or sibling can hold their hand and reassure them throughout the journey.

Tactile Toddler Basics, from Ages One to Three

How the Tactile Toddler Communicates and Manages Emotions

In order to feel emotionally grounded, tactile children need to be nurtured by being held and caressed, and they need to be reassured with a cuddle and a kiss when they are frightened or upset. As toddlers become more independent, it's natural that we hold them much less than when they were babies, so we may forget how much they still need physical contact with us. It is easy to fall into a pattern of communicating with them using words and gestures more than touch, especially if our own orientation is not predominantly tactile. An auditory or a visual child may respond well to these kinds of communication. In the case of a tactile child, however, a pat on the back, a gentle squeeze, or a brief snuggle in your lap will go further than a kind word to help him understand that he is safe.

Sarah, who was visual, came to see me to help sort out what to do with her very affectionate, very tactile three-year-old son, Andrew. "Andrew was always coming into the bedroom and wanting to snuggle up to me; or if I was sitting on the sofa having a cup of tea he would constantly want to sit on me. Wherever we were, he would want to touch me. He'd try to hold on to my leg while I was walking and grab my hand when I was driving. It was making me crazy!" Sarah exclaimed. "While it was all very sweet, I started to feel smothered and was getting frustrated with him always wanting to be on top of me."

After we worked out a few strategies that I thought might help with the intensity of her son's need for affection and physical closeness, Sarah reported back to me about how things were going.

"Rather than getting busy as soon as I get home from work, I have organized my schedule so that I sit with him for a little while, or do something with him that involves a lot of contact, before I move on to preparing dinner or cleaning the house. By spending that time with him and giving him the attention he wants when I've been away from him all day, I can help him relax so that after a while he doesn't have to have so much physical reassurance from me. Then he feels safe enough to play by himself for a time, though usually he stays in the same room with me.

"Though not everything has changed, things are better," Sarah continued. "He still wants a lot of physical contact, but now that I understand that this is what he needs to feel safe, I don't feel as smothered as I did. I am aware that if he has been away from me during the day, he will need a good hour of 'mom time,' just cuddling and holding hands, before he'll go and play on his own, so I simply factor in the time. This has been the greatest benefit to me. Once I identified his dominant sense and was able to understand how it affects the way he interacts with the world, I stopped being annoyed by his clingy behavior and started giving him concentrated doses of what he needed. Now I'm able to fill his 'tactile barrel,' so to speak, and he is more self-assured; the clinging is less of a problem for both of us."

One of the primary developmental tasks of toddlers is to begin to manage their emotions and their behavior when they are facing challenges. This is a huge endeavor, and progress is likely to be very slow and gradual. For tactile children, who have such a deep connection to their bodies, it's often necessary for them to move around physically and be active in order to process their feelings. For the most part, these eminently practical children don't get bogged down by their emotions. However, when confronted with a situation that frightens or frustrates them, they may have trouble verbalizing their feelings and may act out instead. This is particularly likely to happen when they are on overload—when they are tired, hungry, overstimulated (perhaps from having had too much sugar), or all three. If you think his acting out is related to being on physical and emotional overload, it's best to try calming and comforting him with a gentle pat on the shoulder or a warm hug. On the other hand, if the bad behavior seems to be more intentional or a result of his boisterous physicality, the most effective way to stop the behavior is by speaking as simply and directly as possible: "Stop jumping on the couch now."

Of course, it's always possible that neither of these forms of intervention will work. We've all been witness to the resulting meltdowns. Tactile kids can really throw a tantrum! This is their way of telling you that they are angry, overwhelmed, and feeling unable to handle whatever is happening. We have to be careful not to expect too much in the way of self-control from these kids. This is not to say that we can't step in to help them so that they don't have a tantrum in the first place. There is usually a window of opportunity to intervene before a full-blown tantrum erupts. Generally the tantrum will be triggered by some action that threatens to impede the tactile child's freedom of movement or choice, so under these circumstances you'll want to be on the alert for the telltale signs of an imminent explosion. For example, you've just asked him not to play with the flowers in the vase on the coffee table, or you've told him it's time to leave the party, or it would be nice to share his toy with another child, and you can see that he's on the verge of losing it. When you see your child resisting—digging in his heels as you try to pull him away, or holding on to something you've asked him to relinquish—you may be able to distract him, especially if you can think of a way to give him something to do and keep him moving. For example, you might say, "Will you hold the keys while we walk to the car?" or "Do you want to race to the door?"

One mother was in the supermarket with her tactile child, trying to distract him from grabbing the magazines from the rack while she was unloading her groceries onto the conveyor belt at the checkout. At first, she tried to take the magazines away from her son, which of course only made him more upset. She could see he was about to erupt. Then she had the bright idea of trying to distract him by telling him that she needed him to help by handing her things from the cart so that they could get home faster. Of course, this actually slowed things down a bit, but he was delighted to have a job to do, especially one that involved touching everything, and they got out of the store without a tantrum.

If, however, a tantrum has already started, you might try tickling your child or doing something else that is playful in a physical way. As a last resort, simply walking away may get his attention. Your tactile child will not want to be physically separated from you, so he is likely to run after you, which switches his focus from whatever it was that provoked the tantrum to you and his need to be reunited with you. Once he catches up to you, he will tend to throw himself at you for a reassuring hug. When that happens, you should always offer the positive physical attention he craves, rather than withholding it.

When a tantrum erupts, don't throw your own tantrum in response. We need to dial back our own emotional response when our child is turning up the volume on his. In dealing with tactile children, you need to remain calm so that you can calm your child down. As you might expect, tactile children's tantrums are very physical. They throw themselves on the ground with arms and legs kicking. Things get thrown, toys are turned over, and a general whirlwind of physical fury is released. In such situations, it's best to quell his uproar by communicating with him in short, simple directives: "That's enough. We're leaving." The tactile child needs to hear from you exactly what you want him to do. Again, as a last resort, removing yourself from the scene will surely get his attention. Once he begins to calm down, a good long hug might be a very effective way of helping him process his feelings. He won't want to talk about why he is crying or what happened to make him upset. But he will feel "all better" once you connect with him in a physically warm and supportive way.

How the Tactile Toddler Explores the World

Since tactile children learn through the physical world, they rely almost completely on what they can touch and feel as a means of making sense of their environment. This means you'll see them picking things up, touching them, throwing them, and even jumping on them—whatever it takes to get an understanding of how an object works. They will lie or roll on the grass, stomp through any available mud, and splash in puddles, all with intense gusto and enthusiasm. Living with a tactile child can sometimes feel like sharing your space with a miniature tornado. Not only do these kids seem to be perpetually in motion, but they also tend to churn up a lot of mess wherever they go. There's much mischief to get into in this world, and these kids won't miss an opportunity to dig in and spread stuff around, be it your recently folded stack of laundry, your carefully potted plants, or the tube of lipstick in the purse you accidentally left within reach.

As tactile babies become toddlers, their physical development allows them to do much more with their bodies, and you will start to see clear indications that they learn through doing. After taking their first tentative steps and becoming more confident about their ability to get around, they will climb on everything—and that includes you, since you too are part of the environment they are trying to master. They will wake you up by jumping on you and your partner; they will pull on your hair and grasp various body parts.

Being so physical, they love to test themselves, and sometimes this can mean they abandon all judgment and caution. Of course, these are not qualities possessed in large measure by any children this age, but they can be particularly scarce in tactile children. For this reason, parents of these children find themselves childproofing to an extreme. Whether still crawling or beginning to toddle and walk, these kids often stick their fingers in outlets, pull on stray cords, and love to challenge themselves on stairs. You should look at your surroundings with an eye to all possible sources of danger, including not just electrical cords, outlets, and staircases but also sharp-edged tables and counters, knives, pill bottles, matches, toxic substances such as household cleansers and paints, lamps that could topple over, and so forth. You'll want to move, cover, or nail down everything breakable or hazardous that is within reach of your tactile child's roving, busy hands and feet.

Because these kids seem such innate risk takers, it is important that parents of tactile children use very clear language—simple declarative statements or orders—about activities that are off-limits, especially when those activities are dangerous or destructive. For instance, if Johnny is bouncing from one couch to another or about to take a big jump from a piece of playground equipment onto the pavement below, don't try to reason with him or explain why you don't want him to do it. You will have more of an impact if you just say in a clear, unemotional voice, "Stop bouncing" or "Don't jump." No explanations are necessary; they will only distract from the core message.

Use what you know about your child's tactile orientation to help him master cognitive skills. When one boy I worked with was about two and a half, his mother, Pam, noticed that he often pointed to letters and tried to name them. Sensing that he was interested in learning the alphabet, even though it was early for such an interest, Pam began playing a game with Owen in which she would point out letters on the mailboxes they passed when they took a walk. She encouraged his interest in this way because she had also noticed that Owen was much more open to paying attention when he was in motion and while he was holding her hand. Once Owen was familiar with the letters on the mailboxes, he "graduated" to identifying letters on big spongy alphabet tiles that he could play with. He would throw them, stack them high into a tower, and move them around into different piles. This active physical engagement with the letters was a terrific way for Owen to process information through his body. He not only learned his letters quickly but did so with complete enjoyment because of the physical connections he was making.

If you want your tactile child to learn to name body parts, for example, you could follow a similar course. Such a child needs to touch her own arm to identify it as an arm. Showing the child a picture of an arm won't work. For these practical, earthbound kids, a picture signifying a concept is just not real enough. An in-the-flesh demonstration is required for concepts to have meaning. This applies to most aspects of early learning for tactile children.

How the Tactile Toddler Plays and Interacts

Parents of tactile kids will constantly be in search of activities into which their children can pour all their energy and touchy-feely enthusiasm. Since these kids love to play with their hands, when it comes to craft projects, Play-Doh and finger painting are excellent activities. Interestingly, although tactile kids tends to get their hands dirty, they will also want to wipe or wash their hands frequently; it's as if these children need to create a clean slate with each new activity.

Since the tactile child at this age continues to want to be near you and in the midst of whatever the action is—you *are* the action as far as your child is concerned—she is not going to be happy about being asked to play quietly by herself in her room. Even if the "action" is just you and a friend taking a brief coffee break together, your child will want to be part of the scene.

Since tactile children like toys that seem functional, try giving your child miniature replicas of your own belongings—a small mop and broom, doll-sized pots and pans, a toy car, computer, or phone. This way she can occupy herself while you're busy, and she'll feel like she's doing what you are doing, as well as having occasional opportunities to interact with you. If you're sweeping, let your child hold the dustpan. If you're preparing dinner, let your child help mix ingredients. Tactile kids want to help, so it's up to you to figure out ways that will give them the feeling that they're being useful. This is a real self-esteem booster for them.

As you might imagine, these kids enjoy all kinds of physical games and love to engage in imaginative play that involves their whole bodies. One favorite game of my son's and mine was to act out the animals we saw on our trips to the zoo. This kind of dra-

matic play included roaring like a lion, crawling around on all
fours like an elephant, and braying like a zebra. That must be what
was behind Eric Carle's wonderful book *Brown Bear, Brown Bear, What
Do You See?*

In keeping with their love of movement, many tactile kids love
to dance. Although they will break out their dance moves even
without music, playing music makes the dancing all the more fun
and gives them a wonderful physical outlet for their emotions.
This kind of release is an essential part of life for a tactile child,
who finds no better way to express emotion (particularly when
language skills are still undeveloped) than being physically active.
If you decide to jump in and dance with your child, holding
hands and swinging your arms back and forth, so much the
better—tactile kids love this.

For tactile children, music is about the beat, not the melody,
words, beautiful voices, or instrumentals. They get very excited by
fast, rhythmic music and they enjoy bouncing around to it, even
if they're not exactly dancing. Any music that has movement in
four beats and is quite fast, such as songs by The Wiggles, will appeal to them.

Before Kate had identified her daughter, Meg, as tactile, she
would play Mozart for her, thinking Meg would enjoy the same
kind of music she herself enjoyed (and played, for she was a con-
cert violinist). Meg seemed to really come alive when any of the
fast-paced Mozart movements came over the speakers. So everyone in their family thought she was going to be a great musician,
following in Kate's footsteps. But Kate began to notice that during
the slow movements, Meg lost interest and stopped paying attention. She came to understand that Meg wasn't listening to or even
hearing the music in a conscious way; she was simply moving to

the beat of the music. When the music wasn't the kind of catchy, rhythmic piece that she could move to, it didn't mean anything to her.

Tactile children at this age need time and space to work out their physical energies on a daily basis. A tactile child may resort to hitting or pushing if this pent-up energy is not released. This can sometimes cause conflicts in families, particularly among siblings who share close quarters, so parents should try to antic-ipate these conflicts and head them off by thinking of ways to meet the needs not only of the tactile child but also of the rest of the family.

Recently, I met a mother and two daughters who were coping with the challenge of differing sense orientations. Natalie was the visual mother of two daughters, one visual and the other tactile. Her firstborn daughter, Mira, was a visual child, and mother and daughter had always been in sync with each other. Never having known anything else, Natalie just assumed her easy relationship with Mira was the natural, inevitable consequence of a healthy mother-daughter bond.

When Grace was born, three years after Mira, however, Natalie realized that that kind of ease of communication was not a given. "The ways I communicate with Mira, without even thinking about it, always seem to get through to her. She just instantly con-nects to what I'm doing or saying. But Grace and I are on such dif-ferent wavelengths that we just can't seem to see eye to eye on anything."

As Natalie and I talked, I realized that she was concerned not only about her relationship with Grace but also about the conflict that existed between her two daughters, which manifested itself particularly whenever they were together in their playroom. Mira was almost five, and Grace was approaching two. Now that Grace had grown from a wiggly baby to a very mobile toddler, she and Mira began having fights every time they played with each other. Both girls were imaginative, yet their play styles were markedly different. Grace loved nothing more than to throw all the stuffed animals into a towering, squishy pile and then plop herself down right in the middle of the crowd. Being visually inclined, Mira was happiest playing dress-up; she spent long periods of time arranging play clothes in colorful combinations and creating matching outfits. The girls fought over how to use the toys in their playroom—Mira would grow panicky and frustrated when Grace dragged her dress-up clothes into her pile, and Grace would kick and scream when Mira tried to show her how to organize her stuffed animals as guests at a tea party or an audience for an impromptu play performance. Tensions usually boiled over when it came time to clean up, as the girls fought bitterly over how and even where to store their toys.

Natalie watched these conflicts with dismay. "It's hard to see them fight so much, and I never know how best to mediate. I mean, what is fair? Mira is older, but it doesn't seem right to make her give in all the time. And Grace can be so rough with her things."

We discussed the reasons behind her daughters' differences, and Natalie realized how deeply she identified with Mira, who approached life very much the way she herself did. Natalie also began to understand why Grace had such a physical approach to play. Grace wasn't trying to be destructive; she was just acting out her tactile nature.

We then worked on finding some reasonable solutions. We decided that Natalie would reorganize the playroom, keeping an open space in the middle of the room for free play and assigning one side of the room to each child. In Mira's area, Natalie added some open shelves so that her visual daughter could organize her toys and costumes according to color or whatever other visual theme interested her. She stocked Grace's part of the room with a few sturdy, oversized pillows that Grace could stack and topple and throw around to her heart's content, as well as a big open bin where she could store her toys. This allowed Grace to clean up by simply throwing all her toys inside the bin, which proved to be a fun way for this tactile kid to wind down when playtime was over.

"Changing our space has helped with the girls a lot," Natalie told me several weeks later. "Don't get me wrong—they still get into it with each other. But I can see that they both like having their own zone to do their own thing, and they seem to deal with each other better when they do play together."

Tactile children need to let off steam physically, and if there are no ready opportunities for them to do so, they will try to invent some. Fighting with a sibling can be a great outlet for these kids—but not necessarily for the sibling. If you see this kind of dynamic occurring with your children, it's a good idea to try to divert your tactile child's attention by keeping him in motion with lots of activities. If you have a tactile child who always seems to get bored faster than you can find things to keep him busy, you might ask yourself whether anyone in the household is doing something physically active. If his older sister is doing her exercise video, he'll love trying to imitate her, jumping up and down and pretending that he's getting a workout. Is Dad cleaning out the shed? Great—that's what your child will want to do, because the tactile child really likes having a job to do. Dad can put him to use carrying things back and forth. If Dad is reading the paper and Mom is folding laundry, then the child will happily fold towels or match socks, which will keep him busy and content and also teach him the concept of matching.

Remember, as soon as the tactile child gets fussy or destructive, it's a good sign that he is bored. So try to think of ways to put him to use or at least let him feel he's useful. Even if he's still too young to help and is just getting in the way, letting him believe that he's your helper will keep him out of trouble and make him feel good about himself.

The Everyday Life of the Tactile Toddler

Sleeping

The tactile child needs to run out his energy—his battery, so to speak—before he can wind down enough to get to sleep. So you should make sure that your tactile child has enough physical outlets for his energies during the day. Otherwise you may end up with a very cranky child who is so restless and twitchy that it will be hard for him to transition to sleep. As bedtime approaches, you should also build in a very brief period of activity to help your child wind down. Even more so than when they were babies, tactile children need to express the very last bit of their physical energy before they are ready to get into their bedtime routine, which usually includes taking a bath, brushing teeth, and a story.

Tactile toddlers will continue to balk when separated from you and your touch, especially at night. They may even refuse to go to sleep unless you give them some cuddle time before putting them to bed. When they do finally slide into bed, they tend to fall asleep easily if you simply pat them, caress them, or let them hold on to you. The tactile child will often relax more readily if he has a binky, a favorite stuffed animal, or some other kind of transitional object that can substitute for you in your absence and give him comfort.

Thanks to their high activity levels, tactile children need a lot of sleep. Once you get them to sleep, they are likely to sleep long and deeply.

Feeding

At mealtimes, the toddler who is tactile will continue to prefer using his hands to eat. At this point he is likely more than dextrous enough to use a spoon, but for this child, nothing beats the ease and the satisfaction of eating with his hands. Foods that are easy to eat with the fingers will be particularly appealing to him.

As we parents know, all toddlers can be fussy about food, loving mashed potatoes one day and loathing them the next, or eating nothing but refried beans for weeks at a time. For tactile kids, their picky attitude toward food has mostly to do with texture and consistency, as was true when they were younger. They prefer foods with texture and heft, such as crunchy apples and carrots, creamy mashed potatoes, or pizza smothered with cheese, and tend to eschew anything runny or soupy, since such foods are hard to pick up and not as much fun to touch.

These kids tend to eat often and heartily, as their sheer physicality makes them need frequent refueling. For them eating is basically just putting more gas in the tank. They like to eat quickly and be done with mealtime as fast as possible so that they can get back to the activities they enjoy. They are not usually that concerned about taste, flavor, or smell. For tactile kids I always suggest keeping nutritious snacks around—peanut butter, bananas, or carrots—so that their blood sugar doesn't drop too low, because if they get caught up in some kind of intense game or sport, they may forget to eat, and you'll want to have a quick antidote to the tantrum you can see coming from a mile away.

One mom came to me complaining that her two-year-old son wouldn't stay at the table to eat dinner. If she strapped him into his high chair, he would spend all of his time wriggling to get free. Needless to say, he barely ate a bite, given that all of his energy and attention were focused on trying to escape. I suggested using both positive and negative reinforcement: Tell him clearly, while she has her hand on his shoulder or hand, that if he sits at the table and eats, she will sit down with him, but warn him that if he refuses to sit still and eat his dinner, she will leave the room. A week later, the mom called me excitedly: "It worked! It was touch and go at first—I had to leave the room a few times, which was difficult for both him and me—but then he finally seemed to understand that I was serious. He's so compliant now!"

Offering both a positive reinforcement and a negative one is a simple and effective way to communicate with a toddler. It means you're giving options to a child who is hell-bent on exerting some control on his environment (his developmental task, after all) while giving him boundaries, which he absolutely needs. Remember, this strategy may take a few attempts, but if you're resolute and don't waver, your child should respond the way you wish.

Dressing

During the toddler years, our children are beginning to develop their preferences about not only the food they eat but also the clothes they wear. Actually, what tactile children love most of all is to be naked, because it feels so good. These are the kids who come

into my research center and take off their clothes if nobody pre-
vents them from doing so. So don't be surprised to catch your tactile toddler trying to pull off all her clothes, even in public places.
One little girl I know stripped off her shoes, socks, and underpants in a restaurant while her mother and I were having an otherwise civilized lunch. Of course, most of the time even tactile
children do wear clothes, and as toddlers they will start to exhibit
strong feelings about what they wear, which will have everything
to do with how the clothes feel on their bodies. These kids will
choose favorite clothes based on feel and fit, as opposed to appearance. During the fast-growing toddler years tactile children are
moving and experimenting more with their bodies nearly every
day, and what they care about most and respond to best are clothes
that give them room to run, jump, and roll through daily life with
ease. Clothes that feel good next to the skin are also important to
them. Of course, from your point of view, the easier they are to
take care of, the better, because these clothes are going to get very
dirty.

Toilet Training

Though toilet training is very individual, most parents begin this
process when children are somewhere between eighteen and
thirty-six months. The most important factor to keep in mind is
not to put pressure on your child before she is ready to be toilet-
trained, which is good advice for the parents of any child, but especially those of tactile children.

In general, tactile children are resistant to being forced into
change, especially a change such as toilet training, which affects
them in such an intimate, physical way. Therefore, they are often
the last children to officially cast off the shackles of a diaper. This
is not as bad as it sounds, because once they do finally feel ready,

tactile children are actually the easiest to train, and they end up having very few accidents after the job has been done.

Like most children, they tend to learn in two stages. First, they learn to master the urinating stage. The next stage is where you might encounter some resistance on your child's part. Because they are so physically oriented, tactile children tend to be reluctant to use the potty or toilet, which can feel very foreign and therefore scary. So although tactile kids will accomplish the first stage of toilet training early or right on time (that is, at about the same time as other kids), the second stage can take a while. I often hear moms of tactile children complaining that their three- or four-year-old still insists on doing poos in a diaper, even though she has been peeing in the toilet for quite a while. The trick with these children is to encourage them to want to master the next stage. It's a case of mental persuasion rather than physical training. And some kinds of persuasion tend to be more effective than others. Telling her, "Your friend Jenny goes to the potty; don't you want to be like her?" is probably not going to work, because the tactile child doesn't feel the need to be like other kids. Tactile children do, however, like to imitate their parents, so if you're comfortable having your child around when you're in the bathroom, she may learn a lot faster, because she'll want to do what you're doing. Also, since she's trying to be like you, she may want to use the toilet, rather than starting out with a potty.

Goals are another way of encouraging the behavior you want. It's often effective to say something like "I'm sorry, sweetheart, but you can't go to the baseball game with us until you're a big girl, and big girls use the toilet for everything."

Keep in mind, however, that no amount of persuasion or encouragement will work until you've been given the signal that your child is ready for this big change.

Tactile Preschooler Basics,
from Ages Three to Five

The Tactile Preschooler's Emotional Life

As tactile children mature and gain a better understanding of themselves as separate beings, their physical nature continues to influence how they express their feelings. Whether those feelings are positive or negative, they tend to use their bodies to demonstrate them. If they are upset, they will stomp their feet. If they are angry, they may lash out by pushing, hitting, or even biting. If they are happy, they will try to smother you with physical affection, cuddling, hugging, and kissing. Tactile children will need to move physically to process information, cognitive as well as emotional. If they are struggling to master a learning challenge, such as saying their ABCs, they may walk around or jiggle while trying to remember what letter comes next. (This is akin to the adult who needs to fidget or jiggle his leg when working out a problem.)

Even with all their increasing freedom and independence, the new friends they make at school, and all the activities they can now participate in, tactile children will still crave physical attention from their parents. They'll still delight at being cuddled, still respond well to physical cues when you want to get their attention, and still enjoy praise most when it comes as a hands-on message. And when Mom is available, these kids will tend to stick close to her.

At four or five, the tactile child can often be misconstrued as "acting out" or behaving badly when all he is really doing is being the same physically expressive self he's always been. But now that he's bigger, the roughhousing and sheer physicality of his way of relating to the world can be hard on those in the vicinity. He is still the same practical person who experiences his emotions in a straightforward manner. However, when he is overwhelmed by his feelings, the way he expresses them—through his body—may land him in trouble, especially if it involves hurting other children.

One parent sought me out for advice regarding the family's middle child, five-year-old Frank. The family was made up of three children: The oldest was an eight-year-old girl, Genevieve, a visual child who was an angel—well behaved, polite, quiet, and always content; then came Frank, who was clearly tactile and physically oriented; and finally there was four-year-old Sam, who was auditory. All three kids were always late because of Frank, who had become increasingly disruptive, beginning with his resistance to getting dressed in the morning. Frank also had the magical power to make everyone start fighting and bickering. He had become so disobedient and unruly, he was breaking his brother's toys, which of course often brought Sam to hysterics. As a result, most mornings ended with both parents screaming at Frank for the trouble he caused—which was never very effective at stopping his behavior—and his mom leaving the house for work in tears. The father, who happened to be a pediatrician, gave no support to the mom, focused as he was on getting himself out the door in one piece.

After a couple of home visits to get to know the family dynamics, I began to guess that Frank's physical behavior was probably not intentionally disruptive. But it was clear that his rough, physical manner pushed a lot of buttons: His older sister was obviously bothered by his pushing and shoving, and his younger brother seemed to cringe as soon as Frank entered the room.

However, rather than set out to change Frank's nature, I suggested treating the so-called problem child in a more positive way. Appealing to his sense of responsibility and can-do spirit, I suggested to his mom that she give him more responsibility. My first task was helping his mother figure out how to get the kids ready for school and everyone out the door without so much chaos and confusion. I advised her to put Frank in the role of the big boy— he was to be in charge of helping his younger brother get ready for day care. Whereas before she would wake up the kids by taking off their covers and turning the lights on in their rooms, I suggested that Frank be the one who was responsible for waking Genevieve and Sam, dressing his brother, and making sure Sam ate breakfast and put on his shoes. For Frank himself, the day would begin with a quick wake-up cuddle from his mom before he got out of bed.

Tactile kids love being in charge, and Frank adapted to his new role in just a few days. After breakfast, Frank made sure all the dishes were brought to the sink and that everyone had their shoes on and their backpacks ready to go. Frank's mom was amazed at the results that occurred in just one week. The tears, screams, and general chaos had disappeared. An even greater benefit was the transformation of Frank: He'd gone from a frustrated, wild boy to one who was clearly growing into his independence and proud of his new responsibility.

In the past, Frank's mother had relied too heavily on negative reinforcement. When she stressed the positive instead, giving Frank an outlet for his energies and a way to show how responsible he was, he started being much more responsive to his mom's requests. Soon he was giving her hugs instead of pushing her to tears.

The Tactile Preschooler's Learning Style

These children respond strongly to lessons that incorporate tangible items. To teach counting, for example, you can use blocks to show the child that one block plus another equals two. The child can hold the blocks and feel them, so abstract numbers become something concrete. Finding things in your house that start with the same letters—ball, butter, and belt; cat, cup, and carrot—is a way for a tactile child to learn the alphabet by attaching a physical reality to the letters.

One boy I recall from my research was a lively, intelligent five-year-old named Jackson. I met Jackson when his mother, Mariam, contacted me, concerned about her son's performance in preschool. Jackson loved going to school—he greeted his teacher with a hug most mornings, and he'd made a ton of friends since the beginning of the term. He was struggling, however, with learning to recognize and write his letters.

"I know from his teacher that he's behind most of the other kids, and I see how frustrated he is when we work on exercises at home," his mother told me. "He works himself up into such a state that he can't sit still for even a minute. I'm not sure how well he's able to listen or comprehend what he's being taught."

Mariam's words were a key to at least part of the puzzle: "how well he's able to listen" when "he can't sit still for even a minute" was her concern. From this comment as well as other signs I saw during our session, I was pretty sure that Mariam's dominant sense was auditory and that the needs and preferences of a tactile child—we'd already determined that Jackson was tactile—would be foreign to her. For a tactile child like Jackson, listening to a teacher or a parent or looking at a book is often not as effective as literally "feeling his way" into learning, which can't be done while sitting still. Tactile kids will tend to move around a lot in their seats, jiggling their legs or tapping their hands—in other words, some part of their body has to be moving while they are concentrating. As child psychologist Dr. Gretchen Schmelzer says, "For this kind of child, the act of kicking his leg is actually enabling him to process the information. He has a different neuronal path than, say, a kid who has to hear what the letter sounds like for it to make sense."

Tactile children seem to find their focus by creating a physical outlet for the frustration they feel when trying to master cognitive challenges. So what appeared to Jackson's mother (and perhaps his teacher as well) as a lack of concentration during his lessons was, in fact, the very opposite: This was Jackson's way of finding his concentration, in order to put letters together to spell a word or to write out his numbers from one to ten.

Together, Mariam and I came up with exercises for her to do at home with Jackson, ones that were tailored to his specific learning needs. When Jackson was working with numbers, he used small objects—stones and shells from the beach, chunky buttons—to count, and only then wrote his numbers down on paper. When it came time for spelling and reading work, Mariam and Jackson would "act out" their letters with special gestures. Mariam kept these exercises short and allowed Jackson to move from one to the next at his own pace, since he seemed to prefer switching quickly from one project to another. She made sure to communicate with Jackson in ways that made him feel most comfortable: When she needed his attention, she put her hand on his shoulder. When she wanted to praise him for his work, she gave him a quick hug or a kiss on the top of the head. Sure enough, Jackson eventually caught up to his classmates, and he and Mariam both enjoyed their learning play sessions.

"I realize now that I was making assumptions about Jackson's behavior based on my own outlook," said Mariam. "He learns differently than I did as a child, but it's no less valid."

Like Jackson, many tactile children will want to move rapidly from one project to the next, as if constantly seeking a fresh start.

These kids simply aren't wired to sit still or to focus on one thing for long periods of time. Don't be surprised to see your tactile preschooler abandon his painting project in the middle of a brushstroke in favor of making clay figures, only to drop that clay and skip over to his stash of building blocks. As far as the specific types of projects they enjoy, those that involve different textures and sensations will be particularly appealing. Tactile kids will be excited to make sculptures from clay or Play-Doh or to create collages that use a diverse array of craft materials and everyday objects such as glitter, tissue paper, dried beans and pasta, feathers, ribbons, and beads.

The Tactile Preschooler's Social Life

Tactile kids thrive in groups of their peers. Children who are in day care or preschool, and those who participate in various group activities after school and on weekends, will enjoy all these opportunities to make new friends and be social. These kids also love competitive games. At the head of the line for recess and in the center of the huddle in a football game: This is where you will find the tactile child. And don't forget how much these kids like to be given a job. Sometimes that's even more gratifying to them than sports or other kinds of play or games. Outgoing and eager to be involved, tactile kids will often be among the first to volunteer to help out, so you'll see them offering to carry equipment to the sports field at recess or to pass out snacks after returning from the playground.

The parent who expects a tactile child to settle down when he gets to the ripe old age of four or five is likely to be quite disappointed. It's better to channel your tactile child's energies than to try to squelch them, and a great way to do that is to get him or her into organized sports. Whether it's team play or lessons, perhaps in swimming or tennis, sports are terrific outlets for tactile children's need to stay in motion and exert themselves physically, and for their love of being with other kids.

Tactile kids, especially boys this age, seem to naturally seek each other out, and they benefit from having friends who share their deep physicality and high energy levels. Once they identify each other, they will entertain themselves racing to the edge of the backyard and back, rolling down the hill, seeing who can scale the playground climbing wall faster, or doing just about anything that requires lots of energy and motion. But if they don't have peers to play with, they'll be looking to you for entertainment.

One mother I worked with was finding herself exhausted by her tactile son's seemingly endless need for physical activity when he wasn't in school. Since Mary Ellen's five-year-old son, Stephen, was an only child, and the family had just moved and hadn't yet met any of the children in their new neighborhood, Stephen was constantly begging Mary Ellen and her husband, Michael, to run around the yard with him before dinner and during the weekends. "I love playing with my kid, but he can wear me out pretty quickly," she said. "He just goes and goes." When visiting with them, I noticed that they had a terrific climbing wall and play set ready to be assembled, but they had been so busy getting settled after their move that they just hadn't gotten around to it. We decided that she and Michael would make a priority of putting the set together so that they could invite some neighborhood kids over to play on it. Soon, Stephen had a whole new set of local friends to hang out with when school was out, and he no longer needed Mary Ellen and Michael to be his playmates. He was lucky too, because one of the neighborhood kids was a tactile boy who was just as high-energy as he was.

The Everyday Life of the Tactile Preschooler

Sleeping

After a long day of bustling from one activity to the next, your tactile preschooler might find it hard to slow down enough to realize she is tired and to accept the idea of going to bed. Getting these kids under the covers with lights out can take some time: They might zip through their bedtime routine of changing into pajamas and brushing their teeth, so you think they're ready to go down, but turn your back for a minute and you'll find them jumping on their bed—or yours. Making sure these children get enough physical activity during the day will help avoid the problem of their having too much pent-up energy at bedtime. But sometimes no matter how active they've been, they still have a few more laps left in them. A very good way to calm these children before bed is by encouraging them to run around the house or the yard for a few minutes—yes, run! Whereas most kids need quiet time before falling asleep, many tactile children need to exert their last bit of energy as a way to wind down and go to sleep. Remember to wear out that battery!

Feeding

By the time your tactile child is of preschool age, she may be starting to adapt to the ways of cutlery, but she'll probably still want to eat as fast as possible so that she can go back to doing her thing. One of the most effective ways to get an impatient tactile child more involved with food and eating is to bring her into the kitchen and let her help you while you are preparing a meal. And I don't mean to limit this to girls. Tactile kids of both genders gravitate toward the center of activity wherever they are, whether at home, at school, or on the playground, and they do love to have a job to do. In the kitchen, this can mean everything from stirring ingredients in a bowl to whirling the lettuce in a salad spinner or using cookie cutters to make shapes in the dough. Cooking appeals to tactile children on a couple of levels. Participating in anything that involves physical activity is obviously great for them, and getting to do it side by side with you makes it even better.

Being involved in meal preparation also gives the child some feeling of ownership over her food and makes it more likely she'll eat it when it's served. For a tactile kid who is picky about food at this age, encouraging her to work with you in the kitchen may help her view her food more positively once it's on her plate. Of course, she may still have moments of regression when she wants to have at it with her hands. Using a knife and fork and spoon, wiping her mouth with a napkin, and being expected to sit still at the family dinner table until everyone is finished will all present challenges to the tactile child. It's just too much to do when all she really wants is to shovel the food down and go on to the next activity. So try to be patient, even as you attempt to introduce some civility to the table.

Dressing

As your child seeks more independence and control over his daily choices, picking out his own clothes will become one of those tasks he wants to take over for himself. Getting dressed will involve pulling item after item from closet and dresser drawers in search of the most comfortable, loose-fitting clothes he can find. The tactile child's favorite clothes won't necessarily look like anything special to you—in fact, the most preferred pants might be a ragged pair of sweats—but to this child, the more worn-in the better, because they will feel cozy, familiar, and easy to move around in. These are the kids who like to strip down naked or to their underpants as soon as they get home. They don't really like clothes; they enjoy being free and unencumbered. So in choosing clothes for them, think of their comfort and their freedom—pants with elasticized waists that can be pulled up and down instantly so that there are no buttons or zippers to contend with, for instance.

Mismatches with the Tactile Child

Mismatches between parent and child have an incredible potential to ruin daily life. But by being aware of your own dominant sense and your child's, and by making a few relatively simple changes that take into account the differences between you, you can make discord disappear and pave the way for a newfound peace and tranquility in your family life. It's not magic, but it can sometimes seem that way. The following describes some of the typical pitfalls that occur when parents are mismatched with a tactile child, along with a few practical tips on how to minimize the impact of these mismatches. However, I begin by talking not about a mismatch but about a match—because the combination of tactile parent and tactile child can actually be quite problematic in ways you might not expect.

Tactile Child with Tactile Parent

As a tactile parent, you will probably be very inclined to spend many happy hours nursing and cuddling your tactile baby, which is exactly what your baby wants and needs. If, however, your partner is tactile as well, he may get a bit frustrated and even resentful that all your physical affection is being directed toward the baby rather than him. If a tactile father, who needs physical touch as much as any tactile mother, begins to feel left out, a great way to get him involved (and to meet his own tactile needs) is by putting him on burp, bottle, or diaper patrol.

Helping your partner to feel involved in taking care of the baby—regardless of whether your partner is tactile or not—is important in another way. If you don't get sufficient breaks from your baby's constant need to be held or from your toddler's demands to be cuddled and carried around, sooner or later you are going to be overwhelmed. You risk depleting your energy, your patience, and your emotional reserves, all of which we rely on to be good parents. Tactile babies and toddlers can really take a toll on their parents, and it's very important that you take care of yourself during these demanding years. If you run yourself into the ground and end up sick, everyone in your family will pay the price, not just you.

As your tactile child grows into his toddlerhood, his increasing strength and physicality may be a problem for you, because, being tactile, you enjoy being warm and cuddly, while he is trying out other ways of expressing himself through his body. A tactile child will enjoy testing his strength and showing off, which can sometimes involve unpleasant displays of physical aggression. Of course, your tactile child will still want and need affection, but he may also engage in a lot of pushing, pummeling, bouncing, and even biting and kicking, all of which are natural at this stage. While aggression needs to be curbed, a certain amount of good-hearted roughhousing is inevitable. Don't lose sight of the fact that this is the way your very physically oriented child learns and expresses himself, and try to cut him some slack.

Without being conscious of what they are doing or why, parents can sometimes overreact to their tactile child's behavior. This is particularly likely to happen with tactile adults who experienced a lot of strong discipline when they themselves were children. If they were viewed as physically aggressive or destructive during their early years, their parents may have meted out unnecessarily harsh punishments, as if to bash them into submission, and they may in turn be doing the same to their children. Being aware of your own experience and how it may be affecting the way you deal with your child can help you avoid repeating these mistakes.

Tactile Child with Auditory Parent

As an auditory parent, you probably use words, rhythm, and tone in a creative, subtle, often nuanced way that may go right over your tactile child's head. The best way to speak to a tactile child is with straightforward, simple, concrete language—no fancy words, no complicated sentences, and not too much expression or emotion either.

Also, an auditory parent may tend to "overtalk," offering explanations and details that the tactile child will simply tune out. She doesn't need a long song and dance about why you have to go to the grocery store before her gymnastics class or why it's not a good idea to pet the strange doggie. Just the facts, please, delivered in short, declarative sentences.

Because of this difference in speaking style, an auditory parent may have her feelings hurt by her rather direct and straight-to-the-point child. A tactile child won't want to discuss his day or tell you about his trip to the park: He will simply require a cuddle or a gentle squeeze hello when he gets home, and then he's off on his next mission. However, to encourage communication and connection, you might want to establish a regular cuddle time. Your tactile child will be much more likely to tap into his feelings and share the events of his day with you if he's safely nestled in your lap.

Some auditory parents are so sensitive to noise that the sounds of their boisterous child playing with other kids will cause them to refuse to have playdates at their own home. Your tactile child is very social, and it is important to allow her to socialize at home as well as at parks and other places.

Tactile Child with Visual Parent

Of course, the biggest way the visual parent is likely to clash with her tactile child is in the area of how things look—especially her house. The tactile child will tend to be messy, playing with everything he can get his hands on and creating what looks like confusion and chaos to your order-craving eyes. Once you are able to understand and accept that your tactile child has to touch things in order to understand his world, and that in touching he can't avoid generating a lot of mess, you can start thinking about how to create "free zones" where he can play to his heart's content without impinging too much on your highly developed aesthetic sense.

In one situation, a visual mom, Karen, was having a hard time with her youngest daughter, Claire, who is tactile. As a visual person, Karen was rather uptight and particular, and needed to keep her house tidy and neat at all times, especially in the kitchen. Her two-year-old daughter, however, was as messy as can be. She would follow her mother around the house, leaving a trail of toys in her wake as they went from room to room. And no sooner did her mother finish picking up after her than Claire would sit right down and create a new mess. Karen came to me bothered by how upset this situation was making her—she didn't want to keep losing her temper with her daughter. She was especially distressed by the havoc Claire created in the kitchen as Karen was preparing dinner. I suggested that Karen do two things. One was to set up small play stations around the house where Claire could go ahead and make a mess, but in a relatively small area. For the time that they spent together in the kitchen, I recommended that Karen set up a pretend kitchen (she made one out of a big cardboard box), giving Claire small toy pots and pans to play with. This kept Claire occupied while Karen cooked dinner, and contained the clutter within the space of the box. Mother and daughter were both happy with this solution.

Tactile Child with Taste/Smell Parent

As a taste/smell parent, you may know intuitively that your tactile child needs physical comfort, reassurance, and opportunities to express his or her physical energy. Since you tend to be very focused on your child's needs, you probably pay close attention to the somewhat nonverbal tactile child, picking up on his cues and responding to his needs before they get too dire. In this way, this combination is often quite harmonious and close, creating a bond that your tactile child trusts deeply.

However, if the taste/smell parent doesn't give the tactile child clear and strong boundaries, this child can begin to dominate the parent. As you might remember, when my son, Tom, was small and we went to visit my father, Tom would literally push me out of the way because he wanted my dad all to himself. I learned to say no to that kind of behavior, but a taste/smell mom may allow her empathic response to her child to take over, preventing her from responding firmly to such unacceptable behavior. The taste/smell parent needs to remember to deliver clear messages, and to deliver them immediately after any misbehavior occurs. If you wait until later, in order not to make a scene or to embarrass your child, he will have long since forgotten what he did.

Although taste/smell parents (like all parents) want to make sure their child is happy, tactile children can be very aggressive in their demands, and they can overwhelm their eager-to-please parents. So it's important that the taste/smell parent maintain her own boundaries and not lose herself or her sense of priorities to her insistent child.

Tactile children rely on their bodies to guide them through all the phases of development, from their first months in their mothers' arms to their first tentative steps away from their mothers, their first days at preschool, and beyond. They like to give and receive love and praise through touch. They take risks by running—literally—at new experiences and grabbing on with their capable hands. They learn by seeking out real-life, concrete examples to illuminate concepts and ideas—and often by making a mess. Stepping into the world of the tactile child takes us into a place where touching matters more than seeing or hearing. For those of us adults who are tactile, this will already seem familiar. For the rest of us, reminding ourselves to communicate as much as we can through the medium of touch can take us a long way toward connecting effectively with our tactile children.

FIVE

The Auditory Child

Auditory babies live their lives to a rhythm and sound track all their own. Tuned in at every moment to the invisible world of sound, which encompasses (for starters) rhythm, volume, pitch, and tone, these kids take in an enormous amount of sensory information that zips right by those of us with different dominant senses. And yet as these children grow they seem to develop an ability to hear what they want to hear and tune out the rest, which can often be puzzling or downright annoying to parents. For example, auditory children often fail to respond to a parent's request or demands if they are delivered in a harsh or angry voice.

You'll find an auditory child curled up next to the radio, daydreaming contentedly, or flipping through a book near an open window, listening to the sounds of her neighborhood float by. The auditory child will have a lifelong relationship with music; especially in her early years, she'll use songs to give voice to her emotions. And as you'll see below, a CD player or iPod can be the auditory child's best friend, particularly as she gets older. Not only will it enable her to delight in music of her own choosing, but she can also use the device to block out any ambient noise that is too distracting or unsettling to her.

These children don't just take in sound; they also produce quite a bit of sound themselves. You'll know an auditory child when you hear one. He's the baby making all the noise, chatting and warbling away in his own mysterious language long before he learns his first words. He never fails to squeal when he's excited, wail when he's sad, and screech like a wild thing when he's frustrated. He's the toddler who teaches himself how to turn on the stereo so he can sing along at the top of his lungs to his favorite songs. If he can rustle up a few pots to whack in time to the music, that's even better. He's also the little boy who spends the entire car ride home from preschool telling you detailed stories of his day and always has just one more story to tell.

To understand the world of an auditory child, we must attune ourselves, as these children do naturally, to the power of sound, the patterns these sounds make, and the messages that exist in our voices, in music, and in the noisy jumble of our daily environments.

Auditory Baby Basics, from Birth to Age One

How the Auditory Baby Expresses Emotional Needs

The primary emotional task of any baby is to attach and bond to his parent or primary caregiver. As you might expect, the auditory child attaches through sound—specifically to the soothing voice of his mother or other primary caregiver. When this voice is absent or when there is a sudden change in tone or volume, an auditory baby is likely to startle, become frightened, and wail in fear and protest.

From the time they are born, infants recognize the unique sound of their mother's voice because they have become accustomed to it since being in the womb. In fact, a 2001 study by psychologist Dr. Alexandra Lamont at the University of Leicester showed that a baby will respond in recognition to both the mother's voice and to music that was played during his mother's pregnancy, while he was in utero.*

In those first days and nights of whispering and cooing to your child, you are laying the foundation for his lifelong attachment to your voice, which he will use to ground and calm himself. So although it's true that all babies are especially attentive to their parents' voices, the auditory baby is particularly sensitive, and more likely than other babies to pick up on any nuance or change in the tone of those voices. When they are within earshot of the baby, parents should try to speak in warm, pleasant, and loving voices.

Auditory babies need to hear the voices of those closest to them—their parents or caregivers—in order to feel secure and stay calm. In the same way that tactile children seek physical contact with their parents for their sense of security, auditory babies rely on familiar voices to orient themselves in their environment. The sound of your voice transmits to your auditory child the message that he is in a safe place where he will be loved and cared for. This is true even when you are not speaking directly to your baby; just hearing your voice nearby will comfort him.

I worked with one mother, Ashley, who brought in her son, Harry, when he was about six months old and having some sleep

*Whitwell, Giselle E., R.M.T., ed. "The Importance of Prenatal Sound and Music." *Journal of Prenatal & Perinatal Psychology and Health.* Retrieved April 15, 2004 from http://www.birthpsychology.com/lifebefore/soundindex.html

problems. During our first meeting she told me about her labor and delivery. For various medical reasons she had had to deliver her son three weeks prematurely by cesarean section. Ashley was given so much medication for the procedure that she couldn't hold her newborn son for almost three hours after he was delivered, she said. When finally she was lucid and awake enough to have her son brought to her and placed in her arms, she was told by the doctors and nursing staff that he had so far refused to open his eyes. But as soon as he heard Ashley's voice, his eyes shot open. When Ashley recounted to me the story of Harry not opening his eyes until he heard the sound of her voice, I knew at once that he must be an auditory baby and that he had needed to hear that familiar voice to understand that it was now safe for him to enter the world. Of course, there were other indications to support this classification, but the vivid story of his birth captures the power of the auditory reflex in this group of children.

One way of identifying auditory babies is by observing their behavior when their moms are on the phone. Auditory babies are so connected to their mothers through the sound of their voices that they will often get very clingy and fussy if their moms are talking on the phone within earshot. They can sense that Mom is talking to someone other than themselves, and they feel cut off from the magical connection that binds her to them. A frequent complaint I hear is, "My daughter won't let me talk on the phone! She begins to whine or cry every time I try to have a conversation."

An auditory baby is so attuned to nuances of tone and timbre that long before he understands words, he can learn volumes about himself and the world through the voices of those around him. Think of the way we often talk to our pets: We use our tone of voice to indicate our meaning, not really expecting the animal to understand our words. In the same way, a baby won't understand words, but he will understand tone, which is why it's very important to use our voices in an expressive way. A flat, emotionless voice won't communicate the love you feel to this child. Better to use an exaggerated or singsong voice when talking to an auditory baby.

While a gentle, loving voice will soothe and calm an auditory child, a loud and angry voice will have the opposite effect. More so than other children, the auditory baby is easily upset by angry voices and is highly sensitive to people talking in a harsh way. You need not be yelling at your child for her to be affected by the agitation in your voice. Parents arguing in the next room, Mom having a heated phone conversation, siblings squabbling over a toy—these and other common incidents that have nothing to do with the baby herself can nonetheless disturb and agitate an auditory baby.

How the Auditory Baby Discovers the World

Learning for an auditory baby is, not surprisingly, all about sounds. She learns by experimenting with sounds, which means making a lot of noise. The auditory baby learns to speak before babies in any of the other sensory groups, and her babbling to herself is preparation for learning to talk. She can also respond to your directions earlier than some other babies because of her ability to cue into language, even when she is still at the preverbal stage. She babbles constantly in preparation for learning to talk. The auditory baby teaches herself about objects in her world by throwing, dropping, or banging them. Whereas you might observe a tactile child doing something similar with a ball or doll, the difference is in the motivation. A tactile baby throws, drops, and bangs on objects in order to know the physical nature of the object; the auditory child throws, drops, and bangs the objects in order to hear the different sounds she can make with them—sound being the key to how she processes information about her environment.

Your auditory baby will respond strongly and enthusiastically to games and activities involving sound and music. Toys that rattle, jingle, and squeak will delight this child. So will books with buttons that make noises. She'll swoon over puppets that talk (with a little help from Mom and Dad). Singing and clapping to music will get this baby smiling and moving. As soon as she's steady on her feet, she'll be dancing up a storm. This activity is not just about play; it's all part of her cognitive development. She will more than likely show a strong memory for certain pieces of music or songs.

How the Auditory Baby Begins to Play and Interact

The auditory child enjoys music, especially sounds that are rhythmic, melodic, and repetitive. On the other hand, harsh, erratic, or discordant sounds, such as clattering pots, slamming doors, or loud voices, can make this baby agitated and uneasy. Since she can't move herself away from the sound or "turn off" her ears, and noise has a penetrating quality that can be very stressful, she may get fussy when surrounded by a lot of noise, whether from other babies, nearby children or adults, or the environment. If you observe your auditory baby tugging on her ears, then you know she is becoming overwhelmed by the sound.

The auditory baby will generally be content to play on her own if she is within earshot of her caregiver's voice. Even if no one is really paying attention to her, the sound of that familiar voice will make her feel secure and loved. Interaction with strangers will vary, but she will gravitate to voices that are similar to her mother's, regardless of what kind of voice that is.

The Everyday Life of the Auditory Baby

Sleeping

Because of their highly tuned aural sensitivity, auditory children rely on familiar sound patterns for a basic sense of security, especially when they are getting ready to go to sleep. Loud or unfamiliar noises, or changes in the typical sound patterns around them, can trigger their startle reflexes, causing them to go on high alert. They may cry a lot in response, and if it's bedtime, they may either wake up or become too agitated to fall asleep.

This sensitivity to sound is always especially acute at bedtime and nap time. However, how this sensitivity plays itself out differs from child to child. One mother said to me, "I have three auditory kids. The first two were happy to nap anywhere that had a fairly low level of background noise—which was a godsend. It meant I could fold laundry or do some mending while watching my shows, and they would sleep right in the room, where I could keep an eye on them. Not so my new one. There can be no noise whatsoever in the room or else she wakes right up—even from a sound sleep!"

Although some auditory babies do require total silence in order to sleep, many others, like this mother's first two children, can get used to falling asleep to the sound of background noise like televisions or radios. But if the sound stops, they may awaken. For this reason, it's important to be aware of the sounds you might be introducing to your child's nighttime and nap routines: Music, television, singing, even talking in the background can all become part of a kind of "soundprint" that your child relies on to relax, fall asleep, and stay asleep. Once you've developed a pattern of sound during sleep times, you should try to stick to it because your child will want this series of sounds to remain constant, night after night. Any change in that pattern could disrupt his sleep patterns.

Any kind of loud, abrasive sounds, even in the next room, can also be disruptive, though you yourself may barely register the sounds. This is exactly what happened to the child of a woman I met early on in my research.

Tina, a mother of three, contacted me because she was having trouble getting her new baby to sleep. Every time she put the baby down in his crib, he would fall asleep briefly but then wake up and cry. The baby was obviously tired and cranky. Tina was unable to establish a workable sleep rhythm for him and failed to understand why he kept waking up.

At first we weren't quite sure of the new baby's dominant sense. But when I went to see her at her home and she took me around, describing a typical day in her family life and how the baby behaved during the course of the day, I soon identified him as auditory. When Tina put her baby down for a nap, she said, she would then go to the kitchen, which was next to the nursery, to try to get as much done as she could while he was sleeping. She would start washing up or cooking, but almost invariably the baby would soon stir. Because she herself had no strong connection to the auditory sense, it didn't occur to her that the clatter of pots and pans as she did her kitchen chores was a problem. But the fact that the baby always became agitated when she was in the kitchen suggested to me that he was highly attuned to sounds and that the noise she made was triggering his startle reflex, causing him to wake and cry. He was complaining in the only way he could—

with a loud "audible" protest. This protest crying is typical of auditory babies. When a sharp noise causes the startle reflex to turn on, it results in a release of adrenaline, which increases the heart rate and can cause considerable distress to the baby—and the exasperated mother.

Once we identified the problem, Tina was able to make some small adjustments to avoid waking the baby right after he fell asleep. I suggested to Tina that she wait to wash her pots (the loudest culprits) until after the baby had fallen into a deeper sleep, as opposed to at the beginning of his nap. Although this meant a certain amount of inconvenience to Tina, it was a better solution than moving the baby to a room farther away from the kitchen because that too would have bothered him. In order to fall asleep he needed the comfort of being able to hear his mother and know she wasn't far away.

After she worked out a routine that allowed her to get most of her chores done after the baby was in a deep enough sleep to be undisturbed by the occasional bang of a pot, things began to improve. Mother and child were back in tune with each other and both were much happier.

In another case, Emma came to see me after her family had moved in to a new home and she began having trouble with her fourth child, Christopher, who was about three and a half months old at the time. The new place was a very large and well-appointed house, with bedrooms that were spacious and quiet, off in a separate wing from the family areas, and a staff, including a couple of nannies to help with child care. As soon as they moved, Christopher, who had always been an easy and good sleeper, began resisting any attempt by Emma or the nannies to put him down in his crib. Emma didn't understand what the problem was, since it seemed to her that Christopher's new bedroom was a more soothing, restful environment than his old one. When I asked what was different about where Christopher was sleeping now, Emma explained that in the old house, Christopher had slept in a small room right off the main family room, which was exposed to all the noise and commotion of the household. In the new house, Emma had put Christopher in a room that was off on its own, so he wouldn't be disturbed by the sounds of his boisterous siblings and their pets, not to mention the constant stream of friends and cousins coming over to play. I suggested that the sudden change to such a quiet environment might be precisely what was bothering Christopher. So we tried an experiment, putting Christopher down for his nap in the oversized pantry, which, like his old room, was just next to the main family room. Bingo—he went straight to sleep. In order to transition him to his new room (Emma didn't want to let him sleep in the pantry forever), she taped the routine sounds of the household and began playing the tape when he was put to bed in his new room. By the second week, Christopher was happily ensconced in his new room and sleeping through the night. In this case, addressing Christopher's auditory sensitivity involved understanding that a lack of sound can be just as problematic as too much sound.

In a similar example, one mom was very worried about the effect of her returning to work when her baby was about eight months old. Melissa had worked out a plan to drop off her daughter, Angeline, at her mother's house on the way to her office. Because Melissa knew that Angeline was an auditory baby and therefore might be prone to sleep problems at nap time because of the change in environment, this mom planned ahead: She taped the sounds of Angeline's room one day, which included the regular whistle of trains running on the tracks behind their house. Then she brought the tape over to her mother so that it could be played to provide Angeline with a familiar soundtrack to her new daytime situation away from home.

But not all auditory babies need music or sound to fall asleep. Some do require almost absolute quiet. Trudy, the mother of Ava, a one-year-old baby, was at a total loss about how to comfort or calm her daughter. She was very jumpy when Trudy tried to nurse her, seemed to startle easily, and fell into shallow states of sleep from which she was often and easily awakened. Once we determined that Ava was auditory, I asked Trudy about Ava's room and discovered that it faced a busy street filled with the sounds of traffic and children playing. I suggested that Trudy add some sound-absorbing features to her daughter's bedroom, including a fluffy throw rug on the floor, heavy curtains at the windows, and cushions and some stuffed toys on a window seat—all to create a new, softer sound environment in the room, which before had echoed with noise. Trudy also put a white-noise machine in Ava's room to muffle the creaks that the floorboards of the hall outside made when anyone walked past. She made some changes in their day-to-day life too. For example, taking Ava on errands in the car had always been a problem, because Ava whined and fidgeted so much. It turned out that Trudy, a visual person, usually drove in silence, content to absorb the passing scene. But Ava needed to hear her mother's voice. So Trudy now made a habit of chatting softly to Ava when they were in the car, especially at the beginning of a car trip. Ava became much calmer as a result. Nursing became easier as well once Trudy's ability to cue into her daughter's sense gave her a better idea of what Ava needed. Previously, Ava would often stop nursing before she had gotten enough milk. She was just too distracted to continue. After Trudy began the practice of humming a favorite tune whenever she was breastfeeding, Ava would nurse without interruption until she was sated.

Feeding

If you notice that when you are breastfeeding your baby any kind of distraction—a sudden noise, someone walking into the room, the ringing of a phone—causes him to stop sucking and look toward the sound, you probably have an auditory child. Even something as simple as the squeaky rocking chair you sit in while feeding your child could interfere with his ability to relax and nurse. Because auditory children are so easily affected by noise and distracted by the simplest sounds, it is often best to feed them in a quiet, private space, with the door closed. You may find, as Trudy did, that singing softly to your child can help relax him during feeding time. In fact, some auditory babies hum to themselves while nursing. This seems to be a form of self-soothing that they employ instinctively to help themselves concentrate and enter a relaxation zone.

It may seem paradoxical, but while auditory children can be acutely sensitive to noise, they themselves tend to generate quite a lot of it. While still babies they make a lot of noise with their mouths—not just quietly humming to themselves while nursing but cooing, shouting, crying, and babbling, depending on their mood. As they become more mobile and develop their motor skills, auditory children will begin to experiment with making noise in every way they can think of, from banging pots together to throwing toys out of their cribs and splashing wildly in the bathwater.

As your auditory baby grows and you move from bottle-feeding or breastfeeding in your arms to solid food in a high chair, mealtimes may start to get noisy. Like the tactile child, the auditory child will want to experiment with her food. But rather than playing with her food with her fingers, as the tactile child does, she'll want to see how much noise she can make with whatever is on her plate—or, more likely, with the plate itself. Spoons, cups, and plates become noisemakers in the hands of an auditory baby, who will want to bang these things together and throw them on the floor in order to see what kind of noise she can drum up. She'll also play with the food itself for the same purpose, sliding cereal around on her plate and smacking her lips loudly after each sip of milk. This baby will have a vocal response to everything, including food. Her favorite mashed potatoes will make her squeal with excitement, and those peaches she can't stand will set off a screaming fit.

Dressing and Diapering

When it comes to changing and dressing an auditory baby, singing to her as you slip her into her pajamas or fold her into a fresh diaper can minimize her fussing and crying. As she gets older, you'll be able to help your auditory child manage her daily tasks and transitions with songs and sounds—and it's never too early to start incorporating this habit into your routines. She'll be so entranced by your singing (no matter what kind of voice you have) that you'll be able to slip on her shoes or pull that sweater over her head before she has a chance to make a fuss. In one family I worked with, the mother was having a lot of trouble dressing her son. He would squirm and wriggle, and she was always nervous he was going to roll off the changing table. Once we realized he was auditory, I suggested she play some soothing music while dressing him. Now she turns on the music as soon as she begins to change his diaper, so by the time she gets around to pulling on his clothes, he's calm and happy as can be, entranced and distracted by the familiar getting-dressed tunes.

Auditory Toddler Basics, from Ages One to Three

How the Auditory Toddler Communicates and Manages Emotions

The world of an auditory child is dominated by sounds. From the first time she hears her parents' voices, sound has the power to soothe her, excite her, teach her new skills, and expand her knowledge. Sound also has the power to overwhelm this child, either when it is harsh and unfamiliar or when there is simply too much of it for her to experience at once. To hear through the ears of auditory children, we must take new notice of the cacophony of sounds that exists in our environments.

As auditory children grow from babies to toddlers, they continue to rely on the emotional cues they take from the voices of those around them. They also begin at an early age to exhibit strong, sophisticated verbal skills, and once these children begin to speak, you can easily decipher how they are feeling by their tone of voice, even if you can't yet understand the words.

Over time the auditory toddler is increasingly able to express his feelings and preferences vocally—and this will make for quite a noisy household. Although they themselves like to make a lot of noise in the kitchen, the kitchen can be a stressful place for auditory children, especially if your kitchen is anything like mine, where the tile floors and walls of the room echo with all the clattery sounds I make trying to clean up from one meal and prepare for the next. Clinking glasses, whizzing blenders, and banging pots and pans are just the sort of startling noises that set auditory children on edge. Your toddler may do better if he's in a nearby room when you are in the kitchen preparing meals or cleaning up.

Of course, the kitchen is just one of the many settings that can overstimulate an auditory toddler. These children are not able to tune out sounds in their environment the way many adults and other children can. The auditory toddler takes it all in: music playing, people talking and shouting, machines buzzing and beeping. As a result, certain public places—large, crowded restaurants, big department stores or supermarkets, movie theaters—can agitate this child and sometimes lead to tantrums.

Too little noise can also be a problem, as discussed. One mother I worked with was worried that her three-and-a-half-year-old daughter, Sophie, was watching too much television. Having been to their house and tuned in to Sophie's immediate environment, I suggested that, being auditory, Sophie was probably using the TV to add background sound to an otherwise quiet room. So Ann bought her daughter a small CD player and some children's classical music, which she put on whenever Sophie was in her playroom. Ann quickly discovered that Sophie did not miss the TV at all; she had simply enjoyed the sound of the television shows without having much interest in the visual content. With the sound of the music playing in the background, she seemed quite content to play with her dolls and never once asked to put the television on, much to Ann's surprise.

In another situation, Jack, who had just turned three, kept complaining to his father that he was bored. He seemed so unhappy about coming home after day care that he sometimes even threw a tantrum as soon as they entered the driveway. When the father started to think about his son's experience from an auditory perspective, he realized that their house was very quiet. Not only was there no music, since neither he nor his wife was particularly interested in music, but ever since the baby had been born they were always telling Jack to shush and stay quiet so he wouldn't wake his sister. Once he realized how starved Jack must be for some kind of auditory stimulation, he and his wife made a big deal of giving Jack his own CD player for his room at home and bought him some fun children's music. Now Jack can barely wait to get home so he can start listening to his favorite songs.

Music may also be useful as a distraction to help your auditory toddler avoid a tantrum or come down from one more quickly. As one mom recounted, "John used to throw spectacular tantrums, kicking and screaming. And he wouldn't listen to anything I said to try to soothe him. I would have to put him in a room by himself and shut the door until he calmed down, which could take quite a while. After I began doing things to appeal to his auditory sense, I still had to put him in his room, but I tried turning on his music and making it loud enough so he could hear it over the tantrum. After just a few minutes, he would calm down as he lay on the bed and listened to the music. And after about ten minutes he'd come out on his own and say sorry without having to be prompted."

Though these kids are pretty even-keeled when it comes to mood, like all kids they can get very fussy or even melt down into a tantrum if they're tired, hungry, or sick. But auditory kids may also throw tantrums when they feel overwhelmed by too much auditory stimulation. If your child is tired, hungry, or sick, the situation is not going to get any better until you deal with the immediate problem. However, if none of these seems to be the problem and the child is still in obvious distress, whining or squealing in a high-pitched voice, she is asking you for help, even if she herself doesn't understand the problem or have the words to describe it. So check to see if there's a possibility that she's having a bad reaction to too much noise in the immediate environment.

Is there something you can do to lessen the noise? Sometimes moving your child for just a few minutes into a quieter place will help. Often a quick, focused conversation can help alleviate or avoid the tantrum. Putting on an iPod with her favorite music can also be a lifesaver.

Auditory children really like to be read to, from the time they are babies right through their preschool years. Hearing the voice of their mother, or of another person to whom they are attached, is particularly comforting to them and helps ground them emotionally. These children need auditory cues of reassurance in the same way that tactile children need comforting hugs or a guiding hand on the shoulder, particularly during times of stress, such as separation from a parent. In one example, I worked with a mother and her two-and-a-half-year-old daughter, Serena. The mother was a fashion buyer who traveled a great deal. Serena would become so distraught over her mother's absence that the mom reached out to me to help figure out a way to make these trips less painful for both her daughter and herself. I asked her what, if anything, seemed to be the thing that Serena missed most when she traveled. Immediately she replied, "My reading her stories before going to sleep at night." I suggested that she take some of Serena's favorite books with her on her next trip and read her a bedtime story over the telephone. In another case involving somewhat similar circumstances, a mother who had to travel for work several days every month actually tape-recorded herself reading bedtime stories for her auditory child. Both girls were left with their dads at home and missed their moms. But when they listened to the tapes or had the nighttime call, they felt connected to their moms while they were traveling and went to sleep more happily and calmly.

Like all children, auditory kids will have bouts of separation anxiety as toddlers. If your child is having trouble letting go when you drop her off at preschool, a playdate, or any other activity, try playing her favorite music in the car on the way there. This will have a soothing effect as she tries to manage any difficult feelings that arise before having to say goodbye to you.

In one case, a mother even went so far as to ask her child's pre-K teacher to play the same music at school. I have also suggested to parents that they remind their auditory children, "You can always tell the teacher to call me on the phone." Just being able to hear their parent's voice for a moment may be all they need to calm down.

When it comes to transitioning from one activity to the next, including waking up in the morning, getting dressed, sitting down to meals, cleaning up after playtime, getting ready for bed, and so on, an auditory child can benefit from being guided by a consistent, reassuring voice. Music, most of all, can be a great help to auditory toddlers as they move from one task or event to another. If you simply yell, "Hurry, put your shoes on," and expect the auditory toddler to obey, you will be disappointed. But if you play her favorite putting-on-shoes song, she's much more likely to do as asked without any additional encouragement. Not only is the music itself pleasing, but the fact that it gives a clear signal about what the next activity is appeals to the auditory child's early preference for a sense of order and sequence.

This tactic of using aural cues to shepherd your child through changes in her day can also help when you are preparing to leave her in someone else's care. Imagine that you and your partner are headed out for an evening at the movies and you've got a babysitter coming. You could ask her to help you choose a babysitter song, to be played as a greeting when the sitter arrives.

You can also try talking to your child about the fun evening she'll have with her babysitter and how you'll be returning in a short while. But be careful: If you are anxious about how she will react to being left with a sitter, your auditory toddler will pick up on this in your voice, regardless of what words you use with her, because auditory children show a remarkable ability to decipher meaning in the inflections of people's voices.

Your tone matters a great deal to an auditory child, as much if not more than the content of your words. Even if you are not speaking directly to your child, if she hears your voice becoming agitated or tense, she probably will respond in kind.

One woman I worked with, a single mother named Janey, discovered this to be the case with her son, Paul, who was about sixteen months old when I met them. Janey ran her own business from her home, since she wanted to be able to spend as much time as possible with Paul. When we met, she was having trouble coping with her home-work life because of Paul's behavior.

"I bring Paul with me into my office in the afternoons," Janey told me. "I've done this since he was an infant. He used to sleep in a bassinet while I worked at my desk. Now he's in day care in the mornings, but he still comes to spend time with me while I'm working after lunch."

Janey, a tactile person, loved having her son nearby while she worked; she often pulled him onto her lap when she was reading through a stack of papers or scrolling through her e-mail. But over time, her son had become increasingly disruptive during their afternoons in her office. He tended to get agitated and loud and was even showing signs of temper tantrums.

"He just fidgets and cries and makes a nuisance of himself. I will play with him for a few minutes, but it seems that as soon as I turn back to my work or pick up the phone to make a call, he's sobbing or throwing his toys around in a tantrum."

Janey wanted her son to be with her. She also needed to concentrate on her business. But she was beginning to doubt that she could do both. "It's getting to the point where I feel like I might have to make a big change, maybe hire a babysitter for him so I can work," she told me. "I can't really afford this, and I don't really want to do it anyway. But I'm at the point where something has to change." She was becoming more and more exasperated about the situation.

I spent an afternoon with Janey and Paul at my clinic, and a few things became clear. Paul was definitely auditory. He was a verbal child, with a large vocabulary and a strong desire to participate in the conversations between Janey and me. He hummed to himself quite frequently when he played alone. In addition, I noticed that when I accidentally dropped my purse, spilling the contents on the hardwood floor, he was so startled that he jumped and then covered his ears.

When I visited Janey and Paul at home I noticed that at times Paul seemed quiet and content, playing happily by himself, as Janey went about her work. Paul's cries and tantrums corresponded to a very specific circumstance: He acted out when Janey was on the telephone. During her phone conversations, Paul cried, fussed, and tossed his toys around. If Janey spoke on the phone a lot during an afternoon, Paul would cry almost the entire time.

When I explained this connection to Janey, her eyes grew wide. "You're right! I hadn't really thought it through, but part of the problem is that I'm always trying to calm him down while I'm dealing with a client. It's a big part of what's been so frustrating about the whole situation."

I further explained to Janey that since Paul was auditory, he was extremely sensitive to the tone of her voice. The voice she used with her son was soft, tender, and gentle. When she was doing business on the telephone, I observed that her voice dropped in pitch, it became tighter and more clipped, and she frequently sounded tense and serious. This change sounded drastic to her auditory son, and it made him edgy and uncomfortable, which led to his tantrums. As an auditory person myself, it was easy for me to imagine the effect this vocal change was having on her son, but it had never occurred to Janey, who simply isn't sensitive to voices in this way. On the other hand, when she was typing and doing paperwork at her desk, the sounds she made were quiet and repetitive, which were actually soothing for the toddler.

Janey and I agreed that she would rearrange her work so that she could make most of her phone calls during the morning, leaving her paperwork and computer work for her afternoons with Paul.

"What a change," Janey reported to me after a few weeks. "Since I cut back on the phone work in the afternoons, Paul has been so much better. And I am actually getting more work done this way, since I don't have to worry about him screaming in the middle of a business call. I'm glad I understand how my voice affects him, and I can use this to help our communication. It's a very powerful tool to have, to understand how your child interprets what you say and do."

How the Auditory Toddler Explores the World

Language plays a critical role in how auditory toddlers discover and explore the world around them. They are eager to expand their language skills in order to communicate their needs in ever more sophisticated ways. And you'll find that language is the key to communicating your expectations of them. The older they become, the more auditory children rely on words to guide and teach them and to talk them through their activities or your expectations of their behavior.

Auditory children tend to be very precise in their spoken communications, and they expect the same of others, so you need to be careful what you say around them. If there are any inconsistencies in what you say, especially ones that involve little white lies, these children are likely to notice and remember them, picking up on any clues that you are changing your story or not telling the truth. If you tell your auditory child that you are going to stop by the library after school or that you'll treat him to ice cream after dinner, he will hold you to your promise, and at any sign that you may back out he will recite with great accuracy the exact words of your promise. If you change your plan to go out to dinner and tell your auditory toddler a white lie such as "The pizza place is closed tonight; we can't go," don't be surprised if he calls you on it.

As he becomes more mobile, the auditory child explores his world by seeing what kind of opportunities it affords him to make more and different kinds of noise. He also remains sensitive to the noises that others make. And as he becomes ever more adept with language, he also pays more attention to the words that people say. So watch your tongues, Mom and Dad—auditory toddlers tend to be precocious about memorizing what you're saying, and they have the language skills to repeat it. Alas, they also seem to have a penchant for picking up on (and repeating) the most inappropriate expressions that come out of our mouths. On numerous occasions parents have asked me why their small child, just barely out of babyhood, is already using swear words. This is because when we use such language, we tend to speak in voices that convey a lot of emotion and drama—something that the auditory child will cue into. Obviously, the child doesn't know the meaning of the words, but the emotive power they carry ensures that she will remember them and use them herself.

Since toddlers do not yet have a clear or coherent sense of time, they need to be given constant reminders about the plan for the day or the week. But because the auditory child likes order and routine, he will respond well to a verbal description of the events scheduled for the day. And because rhythm and music get through to him easily, you might try reciting a list of the day's activities as a song or even a series of rhymes.

When auditory children resist direction, it often turns out that the negative response has more to do with the tone in which the direction is given than the direction itself. So when a mother complains to me that her child "just doesn't listen" whenever she tells him to come to dinner, get dressed, or whatever, I suggest that she try using a gentler speaking tone and see what happens. In countless cases, I've seen good results from this. Parents who make the effort to speak in a calm, even tone find that their children respond well, listening and following directions readily, instead of seeming to ignore them.

In one case, a mother was frustrated with her three-and-a-half-year-old daughter, Blair's, obstinate refusal to pay attention to even the simplest demands. "When she's playing in her room and I want her to come to the kitchen, no matter how many times I call her she ignores me. Finally, I end up screaming at the top of my lungs, 'Come in to dinner this minute or you won't get to eat!' at which point she dissolves into tears and becomes hysterical. But I don't know what else to do to get her to listen to me." Hearing both the bafflement and the guilt in this mom's voice, I knew she genuinely didn't understand her child's need for a different communication style.

"Instead of yelling from the kitchen," I suggested, "have you tried walking up to her, bending down, and saying warmly to her, 'Blair, it's time for dinner now. Please come to the table'?"

"Could it be that simple?" the mother asked me.

"Yes," I reassured her.

And it was. Of course, it took the mom some time to be persuaded that making the effort to leave the kitchen would be worth her while. But when she did walk down the hall to her daughter's room and speak in a gentler tone, the improvement was immediate.

Sometimes the seeming obstinacy of the auditory child is related to the fact that too many sounds are coming at him at once. If you yourself are not auditory, you might not pick up on how distracting this can be for your child. For example, one mother I worked with, who thought her child was defying her, found that if she turned off the TV while she was talking to him, he was able to follow and pay attention to her with much more focus.

Because of their relatively sophisticated language skills, which give them the ability to recite things out loud, and their sensitivity to the kind of rhythm and repetition that are characteristic of music, auditory children may get an early start on their ABCs and their numbers. One mom said her auditory daughter, Jillian, was able to learn both her ABCs and counting to ten—in Spanish, yet—by merely reciting the letters and the numbers in a songlike, rhythmic manner. These children enjoy repeating out loud any list of numbers, words, or letters. For them repetition is a playful game, one that also happens to enable them to learn more easily. The auditory child also shows a growing propensity for sorting things by color, shape, and size. This is related to her pattern recognition skills; just as she can hear the patterns in music, she can recognize visual patterns as well.

How the Auditory Toddler Plays and Interacts

As when they were babies, auditory children are easily engaged in play that involves sound. Toy instruments, such as drums or keyboards, will give your toddler the chance to make his own music, but hold your ears, since these will be among his most popular toys. Rhyming games, which involve both rhythm and language, are entrancing for these toddlers, as are books that incorporate sound into the story, like those that ask the child to supply the sounds that animals make. To an auditory child, every toy can and should talk out loud. You'll see this child orchestrate conversations among a circle of stuffed animals or between two toy soldiers, keeping himself amused as he chats away, speaking everyone's part. Activities such as building things out of blocks, coloring and drawing, and doing puzzles are enjoyable outlets for his developing sense of organization, order, and structure. He may also like dance, karate, and gymnastics—physical activities that involve rhythm and routine.

In social situations, your auditory toddler will be perfectly content to play by himself. And in some cases your auditory toddler may resist playing with other kids, especially groups. Often this has to do with her tendency to avoid situations that seem loud and chaotic. She might be more inclined to play with one child at a time in a quiet, one-on-one setting in which the noise and general activity level are low.

If there is something in the sound environment that is displeasing to the child—whether it's too much sound or too little—your auditory toddler will try to make changes that give her a measure of control over noise levels. In doing so, this child might behave in what seems a somewhat peculiar way—for example, dragging pillows and blankets into her playroom, or putting all her stuffed animals at the head of her bed before she goes to sleep at night. It's more than likely that what she is doing is trying to adjust the quality of sound in these rooms, whether to dampen the echo of an empty space or to muffle the sound coming from an adjacent room.

The Everyday Life of the Auditory Toddler

Sleeping

Even more than for other children, sleep is crucial for the auditory child's sense of balance, harmony, and energy. Imagine, for a moment, all the effort required by such intense listening, and you'll understand why auditory children tend to be worn out at day's end. After many hours of absorbing auditory stimulation from whatever comes within earshot, not to mention generating a fair amount of noise themselves, these kids need a solid night's sleep not just in order to recharge for the next day but also as a way of getting a break from so much sensory input. But because these children tend to wake up so easily, they might need to spend more time in bed than other kids their age in order to get enough rest.

Auditory children do best when they stick to a regular schedule, going to bed at the same time every night, with a certain amount of time allotted to winding down beforehand. This might involve your reading a storybook to your child or just listening to him talk about what he did that day. Right before they become so exhausted that they're ready to drop off into a deep sleep, these kids can get very wound up, chattering away with great animation, but the outpouring doesn't usually last long. As one mom told me, "I can always predict when David is completely spent from the day—he starts chatting wildly and happily. It's as if he has to express the last thoughts from his head in order to go to sleep!"

Because he is constantly scanning his environment for sound as a way to orient himself, the auditory child sleeps better and more soundly when surrounded by familiar sounds—even Dad's snoring. This child will tend to feel more comfortable and secure, and therefore will tend to sleep more easily, in a room where he can hear a certain amount of background noise, as opposed to being in a room that is completely silent, cut off from these comforting sounds. When sleeping away from home, whether you're staying in a hotel or at Granddad's house, he will feel more calm and go to sleep more easily if he is comforted by a familiar piece of music or a bedtime story.

The auditory toddler can do well sharing a room with a sibling, finding the ritual end-of-day sounds of his sister or brother soothing to his ears as he falls asleep. This child will prefer an occupied room to an empty one for sleeping, provided that the noise is not too loud. If, however, there is too much noise in the room, an auditory child will stay wide awake, avid to hear every last thing. One mother whose son awoke often from the loud thunderstorms that are typical of the climate of Queensland, where they lived, thought that she could solve the problem by keeping him in bed with her until he was sound asleep and then putting him back in his own bed. But she found that the first loud crack of thunder would wake him, and he'd be back in bed with her, crying again. So she installed a stereo in his room and played classical music at a volume that was just loud enough to muffle the sound of the thunder but not too loud to keep him awake, and it worked—he stayed asleep. Bath time was also a big problem, so this same mom put on a CD, explaining to her son, "The first song is for getting into the bath. Three songs during the bath. And one song to get out of the bath." This simple and playful game worked beautifully to help manage bath time and pave the way for bedtime. You might try playful music such as that by Raffi, Jack Johnson, and The Wiggles. The Beatles are popular among children too. Keep in mind that auditory children like a variety of songs—a bath song, a getting-dressed song, a going-to-sleep song, a driving-in-the-car song, and so on. I often recommend that parents choose music they themselves enjoy, or else listening can get quite tiresome quite quickly.

Feeding

Mealtimes for the auditory toddler will remain noisy affairs. From his perch in the high chair, your auditory toddler will continue to make noise as he did as a baby, with anything he can get his hands on—a spoon, dish, or cup—only now he's stronger and more dexterous, and probably has better aim. It's safe to expect that these kids will delight in throwing utensils on the floor and banging their plates and cups on their tray. As your child gets older and you raise your expectations about his behavior, it's easy to forget that he is not simply being naughty in these instances; he's still trying to eke the maximum amount of sound out of every moment. That doesn't mean that you have to just give in. There are techniques you can use to minimize the noise and mess.

One mom was encountering the somewhat typical challenges of feeding a rambunctious toddler. Her son, Judah, who was auditory, would throw his food onto the floor or table or not eat at all. However, she found that if she talked to him while he was eating, he began to eat his food without a problem. If she kept talking, mealtimes went pretty smoothly; if she stopped, he would revert to throwing his veggies around or not eating at all. Once the mother, who was a visual person, quiet and orderly, saw how effective it was to make an auditory, verbal connection with him, she had a technique that she knew she could adapt to many different situations, and she made a point of using it often, even though it ran counter to her own tendency to go about her day in relative silence.

An auditory child needs to be kept engaged; it's not so important *what* you say but that you are saying something, and that you keep up a steady stream of chatter.

Dressing

The daily task of dressing a toddler—no small feat for most parents—is usually not much of a problem for parents of auditory children. Unlike visual children, who love clothes and will have strong feelings about what colors they're willing to wear, or tactile children, who are extremely particular about how their clothes feel next to their skin, auditory children won't generally demonstrate strong feelings about their clothes. If they do have preferences, they'll probably like clothing made with fabrics that create a bit of noise, like the whispery rustle of taffeta or the *swoosh swoosh* sound of corduroy. Noise-making accessories, such as bells on mittens or a whistle attached to an overcoat, will also be appealing.

If there are any problems getting an auditory child dressed in the morning, then talking to her during the process will help move the process along. As you are pulling her clothes out of the closet, talk to her about what she's going to wear that day, where she'll be going, and what she'll be doing. This will help her settle down and focus on the task of getting dressed, both because she likes being talked to and because the information you are giving her about what happens next will motivate her. Playing a favorite song and calling it her getting-dressed song is another technique to help her master this daily task. Think of these routines and your running conversation with your child as part of what you do to help her feel grounded for the day ahead.

Toilet Training

Auditory children are pretty quick at mastering their bowels. Methodical teaching with lots of verbal explanation about how, when, and why will help them understand what you are encouraging them to do, giving them the confidence and know-how to follow through on your directions. Again, you will find that your auditory toddler responds to routines, such as always going to the potty after a meal, before leaving the house, and before going to bed. His progress will be steady, with more mistakes at the beginning and fewer as time goes on. When he does have an accident, it's very important not to sigh or groan or admonish an auditory toddler, which could impede his progress and cause him to regress. Talking to him in an upbeat, cheerful way about trying to remember to get to the potty in time is much more likely to produce good results.

One way you can help to make this process enjoyable for him is by playing special "toilet music" or reading a "potty story" while he is on the toilet. Music and storytelling not only are fun for him but also can be reassuring if he's one of those auditory children who finds the sound of the toilet flushing to be alarming. Placing a bathroom mat down on the floor in front of the toilet can help absorb any echoes in the bathroom, which might also bother your child. In general you'll want to be aware of the many kinds of bathroom sounds that might be troublesome to your child, and to do what you can to minimize them or distract him from them. This will help overcome any resistance he may feel to being in the bathroom. But even these efforts may not be enough, and for a while he may be more comfortable using a potty that is in his room or somewhere else in the house, possibly within earshot of the family so that he can hear the familiar noises of the household.

Auditory Preschooler Basics, from Ages Three to Five

The Auditory Preschooler's Emotional Life

Now that the auditory child is gaining more independence, he will begin to show more inclination to control his aural environment, especially if he is in a situation where too much sound is coming at him. Large, noisy, crowded public places are challenging for these children, who will feel assaulted by the chorus of unfamiliar noises. Supermarkets, for example, are notoriously difficult places for auditory kids to manage because the noise level can seem so overwhelming. The cacophony of sound created by loud voices, the overhead buzz from fluorescent lights, the squeak of the shopping carts, the clatter of footsteps, the crying of other children—all of this can simply be too much stimulation for auditory children. Playing in a large group of kids at school, or even with siblings who get very rowdy and rambunctious, can also stress them. It's not that these kids can't spend time at the supermarket, the mall, the playground, or a sports event. They can. But auditory children may not last as long as other kids in these kinds of environments before becoming tired and cranky. Often the only way to calm them down is simply to remove them from the settings that overstimulate them. When things get too noisy, auditory children will need a break, a little downtime in a quiet part of the house, or outside where the sounds of nature have a soothing effect.

When under any kind of stress, auditory toddlers tend to express themselves by either withdrawing into a shell or having a screaming tantrum. When the behavior of an auditory child is truly out of control or unacceptable, most parents get a very direct and immediate response by simply refusing to talk or listen to him. A parent might say: "I am not going to speak to you until you calm down."

As they get older you might notice another behavioral trait common to auditory children when they are overwhelmed: They show their displeasure by making an audible "hmpf" sound and then crossing their arms in protest, not saying another word. Unable to silence the world around them, they speak volumes with their own silence.

These kids use sound (and occasionally, as noted above, silence) as a way to express their feelings and their moods, and also as a way of managing their feelings. You may find an auditory child singing songs quietly as a way to self-soothe after she scrapes her knee or stubs her toe. She'll also sing to you when she's excited or as a way to tell you that she loves you. When she's happy, she'll want to listen to perky, upbeat music. But if she's in a bad mood and you put this same music on, perhaps to try to cheer her up, she's likely to be irritated, since the music simply doesn't match how she's feeling. Auditory children tend to make a lot of noise, and paying close attention to the sounds that come out of them can give parents insight into their children's emotional lives.

For parents, the best way to manage or direct behavior is by learning how to become better listeners, paying attention both to the words their children speak and the general tone and tenor of their communication. Auditory children tend to be very chatty when happy. If they are quiet, there is probably something going on. At such times, parents can help their auditory children by asking them how they feel or what they are thinking about. Unlike other children, these kids really can articulate what's on their minds, so it pays to ask. And when they answer, try to listen without interrupting. Having the feeling that they are being listened to is extremely important to these kids.

Marie and her husband, Ryan, came to me with concern about their daughter, Vivian. Vivian was a bright, inquisitive five-year-old, well liked by her teachers, who regularly told her parents how well-behaved their daughter was in school. At home, however, Vivian's behavior had become an issue for the family.

As an older sister to a six-month-old baby brother, Julian, Vivian had initially been excited about having a sibling. Before he arrived, she sang songs about the baby and spent hours rocking a doll in her arms, whispering and cooing in the doll's ear. But once Julian became a reality, Vivian's reaction had been mixed, her parents told me. She loved to sit and play near his bassinet and to tell him stories when the family gathered in the living room after dinner. But other times she would behave badly around him—she shouted at him when he cried, and threw loud, angry tantrums when her parents were feeding or changing him or putting him to bed.

"She seemed jealous of Julian, which we had expected to some extent," Marie told me. "After all, she'd been an only child for over four years. But we've also tried to be proactive about this and make sure she's getting plenty of attention, even while we're spending so much time with Julian."

Marie and Ryan had hoped that Vivian's acting out would diminish over time, but unfortunately that had not been the case. As the baby got older, Vivian's attitude toward him seemed to deteriorate even further. Mealtimes were a disaster, they told me. Once Julian had graduated to a high chair and joined the family at dinner, Vivian would refuse to sit at the table. Julian's bedtime was another minefield. Whenever her parents were trying to put the baby down, Vivian would cry and act out in various ways. Many mornings found her refusing to get dressed for kindergarten, even though she loved school. Still in her pajamas, she'd plunk herself down on her bedroom floor with a cluster of her stuffed animals, whispering conspiratorially to them and shouting at her mother whenever Marie asked her to pick up the pace.

After meeting with Marie and Ryan, I spent some time with them at their home, observing the situations they had described. Watching the family's dynamics made several things clear to me. Both Marie and her husband were tactile people—they were active, high-energy, purpose-driven adults who were very physically affectionate with each other and their children. They tended to communicate with each other and their daughter via a kind of "physical shorthand": they tapped each other on the shoulder when one wanted the other's attention; they greeted each other (and Vivian) at the breakfast table with a loving squeeze to the back of the neck; and when they were excited or happy or wanted to express a compliment, there were hugs and kisses for everybody.

As for the kids, it turned out that both of their children were auditory. Julian, at six months, was babbling up a storm, and also throwing every toy and utensil within reach to the ground, in hopes of generating as much ruckus as possible. All of his noisemaking behavior agitated his older sister. Vivian disliked sitting with her brother during meals. When I was there he was banging his spoon and yowling for more peas, and it was clear that she couldn't relax and enjoy her own meal. Moreover, I noticed that Vivian was having a hard time getting her parents' attention. Once upon a time, before Julian came along, she had been used to being the center of attention during dinner. As Marie told me, she would spend most of dinnertime chatting away merrily, filling her parents in on every detail of her day. Now Marie and Ryan were clearly distracted by Julian, as any parents would be by such a noisy child. When I related my observations to the couple and offered the suggestion that Vivian might be feeling shut out, a light dawned on their faces.

"You know, I hadn't bothered to mention it because it didn't seem important," said Ryan, "but when she is upset, one of the things she says a lot is 'You're not listening to me.' It never occurred to me that this would matter so much. I've tried hard—we both have—to give Vivian as much attention as we give Julian."

I asked Ryan and Marie to give me some examples of how they paid special attention to Vivian. "Well, I like to sit with her on my lap and watch television sometimes," Ryan said. "And we both try to make sure she gets plenty of hugs and kisses, since we're holding the baby so much," Marie added.

I explained to Vivian's parents how they were sending all the right messages—they just weren't using the right medium. For an auditory child, hugs and kisses simply don't register as strongly as words do in communicating affection and praise. Vivian's parents were communicating with her in the way that came naturally for them; it just so happens that their daughter's natural communication style operates very differently from their own. If they wanted Vivian to feel particularly loved and praised, they needed to put these feelings into words. In order for her to feel special, she needed to be told she was special.

We also talked about ways to help brother and sister coexist more peacefully. Having two auditory children—both extremely sensitive to noise—presented some interesting challenges and, I believed, some eminently manageable solutions. Julian made a lot of noise during meals, which irritated his sister. Julian also cried and fussed at bedtime and nap time. Vivian was agitated by the baby's cries and responded by making noise herself, such as whining to her parents or turning on the television at full volume. Her noise only agitated her brother even more. These two were in a difficult cycle that needed to be broken by implementing some new habits for everyone.

I suggested to Marie and Ryan that they feed the baby ahead of their own dinner with their daughter, and have him sit near the table in a bouncy seat while the three of them ate together. This way, mealtimes would be somewhat quieter and both parents could direct more attention toward their daughter.

To tackle their other issues, which mostly involved Vivian reacting to the baby's crying at bedtime and in the morning when they were all getting ready for the day, I suggested that Marie and Ryan try to recruit Vivian into their family routine as a helper. For example, Vivian could choose songs to play or sing for the baby while he was getting ready to go to sleep (soft, soothing music) or when he was getting dressed in the morning (upbeat, bouncy music). If she could feel like she was participating in taking care of the baby, and if, within certain boundaries, she could have some control over the sounds in the immediate environment, Vivian was much less likely to feel the need to create some kind of competing noise as a protest. Rather than have these siblings trying to outdo each other with antagonistic noisemaking, I wanted the parents to see if they could bring their two children into some kind of harmony with each other.

Marie called me a few weeks later to report on their progress. "This is really working," she said with relief in her voice. "Feeding the baby separately has helped a lot at dinner—things are quieter and a lot more pleasurable for all of us, especially Vivian. We've been able to devote more of our time to talking with her. And she is doing a great job of helping me with the baby. She loves talking to him and singing to him. These days, whenever things get out of hand, I try to think about how to calm them both down with sounds—whether it's music, or reading a story together, or just talking quietly."

The Auditory Preschooler's Learning Style

As these kids grow older their communication skills—both speaking and listening—become more complex and sophisticated. Their daily environments become more complicated as well as they start going to school, having playdates with friends, and participating in a variety of recreational activities. Exposure to this ever larger, more public world, filled with sounds that need to be interpreted, filtered, and mastered, will be a major challenge for these kids. But through it all, auditory children will continue to rely on sound as their primary guide to experience.

With their rapidly increasing activities involving friends, sports, and school, children ages three to five often have tightly scheduled lives. But the auditory child often resists conforming to other people's ideas about time and schedules, which can drive his parents crazy. This child is striking in his inclination to move through the day at his own leisurely pace, setting his own (usually dawdling) timetable. This can be mystifying and irritating to parents, who spend many frustrating hours trying to shoo their child through the tasks of the morning or the routines of bedtime. As we saw with toddler-age children, this characteristic is related to the auditory child's difficulty transitioning from one activity to the next.

Even at ages four and five, these kids can still benefit from reliable auditory cues, such as prerecorded music or songs their parents make up to signal the time for each activity. The transitions of your auditory child's day can be managed more effectively by playing time-for-school and brush-your-teeth songs, for example, rather than simply telling her what to do. As she is now old enough to have strong preferences about music, one way of increasing cooperation is to include her in the selection of songs you'll use to guide her through the day. An auditory child will enjoy selecting or creating the perfect songs to accompany her getting dressed for school, doing simple chores such as putting her clothes in her drawers or feeding the cat, and getting ready for bed. And praise is always welcome. Short, simple phrases—"Good job" when she puts her clothes on without any prompting from you, for example—are just what she likes to hear.

On the other hand, the auditory child can tune out questions and demands, even if they are repeated several times, if they are not delivered in a warm, friendly tone. She is not being intentionally disobedient; rather, she picks up on negative, hostile, or angry tones so easily—even when the speaker is trying to hide her feelings—that she early on develops the ability to tune out as a defense mechanism, and is often quite unaware that she is doing it.

Once the auditory child starts school (whether preschool at four or kindergarten at five), a teacher may complain that he is not paying attention. If the classroom is noisy, the child may be tuning it out as a protective mechanism. One mother came up with a solution that seemed to work with her son, Michael. Michael attended a Montessori school, which because of its emphasis on freedom of expression was often very noisy. Michael would complain to his mom, "It's too loud in there! I can't think!" His mother suggested that when the noise of his classmates' voices began to bother him, he hum his favorite going-to-sleep song. Once Michael began to do this kind of self-calming, which blocked out some of the sound, he felt much more in control of his environment and more comfortable being there.

Again, one of the best tools a parent can have is a tape recorder, especially as your auditory child gets older. With a tape deck, CD player, or iPod, the child can play his own music and drown out any noise he doesn't want to hear.

Auditory children are good learners and tend to do well in school. Their calm, usually attentive demeanor makes them an easy presence in the classroom and helps them to fall in line with teachers' expectations. An auditory child will sit comfortably, still and rapt, during story time, play companionably but not too roughly with his friends on the playground, and be the first to volunteer to start a sing-along. But he may get into trouble sometimes for being too chatty with his seatmates in class—the temptation to whisper a comment to his neighbor, or even to yell a retort to his friend across the room, often proves too much for the auditory child to resist.

Because their listening skills are so strong, auditory children tend to follow directions well. They will prefer to learn by listening, as opposed to taking information from a book or from visual aids such as flash cards. When learning their ABCs and their numbers, for example, they will respond best to aural cues, such as being read aloud to or being asked to match the sound of a letter with the letter itself. As discussed earlier, rhythm too can help, so many auditory children learn their ABCs by singing them aloud to themselves. This child learns best in a setting where teachers talk students through their work, clearly explaining the lessons and giving precise directions about how to do their homework. Under these circumstances, an auditory child will feel comfortable and eager to learn new things.

The auditory child, so diligent about soaking up the words of others, typically has a terrific vocabulary and excellent language skills in general. He may show an interest—and likely a real affinity—for foreign languages. These children are good communicators, with a knack not only for expressing themselves but also for hearing between the lines of what people are saying, thanks to their sensitivity to nuances of tone.

Whatever the circumstance, these kids simply love to talk. You'll hear your auditory child coming before you see her, chatting away to her dolls or her baby brother, or simply to herself. This child keeps a kind of running commentary going throughout her day. She also needs to get a lot of verbal feedback from her parents so that she knows they are listening to her. Complaints about not being listened to are a typical gripe from the auditory child whenever she feels she's not getting enough attention. For parents who are not auditory by nature and who are coping with so many demands on their time and energy, this plea from an auditory child can easily get lost in the din.

Some auditory children can be rather intense whiners. One technique that a mother and I came up with was to use that handy tape recorder and record the child's whining. When the child listened to himself making that nails-on-the-chalkboard kind of noise, he began to become aware of himself whining and to self-correct the behavior. Another mother, when faced with a whining child, would use auditory cues such as "When you speak to me that way, it hurts my ears."

One mother was having trouble getting her four-year-old son to pay attention to her when she spoke. She was especially concerned about the way he seemed to tune her out when she was trying to teach him to look both ways before crossing the street. Although she was of course holding his hand, she wanted him to notice when there was oncoming traffic so that he would be aware of danger. Instead of shouting at him, "Watch the cars!" she reminded him to look and then said, "Can you hear a car coming?" Again, she cued into his sense of sound to help direct his behavior and make him pay better attention.

The Auditory Preschooler's Social Life

The auditory child loves physical activity that incorporates music and rhythm. She will tend to prefer dance class to soccer or kickball games. She'd rather perform in the school musical than help to build the sets and costumes. On the playground, you'll see her jumping rope, playing hopscotch, and generally gravitating toward games that require her to move to a rhythm.

Auditory kids will continue to love listening to music, wherever they encounter it. As they mature, their musical preferences will sharpen. But individual as their choices may be, they tend to have certain things in common. Gravitating toward music that is simple in composition and melodic, auditory children generally don't like anything that is heavily orchestrated or very complicated. And music that is filled with discordant, harsh, and dramatic sounds can really jangle auditory children. So Mozart will appeal much more than Wagner, and cheerful pop songs and soulful ballads will draw them more than loud rock and roll—not just at this age but as they grow older.

The preschooler can still be quite sensitive to noisy environments, which can make occasions like kids' birthday parties a challenge. Often a child will develop a fear of or aversion to going to big social gatherings because of the intensity of the din created by many children playing in the same room. Keep in mind that your child may experience a real conflict: She probably wants to go to her classmate's party but can't physically handle the sound level there. This was the case with Gaby, a four-year-old child I worked with. When she went to parties, she tended to get overwhelmed to the point that she was cowering in the corner on the verge of tears. Sasha, Gaby's mom, was exasperated by this behavior, and felt that Gaby needed to "just deal with it." Because she worried that if Gaby avoided parties, she wouldn't have friends or develop proper social skills, she insisted that Gaby go, and once they were there she would often lead her away from the corner and try to thrust her back into the action. But when Sasha realized that Gaby was having problems because, being auditory, she was stressed by the volume of sound in the room, she handled the problem differently. When she saw Gaby withdrawing, she would gently suggest that they go outside and have a chat—not to punish her, not even to discuss her being upset—just to give Gaby a break from the loud noise. After a few minutes, Gaby would willingly go back into the party. Soon Gaby learned how to take the initiative. When she felt herself becoming overwhelmed she would pull her mom out to the hallway all on her own. Clearly she had figured out how to make herself comfortable and ask for downtime when she needed it.

In general, the auditory preschooler will continue to be quite content to play on his own much of the time. When he does play with others, he'll prefer one-on-one play to loud, boisterous group play. These children tend to be well grounded in who they are, and as their social lives gradually expand and become more diverse, they will rise to the occasion, always marching to the beat of their own drummer.

The Everyday Life of the Auditory Preschooler

Sleeping

Winding down before bedtime is an important step for this child, who continues to require an abundance of sleep in order to function well. When she gets overtired, you'll know it, because you'll hear it—loud and clear—in her voice. From screaming and yelling to out-and-out tantrums, she'll express her feelings very vocally. However tempting it may be to play fast and loose with this child's bedtime, the short-term convenience of changing her schedule to meet your own needs of the moment is not worth it. Unlike some other children, who might be able to coast through changes in sleeping schedule with comparative ease, the auditory child needs routine and regularity.

As when she was younger, calming bedtime music will ease her transition to sleep; if you choose happy, bouncy music, you might as well give her a shot of adrenaline.

There are a few other strategies that can help get this child to bed without fuss or trouble. Lowering the noise level of her immediate environment in the hour or so before bedtime will help her start to wind down. Playing her favorite songs—for brushing her teeth, putting on her pajamas, and so on—also helps move her toward bed in a familiar, reassuring way. This child will not want to fall asleep in an empty, quiet room all by herself. Reading to her and talking with her quietly as she falls asleep will soothe and calm her; playing music very softly will too. Filling her ears with quiet, gentle, familiar sounds is key to a trouble-free bedtime routine.

Feeding

As auditory children get older, their eating habits are not likely to change. They continue to be easily distracted by sound, so they won't do well eating in front of the television, which will take their focus away from their food. Ordering them to eat their dinner "now" will probably result in their tuning you out, especially if they hear impatience or anger in your voice. Again, they will eat with gusto if you engage them in conversation about their day—whom they played with at recess, what they did in class, where they went with their babysitter after school.

Dressing

Just as with eating, the auditory child's behavior while picking out his clothes and getting dressed is less about the clothes themselves and more about his interaction with you. You can appeal to your child's sense of routine to make this morning ritual fast and easy. For instance, you can discuss the order of events as you pull out clothes for him to wear: "First we are going to get dressed, then we are going to brush your hair, then go downstairs for breakfast, then Daddy is going to drive you to school." Auditory kids love sequence—it's part of their inherently mathematical mind-set—so this kind of discussion will engage them as you help them dress.

Mismatches with the Auditory Child

The auditory child presents some interesting mismatch challenges for parents with a different dominant sense. But let's first address the issues that may occur when an auditory parent is raising an auditory child.

Auditory Child with Auditory Parent

This combination can sometimes be quite explosive, as both parent and child tend to be simultaneously vocal and hypersensitive to sound. If a mother is a chatterbox, always on the phone, always gabbing away, as many auditory people are, an auditory child might feel left out or ignored. And the noise that auditory parents typically make can be overwhelming to a baby or small child. As you may recall, the auditory baby's startle reflex is very sensitive, so a lot of noise in the environment can make for an anxious, jumpy, fussy baby. An older child may just tune it out. In the same way, an auditory parent might unconsciously withdraw. For instance, if an auditory baby or young child is particularly whiny, the mother might "stop the noise" by blocking it out. Or, if driven to distraction by the noise, she might short-circuit and yell at her whining baby or child, almost certainly making a bad situation worse.

Soft music, gentle voices, and patience can all bring the noise level back under control. Giving an older child an iPod or CD player of his own may give him the control he needs over his environment.

Auditory people like to control the sound in their environment, which can set off a battle of wills, with both parent and child competing to assert their preference—loud music or silence, bouncy tunes or quiet classical, and so on. But you can find a compromise. One auditory mother of an infant put the auditory sensitivity of her baby to good use: Every time she sat down to nurse her, she put on her favorite soap opera, which relaxed her and the baby. Why? Because the baby got accustomed to the introductory music of the show and associated it with wonderful "mommy time."

Auditory Child with Tactile Parent

Tactile parents may ignore or fail to take seriously the auditory child's sensitivity to sound, because it just doesn't occur to them that this could be a problem. You might recall an earlier example of a mother who couldn't figure out why her third child could never stay asleep for his nap no matter how tired he was. This mom had not connected her daily routine—the washing of pots and pans, the vacuuming of the living room, and other tasks—with noise that completely disrupted the child's sleep. Although her two older kids were able to sleep through these familiar household noises (they were visual and tactile), her new baby was auditory. Thinking about her children in this framework helped her understand why the baby behaved so differently than his siblings, even though the environment was the same for all of them.

Tactile parents in particular tend to be a bit loud, which can be misinterpreted by the auditory child as hostile. Tone of voice can lead to misunderstandings too. Unaware of how they may sound to a child who is sensitive to nuance, tactile parents often speak in short, abrupt phrases and end up hurting the auditory child's feelings without ever understanding why the child seems so unhappy. One tactile mom would use the expression "Tough!" as a way of cutting off argument or discussion with her three-and-a-half-year-old auditory daughter. For example, she might say, "You can have either an ice pop for dessert or a small bowl of ice cream." If her daughter countered with, "I want a marshmallow pie," the answer was always, "Tough!" and the little girl would invariably burst into tears. One day the girl finally said to her mother, "Don't say 'Tough!'—it's mean!" She had the strength to stand up to her mother and the resourcefulness to teach her mother about her needs, but not every child does, so you'll have to learn to try to hear things through your child's ears.

As a tactile parent, if you try to be more attuned to the way you speak to your child, you'll notice that when you raise your voice, your child will tend to withdraw or act out. A quiet, gentle, even tone of voice and firm but not abrasive language (in other words, not "Tough!") will always work best with an auditory child.

Auditory Child with Visual Parent

As a visual parent, you may tend to go about your day rather quietly, focused on doing your work, organizing your day, making plans, creating order in your house. The quiet, nonverbal parent can be disconcerting to an auditory child who needs to hear plenty of reassurance, guidance, and praise—in words.

The kinds of words used are also important. When visual parents talk to their children, they tend to rely on visual cueing. But "Can you see what I mean?" won't be nearly as effective as "Do you hear what I am saying?" It may seem a subtle distinction, but it really can make a difference.

Visual parents, with their passion for order and their very strong feelings about aesthetics, may be very focused on appearances. The natural messiness of small children can be a problem for such people. The visual parent may have to readjust her standards for tidiness with an auditory child because, believe it or not, a clean room sounds different, more echoey, than a messy room. If an auditory child is making a practice of strewing clothes, toys, blankets, and pillows about, this may be a signal that there are too many hard surfaces, with too few buffers against sound, in the room. The child doesn't know what he's doing when he makes this mess, of course; he just knows that the room somehow feels more comfortable. So a few changes in his room—cushions on chairs, rugs on the floor, extra pillows on the bed, curtains at the windows—might make a big difference for him.

The visual parent's reliance on what she can take in through her eyes means that she will often be unaware of what her auditory child takes in through his ears. The resulting failure of communication can take a serious toll on both parent and child. For example, one mother I worked with had expended great amounts of time and energy to create a stunningly beautiful house. From the crystal chandeliers hanging on high to the wooden shutters at the windows to the highly polished marble floors, her house was a showcase. It was also, unbeknownst to her, an echo chamber that was driving her two-year-old wild, which was why the little girl had become so irritable. For this auditory child, the sound of her mother's high heels clacking across the floors was almost too much to bear. The mother had no idea what the problem was, and she was beside herself with worry and frustration. When I visited their home and heard how every noise was magnified by all the hard surfaces, I explained to the mother how harsh this sound environment was for her child. Simple strategies such as asking people to remove their shoes and buying a few throw rugs helped muffle the noise, and the little girl soon calmed down.

Auditory Child with Taste/Smell Parent

Auditory children often get along quite well with a taste/smell parent. Taste/smell parents tend to be all about comfort, so their homes are likely to be furnished with soft, well-upholstered chairs and sofas, plush, deep pile rugs or carpets, lots of pillows and cushions, and throws on every available surface. All these soft objects and furnishings will absorb sound and help the auditory child feel very safe and secure. In this and other ways, taste/smell parents and auditory children are generally quite compatible.

They do differ when it comes to managing time. Auditory children do well when their days are orderly and well planned. Even though they may have trouble transitioning from one activity to another, they basically like to stick to a schedule. On the other hand, taste/smell parents tend to be loose about planning the day's events. The parents' spontaneity may seem impulsive to the auditory child, causing her to feel uneasy or anxious.

The taste/smell parent needs to guard against the tendency to "overcare" for her child. At the first squeal or cry, the taste/smell parent may rush over to rescue the child, even before it's evident that the sound the child is making is really a signal of any need or distress. Perhaps the auditory child is just making noise because he enjoys it. The parent who rushes in to try to comfort the baby or young child may be stifling the child's means of exploring himself and his world, cutting off what is often a form of play.

The taste/smell parent may be inclined to talk about feelings, always asking her auditory child how she feels. This kind of question can be baffling to an auditory child, who is more practical and concrete and not that inclined to think about feelings. Taste/smell parents also tend to be very emotionally demonstrative—in tone of voice, facial expression, and body language—in ways that can be overwhelming or confusing to an auditory child. I worked with one little girl whose parents were divorced and who didn't want to go to her father's house on weekends, when he was supposed to have custody. When I asked her why, she told me that her dad wasn't very happy to see her, which I found puzzling because I knew he adored his daughter. It turned out that he was so distressed by how limited his time with her was that he became hyperemotional whenever he was with her. The week before I saw her for the first time he had gotten all choked up and teary when she showed him a picture she drew of him, for example. Being only five, she mistakenly thought his tears and a choked-up sound in his voice—which she responded to very strongly because of being auditory—meant he didn't like the drawing and was disappointed in her. Once the father understood how his reactions were affecting his daughter, he began to work on putting his feelings into positive words in an upbeat tone and dialing back the overt signs of emotion, with the result that their relationship improved dramatically.

Auditory children are what I like to call "solid citizens." They like order, routine, regularity—a sense that one activity follows another in a predictable sequence. Because they can be good listeners, they respond well to clear verbal instructions and get pleasure out of behaving well—and being praised for doing so. Their tendency to tune out at times is usually self-protective rather than defiant. So as you try to guide your auditory child through the exciting challenges of this stage, keep in mind that the world of sound is her first point of reference. If you can try to imagine the world as experienced from her point of view—or, more to the point, through her very sensitive ears—you will become much more adept at understanding her behavior and figuring out strategies to shape it. Just listen—to your child, and to everything around you.

SIX

The Visual Child

V isual children feast on colors, shapes, and movement. Highly observant, these children are stimulated—and often overstimulated—by the vast amount of information that shifts constantly before their eyes. From the time they wake in the morning until they manage to close their eyes at night, visual children rely on their eyes to guide them through their days, searching for the familiar (Mom and Dad's smiling faces) and the novel (a new red bicycle in the driveway next door)—though too many new and interesting sights on the horizon can agitate and upset them. These children collect images in their minds as a means to comprehend the world. What they take in has the power to soothe them, teach them, excite them, frighten them, and make them angry. They feel a whole spectrum of emotions in response to the visual landscape. Focused primarily on their parents or primary caretakers, they follow these important people around with their eyes, paying very careful attention to everything in their immediate surroundings. This child is watching you—and everything else—very closely.

As infants, visually oriented children often get labeled as "good babies"—not because they are innately easier than other babies but because their parents are meeting their visual needs even without being aware that they are doing so. Since these babies don't usually make a fuss if they can see Mom or the caregiver nearby, and that is likely to be most of the time during this early period of their lives, most visually oriented babies are calm and contented. They're getting the kind of comfort that works best for them.

The visual child likes order and will organize her room or play space with great attention and care. When visual children come into my office or center, they immediately set about arranging the stuffed animals in long rows, or lining up the trains and cars in neat formations. The ability to create order not only is pleasing to them but also helps them manage their emotions. If, for instance, the visual child has had a difficult day at school or just a long day full of activity, reorganizing her dolls or books on the shelves in her room may be her way of coping with stress and unwinding. It's a process that makes her feel good, a way of self-soothing. We live in a very visual world, and we may underestimate the impact of the visual onslaught that meets our eyes and those of our children every day—the chaos of lights, advertising, television, and the Internet. There's generally not much a child can do to modify this visual landscape. But by rearranging things to suit her own taste, the visual child is able to feel that she can impose her sense of order over her own little piece of the world. The control she exercises over the appearance of her surroundings is like the control an auditory child will try to exercise over the level of sound.

Visual kids express their sense of order in their play too. They play with toys one at a time, they put them in rows, they group things together on the basis of visual links—maybe all the red cars in one area, the blue ones in another. As they get older, their organizing systems will become more extensive and complicated.

In their relationships, they tend to gravitate toward those who look like the people they love: Their favorite babysitter has long hair like Mommy, their best friend has blond hair and blue eyes just like their sister. Even as young children, they will notice people's physical features and have strong and sometimes seemingly irrational responses to them. Out of the blue, they'll decide that red hair means a person is scary. Perhaps somebody with red hair once looked at them in a frightening way, and this experience has made them group together all people with this feature. Rest assured, your visual child will grow out of these particular prejudices. But the way people look will always be of importance. (Indeed, I can spot a visual mother a mile away. These are the moms whose kids are always well groomed and dressed with great attention—the kids are neat and clean, with every hair in place, and their outfits, from hair ribbons to belts to shoes and socks, will be color-coordinated.)

Parents who are not visual may be perplexed or even annoyed by their visual child's intense interest in appearances. For instance, it's likely to matter a lot to the visual child which lunch box or backpack he takes to school, which clothes he wears, perhaps even which plate he eats from. A mom will say to me, "But none of my other kids were like this. Why should I make Tommy the exception?" Well, of course, she doesn't *have* to make Tommy an exception, but if Tommy is so much more comfortable in his own skin because he has a Batman lunch box like his best friend, why not? The rewards of meeting your child halfway on matters of minor importance (to you, not to him) can be considerable.

At school, visual children learn best by looking at books or blackboards, flash cards, or computers. Memorizing letters, numbers, and words comes easily to them because of their ability to "see" all this data in their minds. They may be viewed as somewhat controlling because they are inevitably trying to assert their sense of order in the classroom, the playground, the playgroup, or wherever else they find themselves. As they grow beyond the preschool years, they tend to be very organized thinkers and to do well in school, especially in a traditional setting where the expectations are very clear and subjects are presented in a visual format.

You'll find the visual child hunched over her drawing pad, working with deep concentration on one vivid drawing after the next. She'll be the first to notice if you had your hair trimmed—and she won't be shy about telling you whether she likes it or not. She'll be the toddler who clings to your leg when she first arrives at day care, scanning the room for a familiar face before venturing forth with a smile. She's the preschooler whose books and toys are carefully put away, arranged by color or by some other criterion of her own choosing—and whose closet is more organized than yours.

To spend time with a visual child is to see the ordinary and everyday landmarks of our lives in a fresh new light. The visual child is constantly pointing out details that we, who sense the world differently, could easily overlook.

Visual Baby Basics, from Birth to One Year

How the Visual Baby Expresses Emotional Needs

Recognizing their parents primarily by their faces and their bodies, visual babies will want to see their primary caregiver at all times. When they can't, they tend to feel uneasy. Step out of his line of vision and this child will wail in protest. Unlike tactile children, who constantly want to be held, a baby who is visual is most often quite happy to snuggle into a carrier seat or perch in a high chair as long as he can see Mom or Dad. Comforted by their presence, this baby will amuse himself by checking out all the activity, whether it's watching Mom chopping vegetables for dinner, looking at Dad flip through a stack of bills, or staring wide-eyed at his big sister as she puts on her shoes and coat for school. A visual baby does crave direct eye contact, so he may get fussy if his parents and siblings don't regularly stop what they're doing and take a moment to connect with him, with faces that are smiling and at close range.

Sometimes this child's need to see his caregiver all the time will mean that you'll need to get creative in order to meet his emotional needs during the course of an average day's activities. For example, you should think about what kind of visual distraction you can provide your baby when he's in his car seat, since for the first year the car seat will be rear-facing. Perhaps you can tape a picture of a scene or a photo of you and your child together to the surface he'll be looking at. However, I don't suggest that you put up a mirror, as this could be dangerous. If there were ever an accident in the car, the glass could shatter and hurt your child.

On a walk to the park or to a bustling part of town, the visual baby will be entranced by all the activity around her, whether it's the trees and flowers and playgrounds filled with children running around or the stores and shoppers in a mall. The stimulation of all this novelty will keep her eyes wide with interest. But in order for her to relax and feel safe enough to enjoy herself, the visual baby also needs to be able to see her caregiver whenever she wants. Being aware of this simple fact will enable you to make adjustments that can result in a profound difference in daily life, as it did for Terry, a woman I met during my research.

Terry came to me feeling frustrated because she could not understand why her baby, Stephanie, seemed to dislike being in the stroller so much. Terry was very social and loved to hang out in her neighborhood café, hoping that Stephanie would sit comfortably in her stroller (as her other children had done) and allow her to enjoy a much-needed coffee break with her friends. But Stephanie would whine continuously, no matter what Terry tried, and the only time she would quiet down was when Terry stopped talking to her friends and paid attention to her. Terry was becoming increasingly upset by the demands of her baby. She thought the problem was that Stephanie was so possessive of her that she didn't want to share her with anybody else.

I met her in the waiting room of the center and quickly noticed the dynamic Terry described. As Terry and I talked and Stephanie sat in her stroller nearby, Stephanie began whining. The first thing that I noticed was that the stroller was facing away from Terry, so Stephanie couldn't see her mother. When I asked, Terry confirmed that this was how she always set up the stroller when they met up with her friends. Terry thought that having Stephanie face away from her, so that she could see the park across the street, would help to distract the baby from her seemingly incessant need for her mother.

My very first suggestion was to reposition the stroller so that Stephanie would be facing her mother, not turned away from her. From this reassuring vantage point, with Mom right there in front of her, she could take in the rest of the scene with pleasure. Terry agreed to try this as an experiment and discovered that when she met her friends for coffee Stephanie was now much calmer. And if Terry just made a point of glancing her way occasionally, giving her the eye contact she needed to feel secure, Stephanie seemed delighted. The activity in the park had little appeal compared to her mother's face. Their outings became much more fun for both of them once Terry understood that Stephanie was happiest when her mother's familiar face was directly in her line of sight.

By making one simple adjustment to the positioning of Stephanie's stroller, this mother began to build a better relationship with her baby. She learned that her baby wasn't trying to take her away from her friends. She was just processing the world in her own unique way. (As you will see below, during the toddler years, a child may prefer to have her stroller facing outward in order to view the passing scene. But when she is tired and needing a nap, she may still need to see Mom's face in order to settle down. Or she may need to have all visual input blanked out.)

When a child is navigating a milestone such as stranger awareness or separation anxiety, her distress will often be visible in a heightened sensitivity to input from her dominant sense. While an auditory child may cry when she hears new voices or when she can't hear the familiar sound of her parents' voices, the visual child might react badly to the sight of an unfamiliar person or fall apart when Mom or Dad leaves the room.

To help your child work through this phase, you'll need patience and a strategy that corresponds to your child's dominant sense. There's no way to rush her through coping with stranger and separation anxiety, but you can help ease her difficulty (and your own frustration) by being thoughtful about how you introduce her to new people coming into her environment and how you engineer your own departures.

Let's say you've hired a new babysitter and you want to prepare your visually oriented baby to accept this new caregiver and to be able to tolerate your absence for a short period of time. You'll want the babysitter to spend some time with your child in your presence so they can get to know each other before you actually leave them alone together. This way you can help your baby overcome her natural fears of separation and of strangers. So rather than drop her immediately in her new babysitter's arms, spend some time sitting quietly with your child in your lap, with the babysitter nearby. Let your baby see you interacting with the babysitter, chatting happily and smiling. Your baby will look to you for visual cues as to how you feel about this new person. The babysitter can also provide reassuring cues by smiling at the baby and using a lot of eye contact. Gradually, as your child grows more relaxed, put your baby in her car seat or on the floor on a play mat or rug and experiment with leaving the room for a moment or two and then returning, so your child grows familiar with the pattern of your leaving and coming back.

Sometimes a visually oriented child will have a strong negative response to someone who looks very different from the people she is used to. In one case, a six-month-old visual baby demonstrated an intense fear of one of her grandfathers. She liked one grandfather but not the other, though from what the mother said the grandfather who was the problem was a kind, loving, gentle person who had gotten along just fine with the other babies in the family. Not knowing what the problem could be, I asked the mom to bring in photos of the two grandfathers. Sure enough, the grandfather the baby was afraid of had an enormous moustache, wore big glasses, and was bald. These features were very foreign to the baby. So in preparation for his next visit, I suggested that the mother take out family pictures that included the grandfather and show them frequently to her daughter so that she could become familiar with his face. The mom also bought a Mr. Potato Head and played a game with her daughter, putting glasses and a moustache on the bald head. Silly as it might sound, this game actually helped the baby get acquainted with the facial features of her grandfather.

By the time the grandfather came back, she had grown accustomed to the sight of him and exhibited no fear or dislike in his presence.

How the Visual Baby Discovers the World

As visual children begin to comprehend the world around them, they will point at things and make noises. This is their way not only of identifying people and objects but also of communicating their feelings about what is happening around them. Pay attention to your child as she points to the people and objects in your home or on your daily walks to the park, and you'll open a window into her cognitive and emotional life, her preferences, the things that excite her, and those that make her fearful or unhappy. For visual children, this inclination to point at objects and people instead of using their voices to name things may delay the development of their speech. Since they are processing the information in their brains in a visual way, they don't yet feel the need to hear themselves say words, unlike the auditory child who learns through his sense of hearing. Not to worry. The words will kick in soon enough.

Again, the visual baby seems like what we often refer to as an "easy" baby because parents often unconsciously and routinely meet their baby's need for their visual contact merely through their presence. If, however, this happy, smiling baby suddenly starts to cry and get upset and you have no idea why, it may be because there's just too much visual stimulation in the environment, even though you yourself have not noticed it. In fact, it's because parents think of these babies as easy and therefore take them on outings more frequently that they put them in situations that can trigger visual overload. So keep this in mind as you and your baby begin to explore the world around you.

How the Visual Baby Begins to Play and Interact

Playtime for visual children is neither as loud as it is for auditory kids nor as rambunctious as it is for tactile children. These children are stimulated and engaged by a wide spectrum of toys, as color is the primary attraction for them. They may gravitate toward playing with toys of a particular color or may simply enjoy arranging their toys as if to display them. They love picture books and will happily point out all the animals and characters in their favorites.

Peekaboo and hide-and-seek games with her parents and siblings are among this child's favorites, since these games bring her in close contact with the smiling, happy faces of those she loves best. This kind of intimate visual contact is particularly important to visual children, who learn about communication and emotions by watching for signs in the faces of the people they know and trust.

Visual children can be strongly attracted to television, with its powerful imagery. As parents, most of us have relied on a television program or a DVD to entertain our child while we cleared the sink of dishes or changed into a clean pair of pants. A little bit of television goes a long way with visual children, who will be deeply affected by images on a screen. Regardless of the content of these images, television watching is an intense experience for visual children, one that can easily overexcite them; in general, it's best not to allow them too much of this, especially near bedtime. Colorful picture books will comfort your child and hold her

attention without giving her too much visual information to process at once.

The Everyday Life of the Visual Baby

Sleeping

Visual children are generally able to settle into a routine of sleeping through the night quite easily because a schedule that is organized around light and dark gives them the kind of signals that
work best for them. The rising and setting of the sun help the visual baby wake up in the morning (sometimes before you wish
she would, to be sure) and go to bed at night. Similarly, darkening
the nursery at nap time with light-blocking curtains or shades will
help with daytime sleeping. However, a visual baby can be easily
overstimulated if you're not careful. This means you need to pay
special attention to the visual cues that seem to excite your child
and keep her brain in high gear. No matter how tired she might
be, a visual child will have difficulty falling asleep if there are
bright colors, moving shapes, or other kinds of visual activity in
her line of vision. There will be many circumstances when you
will want to surround your child with lots of exciting visual input
because it distracts and entertains her. Sleep time, however, is not
one of these times. Mobiles moving through the air over her head,
splashy murals on the wall near her eye level, brightly colored
padding and bedding inside her crib—all these vivid details,
which could be soothing to another child, will keep your visual
baby wide-eyed and watchful late into the night.

    In general, you want to keep stimulation at bedtime to a mini-
mum with a visual child in order to help her fall asleep. It is so
tempting to decorate a child's bedroom with bright, playful colors and designs full of patterns and contrasts. Many of us moms

dreamed about these rooms when we were pregnant and designed them in our minds with floor-to-ceiling whimsy and color. The reality for many babies, especially these visually sensitive children, is that all this visual pizzazz can distract and agitate them at critical times—such as bedtime and feeding time—when they need to relax.

If your child is visually dominant, consider starting out with a nursery that will provide a kind of blank slate. A bedroom that has light-colored walls and fabrics and furniture in simple, muted tones would be soothing for a visual baby. If you hang artwork in your child's room, consider choosing pieces that blend with or complement the wall color, as opposed to being in sharp contrast. As you better understand how your baby reacts to the visual stimulation around her, you can slowly add color to her bedroom, one dab at a time. In the meantime, other spaces in your home—the kitchen, the playroom—are great places to hang the vivid pictures your child will love. But the bedroom needs to be a stimulus-free zone, where she can rest her mind and her body.

Feeding

Feeding a visual baby often requires a similar approach. Too much visual stimulation can distract this baby while he is nursing or bottle-feeding. The visual child will lock eyes with Mom or Dad when he is feeding. This is how he establishes the connection he needs to make him feel secure. Being able to look at the person feeding him is all the visual activity that this baby needs. Just as with auditory children, it's best to feed a visual baby in a low-key setting—only in this case, rather than being concerned with noise level, you should be careful about the level of visual activity in the room. If it's nighttime, for example, and you decide to turn on the television while breastfeeding, the light and color emanating from the TV might distract your infant. Feeding a visual baby in a room where older children are playing or other kinds of activity are taking place may also detract from his ability to focus on the task of eating. The same is true of public places. Giving a visual baby a bottle at the playground or in a busy café puts him in a situation where too many things are competing for his attention, which can make him fussy and distracted. These children are best fed in calm, visually soothing environments, where there is not a lot of movement and activity.

As you introduce solid foods to a visual child, he may appear to you to be playing with his food, when what he is actually doing is arranging it to his own satisfaction. You might find this child stacking his cereal in one corner of his plate or pushing his peas away from his potatoes. From the time they are very young, visual children enjoy making their own arrangements of things, and food is no exception. The visual child may demonstrate preferences for certain foods based on their appearance. He might even reject certain foods because of their color. I've encountered visual children who refused to eat anything yellow, turning up their noses at corn and squash, or anything brown—so much for beans and whole wheat bread! Be prepared for your visual baby to make some dramatically unpleasant faces when he sees the wrong-looking food on his plate.

Dressing and Diapering

Visual babies usually enjoy being dressed and changed because they get to look at you so closely. As you change, bathe, and dress them, they will simply want as much eye contact as possible. If your baby happens to be a bit squirmy during changing or dressing, try sticking a mirrored square (not an actual mirror, which may fall and break) on the wall next to her changing table. The visual baby loves to catch sight of herself. Also, if you find her a bit fussy, you could position a mobile to help distract her.

Visual Toddler Basics, from Ages One to Three

How the Visual Toddler Communicates and Manages Emotion

As visual children grow from babies to toddlers, they begin to explore the world around them with great gusto. Now more sturdy and agile on their feet, they become ever more observant of their surroundings, but they will continue to need to be able to see their parent or caregiver in order to feel secure and safe. Looking at the faces of the people who are important to them is how they ground themselves.

Visual children have an uncanny way of reading the faces of others, always on the lookout for clues as to how a person is feeling. Just as the auditory child is tuned in to his mother's state of mind through her voice, the visual toddler is looking for clues to his mother's emotional state written on her face, which can sometimes cause him to misinterpret a parent's mood or feeling. If, for example, Mom is crying in relief or joy, a baby may incorrectly respond to his mother's tears by becoming upset.

Visual toddlers continue to have strong reactions to people based upon physical looks and expressions. In one case a two-and-a-half-year-old boy who was visual, developed a distaste for his aunt, whom he saw infrequently. It was very distressing for his mother to watch her child squeal and run away from her sister during visits. When she determined that her son was visual, she guessed that the reason her son was put off by his aunt was the woman's exaggerated makeup and long, red fingernails. Being careful not to offend, the mom kindly asked her sister to tone it down a bit. At the same time, she began showing her son pictures of women who wore lots of makeup in order to familiarize him with that look. She even did a face painting on both of them in order to create more positive associations with makeup. It took some time, but the next time his aunt visited, the little boy was much less standoffish, even consenting to sit on her lap after she had been there for a while.

When it comes to comforting and soothing the visual toddler, you need to be sure that your child can see you. If your visual child is frightened by a neighborhood dog coming into your backyard, for example, calling out to her from inside the house with reassuring words won't do the trick. She needs visual contact with you so that she knows you are watching over her and she is safe. The same holds true for setting boundaries for your child and disciplining her. If she grabs a toy from another toddler at playgroup and you want to communicate that this is a no-no, she needs to see your face, preferably up close, looking her in the eye, as you lean down to her level to speak to her. These children are very sensitive to facial expressions, so a grave look will send a very strong, clear message.

Visual toddlers' fears can be calmed and managed if parents think about using imagery to reassure them or to desensitize them to the things they find scary. In one case, a mother and I addressed a child's deep fear of spiders by exposing him to pictures of them in a storybook so that he would get used to the sight of them. This four-year-old boy was so terrified of spiders that even a rubber spider in my center sent him into hysterics. One time, the sight of a real spider actually made him vomit, he was so afraid. I suggested to his mother that she read him *Miss Spider's Tea Party* and then have a pretend tea party to which she and her son "invite" spiders and other insects.

I also suggested that anytime they spotted an insect—a spider, a cockroach, or even an ant—the mother jump in and say something about how it must be on its way to the tea party at Miss Spider's.

A few weeks went by, and the mother called me to report: "The other day we were in the kitchen and a huge flying cockroach came in. Rather than crying or running away, he just said, 'Oh, Barry, you're late for Miss Spider's tea party! Hurry up!'"

It's important to try to be creative about using all aspects of visual imagery, which can include color, to help visual children overcome their fears. In another case, a twenty-four-month-old girl, Mary, was resisting going to preschool because of her anxiety about separating from her mother. When Mary and her mother visited the center, it was clear to me that Mary's favorite color was yellow: In my center she picked out the yellow flower on the wall, put the yellow truck with the yellow cars, and pulled out all the yellow pencils and arranged them in neat rows. When I suggested that transitioning to preschool might go more smoothly if Mary was able to wear something yellow, the mother was quite resistant. She too was visual and had very strong visual likes and dislikes. Yellow was not, as it happened, one of her favorites. "But I don't like yellow! I would never choose clothes in that color for her." After she got home, however, she started to think how she could use yellow to comfort her daughter without offending her own highly developed visual aesthetic. When they returned in two weeks, I read in the mother's diary that she had put together a photo book and covered it with a soft yellow material. She filled it with pictures of Mary with her dad, her mom, and her sister, all of them together in each of the photos. Mary was now taking this special book to school with her, leaving it in her cubby, and saying goodbye to her mom with a smile on her face. Whenever she needed reassurance, the teacher would show her the yellow book.

Although separation anxiety can be triggered for any toddler when a parent or caregiver leaves the child at preschool or day care, the visual child gets very upset if she actually sees her parent leave. A simple solution is to arrange to have the child be distracted so that she doesn't notice your departure. Perhaps the teacher could read her a book or engage her in another activity while you slip out. Even though you may feel this is a sneaky way of behaving that will make her fearful and anxious, watching you walk out the door is actually more disruptive than discovering your absence later.

As is the case with most children, visual children have tantrums when they are tired, hungry, or both and don't have any reserves to cushion them. Since we live in a visually stimulating world, which can be experienced as overwhelming, even assaultive, by the visual child, reducing the stimuli in the environment when you sense that she's running on empty may help you to prevent a tantrum before it occurs. The visual child's tantrums are dramatic, with angry, red, distorted faces and of course copious tears. These kids definitely play to an audience, so if you're watching, the hysteria may escalate, although sometimes it's manufactured for the occasion. You may be able to tell whether it's a real tantrum by the child's eyes. If she averts her eyes and won't look at you directly, then she is truly in an unmanageable place; however, if your child is in the throes of a hissy fit but is looking straight at you, this is a signal that she is much more in control of what she is doing than she is letting on. A good way to undercut the drama of the moment is to look away from your child.

Even once your child gets herself worked up into a full-blown tantrum, you may be able to cut it short by offering her a visual distraction. Try pointing out the window at a funny scene, a dog on the street corner, or a bird flying above. If distraction doesn't calm her, try looking away from her entirely. Depriving her of an audience often causes the tantrum to die down fast.

The visual toddler will continue to be a bit fidgety in the car if Mom or Dad is in the front driving and his car seat in the back of the car is situated so that he can't see his parent's face. It's much better to position him so that he's on a diagonal, with the side of the driver's face visible to him from his seat, unless of course there's somebody else in the car who can provide him with the eye contact he needs. Some mothers with whom I've worked have found that their toddlers do much better on car rides with something visual to do, so they bring along picture books, an Etch a Sketch, or other drawing materials to keep the children focused and engaged. Although some parents may want to put up screens on the windows to block the sun, it might be better not to, because they interfere with the visual child's ability to look out and enjoy the passing scenery.

How the Visual Toddler Explores the World

When it comes to language development, visual children may be slower than some of their peers. For parents who are not visually oriented, particularly those who are more comfortable communicating to their children with words, it can be hard to remember that for some children showing is better than telling, and words may just not seem necessary to a visual child in the early years.

Marisa was one of those parents who think something is wrong if a child is not speaking by the age of one. "My first child said her first word at ten months," Marisa told me. Her second child, Bella, at thirteen months was happily babbling away in nonsense syllables but, to her mother's consternation and concern, seemed to show little interest in learning to speak. "I'm driving myself crazy trying to get her to talk to me," Marisa said. "I'm like a parrot in my own house, saying 'Mama, Mama, Mama' and 'apple, apple, apple' over and over again." The frustrated young mother threw up her hands. "She doesn't seem to care a whit."

I spent a few afternoons with the family and discovered that Bella was a bubbly and vivacious, visually oriented child. As her mother indicated, she babbled quite animatedly and frequently accompanied her chatty "baby speak" with pointing. She watched her mother and older sister, Erin, carefully, and was happiest when they were both in the room and in her line of sight. Marisa was clearly auditory—she expressed her interest and affection to her girls through language, keeping up a constant patter of conversation with both of them as they went about their day.

After a few sessions observing Erin and Bella together, I realized that five-year-old Erin was acting as a kind of facilitator for her younger sister, as taste/smell children often do for younger siblings and playmates. When Bella grasped her hands in a certain way, Erin said, "Mom, I think Bella wants a cookie." When Bella made a particular, fussy sort of noise, Erin pulled a box of toys within her little sister's reach. No wonder little Bella didn't feel the need to speak—her big sister was such a good interpreter. Between her mother's regular patter of conversation and her sister's intercessions on her behalf, there wasn't much need or incentive for Bella to enter the speaking world herself.

As I explained to a relieved Marisa, there was nothing wrong or even unusual about these family dynamics. Each individual's sensory preference influenced the way they all related to one another and probably had some influence on the baby's language development. Bella would speak very soon, I reassured her. Her internal developmental drive would push her inevitably toward speech, even if there weren't yet any signs that this development was under way, and a few months' delay was nothing to worry about. In the meantime, rather than just relying on her voice to stimulate Bella's interest in speaking, I encouraged Marisa to spend time talking with her daughter face-to-face, at close range, so that Bella could absorb all the visual information that speaking involves. Talking their way through colorful picture books could also help Bella move forward with her speech, particularly if Marisa curbed her impulse to do all the talking and left openings for Bella to take the lead. Marisa's emphasis on sound had probably worked with Erin, who, as a taste/smell child, was inclined to adapt to others' sensory preferences—just as she was now doing with her sister's visual messages. But Bella was a different child, with a different set of challenges facing her. With a mother and a sister doing all the talking (and fetching) for her, it was hardly surprising that the baby was taking her time learning to speak on her own. I figured she would respond well to some visual prompting.

I didn't see any need to try to curb Erin's habit of interceding on her baby sister's behalf; this was a natural inclination for the older child, and neither child was harmed by this loving attentiveness on Erin's part. But I did suggest that Marisa could encourage Erin to engage with Bella in a verbal way as well, perhaps by reading a storybook to her with lots of facial animation and hand gestures or by talking to her and trying to get her to respond. Children love to imitate their older siblings, and Bella clearly adored her sister.

I wasn't surprised to hear from Marisa a few weeks later. "Two words in one week," she told me excitedly. " 'Mama' and 'banana.'

Well, actually it was more like 'anana,' " Marisa laughed, "but she said it three times!"

Visual children learn by imitation. If they can watch someone else doing it, they will be more likely to succeed, whether it's talking, following directions, or mastering a new game. So, for example, when you tell your visual child to pick up his spoon, pick up a spoon yourself—he'll make the connection more easily if he can see what it is you're asking him to do.

Again, visual children often learn by mimicking, so when they are first getting acquainted with their letters or numbers or seem interested in learning about the natural world or their own bodies, an effective way to engage and teach them is by looking at picture books together. Any kind of visual depiction of a skill they are trying to acquire, from brushing their teeth to putting on their socks, will help them master it.

When you want to give a visual child direction, it is best done at close range, with lots of eye contact. This way, your child can pick up your meaning through your facial expressions, not just from your words, which won't mean as much to him at this age. When you're warning your visual child away from a hot stove or an electrical outlet, for example, make sure your facial expression matches the seriousness of your voice—he's more likely to comprehend the message of danger, and make the connection to the word "no."

How the Visual Toddler Plays and Interacts

Visual children at this age will discover ways to express themselves in drawing and painting. When they draw, these children will create elaborate, colorful scenes often taken from nature. Trees, flowers, and animals are favorite subjects for the visual child.

These children may also begin to demonstrate strong feelings about how their toys are presented and stored. Your toddler may suddenly decide that he wants his stuffed animals to be kept on his bed, not on the floor or in a storage chest, and he may have a very specific arrangement in mind, perhaps lining them up according to size, color, or some other principle of order that you may not be able to see (and which he probably can't articulate). Invisible as it may be to you, that concept of order will be very important to him. He may need to show you how to put his picture books away after you've finished reading them together, since only he knows the "right way" to do it. And he may come into conflict with his siblings or playmates if they interfere with his way of doing things, so you may have your hands full mediating these struggles.

Visual children can be a bit single-minded. For example, at three to four years old, when children are becoming more aware of gender differences, they can be adamant about the visual markers that signal these differences, taking their cues from the society around them, because kids at this age are often very concerned about conforming to gender stereotypes, even if their parents are trying to reject conventional ideas about gender. Thus, a visual girl might suddenly be insistent on wearing pink frilly dresses. And she may try to impose her ideas on others. "I didn't want my daughter to be wearing pink," one mother said. "But she wouldn't give it up. In fact, she kept trying to get me to dress in pink too." The same thing can happen with visual boys. Some parents want their boy to play with dolls in order to encourage their empathic, caring nature. But a visual boy might refuse because he doesn't see the other boys playing with dolls. If in fact one of the boys in his day care does have a doll, he may be very disapproving. In one incident, I observed a little boy become very upset watching a Mardi Gras parade in which some of the men were dressed in drag. The boy was three and a half, and he just couldn't handle a man with a beard wearing a dress and vampy makeup. My son, Tom, was with me at the time and said, "Oh, don't worry—his cape is just like Superman's," to console his hysterical friend.

The Everyday Life of the Visual Toddler

Sleeping

As toddlers, visual children are still usually good sleepers, if their rooms are kept dark at nap time and bedtime. However, if a visual child does wake up in the middle of the night and if there are a lot of potential distractions in his room, he may become too excited to get back to sleep. This was the case for one mother whose child kept getting up at night to play. The mom was very imaginative and had created a lively room complete with a rocking horse, brightly painted bookshelves filled with picture books, and storage cubes stuffed with toys. This was far too much stimulation for her visual child. So I suggested that the mom cover all the temptations at night. She installed curtains that could be closed over the bookshelves, and as part of the going-to-bed routine she put sheets over the rocking horse and the toys. After she'd covered everything, she'd have the little boy say, as part of their bedtime ritual, "Goodnight, toys—see you tomorrow!"

It's very common for these children to be so sensitive to visual stimulation that they need to be removed from it in order to quiet down and be able to get to sleep. One day I came across a grandfather wheeling his toddler grandchild around and around the park, attempting to use the motion of the stroller to lull the child to sleep. We chatted for a few minutes and he complained to me, "I just can't get him to sleep. This is his nap time and I know he must be tired, but he just won't close his eyes."

From the sounds and gestures the child was making, I could see that he was showing all the signs of being tired. But I could tell from the way his eyes were darting wildly about that he was a visual child and that he was too overstimulated to get to sleep. The endless variety of shapes and colors he could see from his stroller was just too exciting for him.

I suggested to the grandfather that he recline the child further in the stroller and drape his blanket over the top so that he couldn't see his surroundings. In this way he could create a blank screen for his grandson, much like a boring show on television. Within minutes the little boy was asleep.

One mom said that the biggest issue for her was that their visual child didn't like the dark but wouldn't sleep with a light on, even if it was a night-light. Night-lights, which help so many children cope with falling asleep in an otherwise dark bedroom, may actually have the opposite effect on visual children, keeping them awake rather than comforting them. The issue in this case turned out to be the boy's concern about how far down the hall he was from his parents. So I suggested she put the night-light outside in the hallway. "The light will help you find Mommy in the middle of the night if you need me," she'd tell him at bedtime. Knowing that the light was there, "just in case," he slept soundly thereafter.

Another mom was very anxious about an upcoming vacation because her child had never been able to sleep anywhere except in her own bed in her own room. So, weeks in advance, the mom took the travel bed that they would be using on vacation and moved it into her daughter's room. By acclimating her daughter to seeing the travel bed in her room every day and sleeping in it at night, she helped prepare her for the changes that she would face over vacation.

Though they enjoy all kinds of visual stimulation during the day, visually oriented toddlers need the stimulation to be dialed back dramatically before bedtime, as it will be too distracting to them. You shouldn't place a television in any toddler's bedroom, but especially not in a visual toddler's. Furthermore, it's best to turn off the television in the family room at least half an hour before bed. This may require a shift in the family's television habits, but more than likely everyone will benefit from less television watching. Planning your child's pre-bedtime routine to include activities that relax him, rather than excite him, can make getting him to bed—and to sleep—much easier.

Sally, a busy mother of three, found this out after months of bedtime battles with her toddler. When she brought her three-year-old son to see me, Sally explained that during the past few months Kevin had gone from being a "good sleeper" to a kid who refused to go to bed without a fight. Even after his parents managed to get him into his pajamas and under the covers, Kevin would get up repeatedly at night. He wound up overtired and cranky during the day, easily upset and prone to tantrums over the slightest mishap.

"For so long, I felt so lucky," Sally told me. "He slept great as a baby, and he's always been easy to put to bed. Once he gets there, he stays there—at least until recently. These days, every night is a battle. He races around a lot and jumps out of bed five times after we've said our goodnights. It's affecting his mood during the day, not to mention mine, since he's so irritable!"

Kevin showed many characteristics of visual children during our meeting at my office. While his mother and I were talking, he wandered over to my bookcase and pulled out one picture book after another, thumbing through them contentedly. On one of the shelves, I keep a collection of beach stones my son and I have gathered on our trips to the ocean. When Kevin finished with the picture books, he spotted the stones on the shelf—and promptly rearranged them from what I thought of as an artfully casual cluster to a neat and tidy straight line. This kind of attention to detail and organization is typical of visual children, who prefer clean lines to anything that looks random.

I asked Sally to tell me about the activity in their house during the evenings and whether there was anything that had changed in the last few months. Kevin is the youngest of three children. His brother and sister are seven and nine years old, a big enough age difference that Kevin had been on a very different nighttime schedule from them—until recently.

"A few months ago I decided to let Kevin stay up and play with the other kids for a little while before bed," Sally said. "He loves to be with the 'big kids' and they are very good with him, most of the time. I figured that playing with his brother and sister before bedtime might tire him out a bit too."

When I asked Sally to describe the kind of playing that the kids did together, she said, "They love to play video games, so they do that a lot. Sometimes they'll watch a DVD together, or wrestle around a bit in front of the television. Nothing too wild."

The kids' play might not have been wild, but it was exactly the wrong kind of activity for a visual toddler to be engaged in before bedtime. There was absolutely nothing wrong with Kevin playing with his siblings in the evenings—it sounded like a wonderful opportunity for the children to have fun and deepen their bonds to one another. But Kevin, as a visual child easily stimulated by images, needed to be kept away from the TV and the video screen, particularly so close to bedtime.

After our meeting, Sally decided to adjust Kevin's evening routine to help him wind down so he'd be ready for bed. And she enlisted the help of her two older children to make some changes to their playtime with their younger brother. Video games and television were out until after Kevin was in bed. Instead, Sally and her kids came up with some activities that would be fun for Kevin and appeal to his visual nature without making him too excited. Puzzles and board games replaced TV and video games.

During a follow-up session, Sally reported significant improvement in Kevin's sleep habits.

"At first I had to hide the video games and the remote control," she said, "but after a couple of weeks Kevin was pretty used to his new evening routine, and he didn't seem to miss the TV anymore. His sleeping habits changed almost immediately; it was amazing. He's happier during the day, and we're not fighting to get him calmed down at night."

She was also excited to tell me about some unexpected benefits. The simple changes they had made had had an impact on the entire family, it turned out. Sally's older children embraced the new routine. "I think they feel grown-up when they're helping their brother," she said. Before long, the whole family—parents too— were spending an hour or so in the evenings sharing "game time" together. And Kevin wasn't the only one to become less dependent on TV.

"There are times that the TV doesn't even get turned on, even after Kevin has gone to bed," Sally said. "We're having fun."

Feeding

Feeding a visual child is never just a matter of shoveling food onto a plate. These kids love a good design, and mealtimes are no exception. As your child becomes a more proficient, independent eater, he will probably develop a fondness for a special plate and favorite cup, and ask for them over and over again. Those decorated with animals and cartoon scenes are likely to be big hits with these visual kids, so it's worth keeping a few extras on hand so you don't have to keep raiding your dishwasher to dig out his favorites.

Visual children are also quite fussy about how the food is arranged on their plates. They may want a sectioned dish so that the different foods don't touch each other. And they may strongly object to food combinations. For example, they might prefer a serving of peas and a serving of carrots, not a mixture of peas and carrots. If the pasta is spaghetti but they prefer spirals (or vice versa), it might go uneaten. Visual children can develop aversions to food based on appearance and texture—macaroni and cheese that's too gloppy, an egg that is too runny, meat that is a color they don't like. This may seem a bit excessive to you, and therefore something you might be inclined to ignore. But to a young visual child, it's just this kind of "disorder" that can cause him to push his plate away. Richard, a one-and-a-half-year-old boy, wouldn't eat fruit until his mother cut the cantaloupe into "fruit fries," which meant cutting it into long pieces. With a simple change in the presentation of the fruit, the child's attitude shifted from negative to positive immediately. Another mom I know finally got her three-and-a-half-year-old to eat his peanut butter and jelly sandwich when she cut the bread into star shapes, using a cookie cutter.

Dressing

Sooner than you can imagine, that visual baby of yours will begin to show strong preferences about his clothes. As toddlers, these children start to care a great deal about what they wear, and they will state their sartorial preferences loudly and clearly. This trait begins when they are quite young and will only strengthen as they get older and become more self-aware, as well as more aware of others' appearances. Make no mistake: Even at this young age, a visual child is very interested in how she looks. For visual children, how they present themselves is closely connected to their becoming aware of themselves as separate, individual beings, and their clothes are a meaningful part of this process. Clothes may also become an important part of your visual child's playtime, as these kids love to engage in dress-up play. Just don't be surprised if your visual child fights to keep wearing her dress-up clothes when you head out to run errands.

The visual child might already have a favorite color (yellow? blue? pink?) or pattern (stripes? plaids? flowers? trucks? trains?). The mother of one-and-a-half-year-old Richard always had trouble getting him dressed until she cued into his visual preferences. As the mother recounted, "One day I told him, 'If you get dressed now, you can wear your favorite monkey T-shirt.' He thought about it for a second, then looked at me and walked right over and got dressed. That had never happened before."

An activity such as brushing teeth may become easier if you can figure out a way to make it visually appealing, perhaps by letting your child choose his own toothbrush. One mom motivated her visual child to brush his teeth by getting him to watch himself in the mirror, and still another mother with whom I worked showed her daughter pictures of yucky teeth (what will happen if she didn't brush) and pictures of nice teeth (what will happen if she did). Your child may be willing to wear his snow boots if they have a favorite cartoon character on them, so buy some decals ready to be slapped onto whatever needs to be made more engaging to your child. We are all quick to label our toddlers' obstinate behavior as the inevitable result of the "terrible twos" or some such, but some of this stubbornness may be remedied quite easily by appealing to your child's dominant sense, in this case, visual.

Toilet Training

Visual children will tend to master the action more quickly than the other children, but this doesn't mean toilet training should be started prematurely (bladder and kidney problems can occur in adult life as a result). The visual child can be a little more self-conscious than others when it comes to toilet training, so it's important to start the process at home and remain there for a few days, with only short trips out. By avoiding situations that ask him to control himself in public and helping to minimize the possibility of accidents in places where he's less comfortable than at home, you set him up in such a way that his pride can remain intact. If you do need to be away from home for any length of time, keep a couple of changes of clothes available in case of accidents, and change him immediately with a minimum of fuss; your visual child will not want to look messy or let others see that he's had an accident.

Being good imitators, visual children may be toilet-trained more quickly by mimicking their parents' behavior—if the parents feel comfortable being watched while they are on the toilet. If your visual child is truly physically ready to control himself, you may be able to encourage him by pointing out other children who are not wearing disposable training pants and are using the potty, because he will not want to appear different from his peers.

Illustrated children's books about toilet training are a great help and simply pointing out the fact that everyone else uses the toilet speeds up understanding. Visual rewards such as stars for every time he uses the potty will encourage your child too. Or you can create a chart onto which you put stickers in your child's favorite color. The goal, obviously, is to do everything you can to make using the potty a positive experience. For the same reason, you should try to avoid ever taking your child into an unclean restroom, for the visual child may have a very strong negative response to such an environment.

Visual Preschooler Basics, from Ages Three to Five

The Visual Preschooler's Emotional Life

As they become increasingly independent, visual children have new opportunities every day to explore. They interact with peers, they learn new skills and acquire fresh knowledge, and they begin to make sense of what they see and observe. They will make their way through this ever-expanding world of theirs by taking their clues from the visual environment that surrounds them.

Since these kids are highly attuned to facial expressions, they use this skill to read the moods of people around them, and they can be very affected by those moods. For example, a visual child may tell you, "I feel bad when I see Johnny because he always looks sad." They are so aware of people's facial expressions that a stern look will be enough to make them self-conscious and curb any inappropriate behavior. And they show their own emotions very clearly. What they are feeling will be written all over their faces. If they are making eye contact, it's usually a sign that they are feeling comfortable and grounded; if they avoid eye contact, it's a clue that something is bothering them, something they feel unable to express.

They tend to be "quick studies," recognizing people, places, and situations on the basis of very little information. For example, your visual child will be able to identify a friend of yours from far down the street sometimes long before you do—perhaps by her gait, hairstyle, or some other characteristic that has imprinted itself on the child's mind.

Like both their adult counterparts and their younger selves, preschoolers who are visual like to arrange their rooms and their belongings in an orderly and tidy way. Everything has its place, and woe to the person who messes with their picture-perfect arrangements. Children at this age also become even more conscious of gender differences, and they will have very definite ideas about how boys and girls should behave and how they should dress.

As these children develop both their observation skills and their language skills, they will continue to take a keen interest in what people look like and won't be shy about expressing their opinions. For better or worse, it's not unusual for a trip to the store with a visual preschooler to include a vivid running commentary on how people look—pretty, ugly, weird, scary, et cetera. Parents of these visually inclined children will recognize this trait and may have witnessed their children shouting out their uncensored thoughts for all to hear: "Wow, look at that bald man!" "That lady is really fat!" "That man looks all wrinkly!" Such moments are typical in the lives of visual children. They are describing what they see, not meaning to be insulting of course, so it's important that you guide your child to understand that some of these observations need to be kept to himself or said in a very quiet voice. You could also use these opportunities to help the child develop empathy, to understand how what he says and does makes other people feel.

The Visual Preschooler's Learning Style

Visual children process information based on what they can see. They tend to use visual cues to remember and organize information. Indeed, their ability to learn often depends on a concrete sight association. This trait makes these children very good at memorization. They learn well by taking information from books and from flash cards with pictures or photographs. When their teachers use blackboards or projectors to display information, they absorb it readily. Unlike tactile children, who need to touch the letters of the alphabet in order to learn them, perhaps by moving their fingers over sandpaper cutouts of the letters (such as used in Montessori-style classrooms), visual children need only to look at the letters to remember how they are shaped and come together into words. Being able to see with complete clarity is vitally important to them. In one case, a visual child with dyslexia made strong improvement in learning the alphabet when his desk was moved nearer to the window, where there was more natural light. The teacher also gave him pale blue paper to write on, which further enabled the child to see his work more clearly.

On the other hand, these kids have a more difficult time digesting information that they hear. Whereas an auditory child will sit contentedly while being read to in class, a visual child will quickly grow impatient and might demand to see what's in the book. In later years, the visual child will be able to convert auditory information into a visual form by taking notes, but that obviously doesn't occur at this age. If this child can't see something that you are trying to tell her about, she may find it hard to understand what you are saying.

The Visual Preschooler's Social Life

Rather than finding this child in the middle of a raucous game on the playground, you're far more likely to see her collecting flowers to bring inside after recess. She won't be the child who jumps up to dance when her teacher plays music, but if you look to the arts and crafts corner of the classroom, you'll find her painting diligently with a group of like-minded peers, surrounded by colorful paints and papers. The visual child will be neat at play. Even boys will not want to get dirty and will choose their sports accordingly, opting for swimming or karate instead of soccer or football.

One way to get these children involved in activities is to choose those that involve dressing up in some way—wearing a tutu or leotard for ballet, a smock for arts and crafts, or a uniform for Scouts. You can bet your visual child will be thrilled to sign up for any activity that requires some kind of costume—unless, of course, she doesn't like that particular costume.

Once this child has found pursuits that appeal to her, she will pursue them with concentration, discipline, and tenacity. These children may not be the obvious extroverts that their tactile peers tend to be, but they are no less enthusiastic about or devoted to their passions. This is a lesson that one client of mine, a young mother named Josephine, learned with her preschool daughter.

Josephine came to see me when her daughter, Darcy, was four years old. Darcy had been exhibiting some "destructive" behavior, Josephine told me, and she was at a loss as to how to correct the problem. A couple of months before, Darcy had started drawing on the walls of their home, using crayons and markers to scrawl colorful pictures across the white walls of the living room and her own bedroom. "I punished her the first couple of times by giving her a time-out, but she just keeps doing it. I'm angry with her—this stuff is incredibly difficult to clean—and I'm also worried. I mean, she's being so defiant. I worry about what's behind this behavior of hers."

I started by asking Josephine a few questions about herself and quickly discovered that she and I had a few things in common. Josephine, like me, was a singer, and like many musicians, she's an auditory person. She began taking music lessons at the age of four, and studied piano and violin before taking up voice lessons as a teenager. She loved jazz and sang regularly at a local cabaret venue.

Josephine had played music for her daughter since she was born, hoping that Darcy would find the same kind of passion for music that she had and that it could be something for the two of them to share. She regularly took Darcy to hear a local children's singer perform at their town library and was encouraged to see that Darcy looked forward to these outings and always seemed excited by the performances. Shortly after her fourth birthday, Josephine had enrolled Darcy in piano lessons—just as she had been enrolled when she herself was a preschooler.

I asked Josephine how Darcy's piano lessons were going. "Not great," she confessed. "It's a struggle to get her to the piano to practice, and she complains when we go to her weekly lesson."

Observing Darcy, it was clear to me that the little girl had strong visual inclinations. The story about drawing on the walls seemed to indicate this, but there were other signs as well. Darcy was highly organized. When I visited their house for a visit, Darcy proudly showed me her room, which she kept in pin-perfect order, and led me directly to her doll collection, which was her most prized possession. The dolls were arranged in what Darcy thought of as family groups. Here were sisters and mothers and their children, and a father and a son and their dog. She loved fashion and clothes, and her favorite activities in school were art and gymnastics.

I explained to Josephine that I thought Darcy's dominant sense was visual, and my hunch was that her drawing on the walls was an expression of her frustration at not having enough of an outlet to express herself in a visual medium. I asked her whether she would be willing to consider switching her daughter from a weekly piano lesson to a weekly art class. At first Josephine was reluctant, not wanting to give up on the possibility that her daughter would come around to loving music as much as she did. But then I asked her to imagine how she would have felt if someone had tried to turn her away from music in favor of playing soccer or joining a swim club.

"I would have been angry, I'm sure. And I'd have done anything to make it possible for me to play music," she said.

"Would you have broken your parents' rules?" I asked.

Josephine broke into a smile and laughed out loud. In that moment, she made the connection between her own feelings about music and her daughter's desire to draw and paint. "Yep," she nodding. "I loved music so much that I'd have been really determined to have my way, even if it meant being really bad."

Josephine agreed to have her daughter try an art class and hold off on music lessons for the time being. When I heard from her a couple of months later, she was thrilled about the effects of this change. "Darcy is loving her art class. She can't wait to go every week," said Josephine. "She's making these wonderful murals with her teacher. And she's no longer drawing on the walls!"

Josephine and her daughter were continuing to enjoy music together—in a manner that suited both their sensory preferences. The concerts they attended together were a great way for them to do this, since Darcy was drawn in by the visual component of a live performance.

For Josephine, like so many parents I meet, the process of understanding her child was twofold. First she needed to identify and understand her daughter's dominant sense. Next, she needed to put herself in Darcy's position in order to help her daughter develop her own interests and skills.

Visual children tend to be well behaved and easygoing. However, when they feel under stress (if they're tired, for example), they tend to exert a stronger need for order and can become more high-strung. At such times, their insistence on controlling their visual environments can cause conflicts when they're playing with children who take a less structured approach to life. Stress can also cause them to become very bossy as a way of trying to exert more control over their environment. In my clinic, if I observe a child bossing other kids around, I always suspect that he might be visual, and also that he may be upset by something going on at home or at school. I suggest to parents that when they see their visual child trying to dominate other kids in this way, they try appealing to the child's natural talent for leadership (the other side of bossiness). Encourage him to set a good example by doing the "right thing" so that others will look up to him. Visual children care about what others think of them, and you can put that concern to use to redirect their behavior.

The Everyday Life of the Visual Preschooler

Sleeping

Getting the visual preschooler to bed will continue to require a kind of decompression period, during which visual stimulation is kept to a minimum. This child should definitely not have a television in her bedroom, because she won't be able to wind down if she watches it at night. To avoid having this battle at bedtime, set aside a time for TV earlier in the day. Drawing pictures and reading books are fun activities that your child can do without becoming overexcited at bedtime.

Some visual kids are so dependent on being in an orderly environment that they may need to clean up their room before they can go to sleep.

As she gets older, the visual child will have an increasing need to organize her space her own way. She will want to pick out the paint color on her walls, her bedspread, rug, and other visual furnishings. So be prepared for her wanting her own room. If that's not possible, a room divider, a screen, or even just a curtain that can be drawn to delineate a space that is hers will minimize conflict.

If you have moved recently or there have been any other major changes in your child's life, a visual child may suddenly become afraid of the dark at night. Shadows may seem scary, she may have nightmares, and even the furniture in her room could upset her if it's new and she hasn't gotten used to it. Take her seriously. These fears are truly disturbing to her and should not be dismissed.

Feeding

Visual preschoolers' fastidiousness also applies to their eating habits. Visual children will continue to be very picky about the appearance of their food. I remember one visual child who wouldn't eat pasta when his mother cut it for him so it would be easier to eat—the spaghetti had to be perfectly intact! These children may also have particular visual rituals they want observed during meals, such as eating their sandwiches only if they've been cut in a certain way, or drinking their milk from the same cartoon-character glass every time. Visual children will be easily upset when other people don't take the same care with their food. Younger siblings who are messy with food, smearing it around their plates and throwing it across the room, will agitate the visual preschooler. Parents may find that feeding these kids separately—or at least positioning them so that the visual child doesn't have to see the mess being made—will make for more peaceful mealtimes for everyone.

Because the visual child takes a lot of pride in presentation, by the time he is five he'll probably eat with good manners and may enjoy setting the table too. And though he may still be picky about what kinds of food he eats, he'll gradually become interested in a wider array of foods, so long as they are visually appealing to him.

Dressing
Visual children continue to be concerned about their clothes and their appearance. As they expand their social world, through school and other activities, these kids will begin to take careful note of how other children look, and will often want to dress or wear their hair like someone they admire. A new friend from preschool has bright blue sneakers? Your visual toddler will come clamoring to you with requests for the exact same pair. All the girls in class are wearing jeans with patches on them? Your child must have the same style right away. These kids will also be attuned to how their parents dress, so be prepared for commentary.

Again, gender is important, not just in terms of how the child dresses but in regard to how you dress too. A flowered shirt on Dad or pants instead of skirts on Mom may not please your little fashion critic.

Mismatches with the Visual Child

Visual Child with Visual Parent

Ironically, this parent-child combination can result in a mismatch if the parent and child possess different visual sensibilities—like the mother and daughter described earlier who had different but equally strong reactions to the color yellow. Such problems don't usually present themselves until the child is older, when the child begins to have much more defined preferences about clothing, room decoration, and other aesthetic choices. When the child is a baby or toddler, parent and child usually see eye to eye (excuse the pun).

But once the child does start to exhibit strong preferences, the parent should watch for signs in herself that she is not letting him express his own sensibility and make his own choices. Kids need to experiment, and no matter how particular you are about how you want your child to look, that means you need to give up a bit of control. If he insists on wearing all purple and growing his hair long and you think little boys should wear navy blue and have crew cuts, try to remember how you felt as a child when you weren't allowed to dress as you pleased.

If your child thinks she has "cleaned" her room but it's not up to your high standards, rather than judge her job as imperfect, try to admire her effort. (And when she's out of the house, go ahead and tidy it to satisfy your own craving for visual order.)

In general, try to give your child as much freedom as possible to express his individuality. If the price is clothes that you don't like and a room that isn't arranged the way you yourself would do it, it's worth it for the feelings of self-confidence and autonomy you'll be building in your child. And of course there are always compromises that can be made. "You can wear those clothes to school today, but when Grandma and Grandpa come and we go out to dinner, you have to wear the new pants and sweater I bought you last week."

Visual Child with Tactile Parent

The biggest stumbling block for the tactile parent of the visual child is that you may not understand your child's need for visual order. And for the tactile parent, who is eminently practical as well as tending toward the messy, this visual fastidiousness might make you jump to the conclusion that your child is a bit obsessive or compulsive. For example, I worked with a mom whose response to her daughter's need for cleanliness and order was: "Doesn't she have anything better to do than worry about being tidy?" As a tactile person (and a committed feminist), she viewed a clean house as the sign of a boring person with too much time on her hands. Remember, order to your child is as important as a hug is to you.

The visual child organizes her belongings with great precision as a way to control her environment and to manage her stress; order calms and grounds her. You need to realize why this kind of visual order matters so much to your child. As a tactile person, you are practical and goal-oriented—doing the laundry and throwing it in a basket is good enough for you. Your child, however, will want to see her laundry carefully folded before being put away, in neat piles, in her drawers.

You may also overlook the importance of your visual child's preference for a favorite red plate at dinner, or a bed that is neatly made, or food arranged in a certain way on her plate. A tactile parent may also forget exactly how to tie the bow on a dress the way her daughter likes it, how to arrange the sandwiches and fruit in her son's lunch box, or how to re-create the arrangement on his train table exactly the way it was before she dusted it. You may think these things are trivial, but I can assure you that they can matter a lot to your child. Since they don't take much effort and can help keep the peace, it's worth keeping these in mind.

Visual Child with Auditory Parent

The auditory parent and the visual child are usually a congenial match, but there may be a certain distance between them because of the way they run on parallel tracks. There's the child, quietly going about his business each day, focused on bringing order into his visual environment, and the parent, chatting away to her child, not noticing that the child has tuned her out because he is so focused on his own world. Subtle shifts in tone of voice and expression are not going to be picked up on by this child. To get his attention, you may have to stand right in front of him and establish eye contact as you speak to him. It's the look on your face that will matter more to him than the tone of your voice.

Since the auditory parent and visual child can both get very wrapped up in their work and their play, happy to function by themselves, it's important to find as many ways as you can to connect. Reading aloud from a colorfully illustrated children's book is certainly one of the best, because it plays to the strengths in both parent and child. The child will enjoy looking at the pictures while the parent reads to him, and both will feel good about the closeness that envelopes them as they enter the imaginary world of the storybook together. And when you're explaining something to your child, always remember to *show* her examples instead of simply *telling* her.

Visual Child with Taste/Smell Parent

Many taste/smell parents tend to give too much of themselves—their time, their energy, and their attention. They can get so wrapped up in doing what they think will make their child happy that they often lose sight, literally, of their child's more basic needs. This happened with one mom who was a real foodie and went to elaborate lengths to make nutritious, home-cooked meals. One time, she cooked a delicious spaghetti Bolognese and proudly served it for dinner. The visual child, all of four and a half years old, looked in horror at what appeared to her as a messy pile of red, brown, and white food on her plate and pushed it away. "I don't want it, Mommy; it looks icky." The mother was crushed since she'd put so much time and energy into the meal. But Sophie wasn't at all interested in her mother's feelings. Visual children tend to develop empathy a bit later than is typical (around five or six rather than four or five years old).

In the above example, the mother lost sight of who she was actually making dinner for. If she had kept in mind that Sophie liked her food plain, simple, and arranged neatly on the plate with all the parts of the meal in separate little piles, she might have saved herself the disappointment.

The taste/smell parent and the visual child can sometimes clash when it comes to how the child wants to dress, with one focused on comfort, the other on aesthetics. The child might want to wear her pretty pink princess gown to school, but the mother sees that it's forty degrees outside and believes the child needs to wear long pants and a heavy sweater under a snowsuit. You'll have to be creative about negotiating these situations, trying to see your child's point of view while doing what you have to to keep her warm and healthy.

Since taste/smell parents are quite expressive, often wearing their feelings on their faces, they have to be careful not to send confusing signals to their child. For instance, a taste/smell mom might be moved to tears watching her daughter in her first ballet recital. The visual daughter, catching sight of her mother's tearful face, could come to the conclusion that her mother is sad, not proud. The visual child runs off the stage, now crying herself. The visual child does not have the emotional sophistication to understand that tears can be shed at moments of great pride or love, so misunderstandings can arise that cause unnecessary hurt feelings.

Hurt feelings can also arise when the visual child begins to explore his world and push for greater independence, a move that many taste/smell parents find painful and try to resist. As a taste/smell parent, you may need to be more sensitive to your child's need for autonomy and separation. Hard as it can be to see your child pulling away from you, it's one of the many developmental tasks that he must negotiate. The more you can support him in these efforts, the better for both of you.

Visual children see things that many of us miss. They watch us for clues—and cues—about how to feel, behave, and manage the challenges of their world. They take in the smallest of details to create vivid pictures that they carry in their minds and recall with remarkable clarity. From their earliest infancy, they look to us parents for visible signs of love and guidance. They rely on their powers of observation to recognize what's familiar and explore what is new. To understand these children, we must take a fresh look at the world through their eyes.

SEVEN

The Taste/Smell Child

The fourth of the sense mode classifications is taste/smell. Children in the taste/smell group are sometimes hard to classify because their sensitivity to other people and their ability to tune in and adapt to those around them can make them so chameleonlike that they are often misidentified as belonging to another group.

Taste/smell children are such sensitive creatures, deeply affected by all sorts of intense stimuli, including loud noises and angry voices, bright light, strong or unpleasant smells and tastes. Their sense of taste is acute, and they are very clear about their likes and dislikes in food; their preferences tend toward the bland (to an adult) but often are quite unpredictable and hard to understand. This is the baby who refuses previously frozen breast milk because once the milk has been frozen its chemical composition has changed and it is subtly different in taste. If on formula, this is the baby who will drive you crazy by refusing all but one brand of formula, which you arrive at only after nerve-racking trial and error. Later, this is the child who refuses to eat leftovers because they "taste different," who will not eat yogurt from a silver spoon because the taste is too "metally," and who is the last to try a dish made up of a combination of foods.

This acute sensitivity to taste and smell can result in behaviors that are very puzzling to those around them. I worked with one family who were mystified by the fact that their two-year-old seemed to have taken a strong dislike to her aunt, which was upsetting to the whole family. When I first met the mother, Mary, and daughter, Sara, in my office and was trying to figure out the sense mode of the little girl, the mother shared with me several stories that highlighted Sara's intense sensitivity, including not nursing if the mother had eaten spinach and being very sensitive to any slight change in her sleep routine. As I watched, Sara sat in her mother's lap completely at ease—not squirming, not bothering to look around her, and not following her mother's or my voice. To me, these were all indications of a taste/smell baby.

According to Mary, there was no apparent reason why Sara would pull away and refuse to be held by her aunt. We decided that it might be helpful if I came to their home on a day when the aunt in question was visiting.

The first thing I noticed was that the woman wore quite strong perfume. I asked the aunt if she wore it all the time. She said yes, she did. This lovely woman then explained to me that she always made a special effort when seeing her niece to dress up and put on perfume. "I like to be well presented and I like to smell good," she said.

There were actually two problems here. First, the aunt smelled unfamiliar, not like the child's mother; and second, the perfume masked the natural scent of the woman, making it impossible for the baby to "know" her aunt in the way that taste/smell children like to do.

I suggested that the aunt start using the same soap as the mother and avoid the perfume for a while. She was a bit skeptical at first; she hadn't had this problem with any of her other nieces or nephews, who were all affectionate toward her, and who ever heard of a baby caring about how a person smelled? She had decided the child just really didn't like her, and admitted that she even suspected her sister of turning the child against her.

With a little convincing, however, the aunt agreed to try the experiment, and things changed dramatically. The familiar smell of the mother's soap made the child more relaxed and comfortable around her aunt. This simple change enabled the natural affection between aunt/niece to develop easily and quickly.

Because of their sensitivity to all types of sensory stimulation, taste/smell children have a tendency to retreat to an active inner life that helps to shield them from the sometimes overwhelming barrage of information they receive from the outside world. Often happy to play alone, taste/smell children have vivid, wild imaginations that enable them—especially in their early years—to inhabit fanciful realms where fairies, goblins, or other imaginary creatures live. Stuffed animals are not mere ornaments for their rooms or plush toys to cuddle at night; taste/smell children will attribute complicated personalities to these toys, making them companions they can bring along on elaborate fantasy journeys.

These children are sensitive not just to all kinds of sensory input but also to their own and others' emotions. They may alternate between being intensely involved with the people who are close to them and retreating to their inner lives when the emotional connection becomes too much for them. Protective and loyal, these children will do anything for those they care about.

They make close friends and will always have a "best friend," preferring one-on-one intimacy to group socializing.

As they get older, they show an uncanny capacity for empathy. This emotional sensitivity can result in such a blurring of boundaries that they take on the feelings of others, especially those to whom they are close, confusing their loved ones' feelings with their own.

In the social realm, this sensitivity makes them very vulnerable to embarrassment and hurt feelings. To protect themselves, they generally prefer not to be singled out in any way. This means that in her early years the taste/smell child will rarely misbehave and will probably be very obedient at school. But as she gets older, beyond five, this same desire to fit in may make her especially sensitive to peer pressure. And, as you will see below, it's for this reason that parents need to pay special attention to helping their taste/smell children develop their ability to recognize and respect their own opinions, preferences, and desires. In other words, the taste/smell child really needs to be supported in learning how to stand up for herself, whether it's about something as simple as choosing a flavor of ice cream (what she really wants instead of what Mom or her sister is having) or something as challenging as having the strength to resist inappropriate peer pressure.

With taste/smell children of any age, it is important to observe them carefully in order first to recognize and then to accept their preferences—even before they are able to articulate them, and even if those preferences don't quite make sense to you. You may not understand exactly why your child always likes to be put down in his crib facing one direction as opposed to another, or why he feeds calmly and contentedly in the rocking chair but not on the couch. What is important is that you recognize that these preferences exist and that they have meaning and resonance for your child, who relies on them to ground him throughout the many transitions of his day. It may seem like a hassle, but a bigger hassle is a baby who is not eating or sleeping.

Taste/Smell Baby Basics, from Birth to Age One

How the Taste/Smell Baby Expresses Emotional Needs

As babies, taste/smell children crave the closeness of their primary caretakers. Similar to tactile babies, who don't like to be put down, taste/smell babies are those who are happiest in the Baby-Björn carrier or sling, asleep on their mother's chest or in her arms. However, unlike tactile babies, taste/smell babies are not calmed simply by being held; because they are so sensitive to the moods of their caretakers, they can take on that person's emotional state. If the mother is nervous or fearful, the baby will often become agitated as well. If she is angry or irritable, the baby will pick up and express a similar mood. If she doesn't like her next-door neighbor, the baby will intuit this feeling and become agitated when the neighbor comes near him. If at the end of the day the mother is upset or distracted over a squabble she's had with her partner or a problem at work, the taste/smell infant will sense these feelings and may balk at going down in his crib. This applies to positive feelings as well: When Mom is feeling calm and happy, her infant will mimic this contentment and go to sleep with ease.

This emotional contagion can have a big impact on breast-feeding. If an infant's mother is tense about nursing her child, the baby also will be tense and may have a difficult time settling down to feed. Babies will be especially tuned in to a first-time mother's natural and understandable nervousness when beginning to breastfeed.

If you use what you know about your baby's emotional sensitivity, you can help her learn to self-soothe, an important part of emotional development at this stage. Megan, the mother of ten-month-old Jasmine, found this out somewhat by accident. Jasmine, a taste/smell baby, was resisting going down for her naps. "She cried and fussed herself to exhaustion, but she just wouldn't sleep when I put her in her crib," Megan recalled. "I was wiped out too, since I couldn't get a break. I would get stressed out and anxious every time nap time came around. The very thought that I would have to go through the routine was making me feel crazy." Megan finally reached the point of giving up—and that's what changed the situation.

In desperation, one afternoon Megan pulled out a portable baby bed that she'd received as a shower gift. Rather than putting her daughter down for a nap in her bedroom crib, she plunked her tired baby into the soft, fleecy portable bed next to her and sat down to read a magazine. To her amazement, Jasmine dropped quickly off to sleep. Soon this became their routine: Jasmine would nap in her portable bed near Megan while Megan did quiet tasks or just relaxed. Yes, the proximity to her mother was part of why Jasmine was calm enough to go to sleep, but more than that it was Megan's obvious shift into relaxation mode.

"She seems to need to be near me to fall asleep. So I stopped fighting that, and things improved. I just hope that over time she'll be able to soothe herself to sleep in a crib or a bed without me nearby," said Megan. I suggested that after Jasmine got a bit older and more accustomed to her nap-time routine, Megan could try introducing a teddy bear or some other soft, cuddly object that the child could begin to "take care of." This transitional love object would eventually help Jasmine learn how to self-soothe in her mother's absence—an ability that will stand her in good stead when she is apart from her mother for longer and longer periods of time. (As you will see in the next section, the taste/smell toddler, and even the preschooler, tends to have a difficult time separating from her loved ones. She feels so close to these people that they are like extensions of herself; she simply can't imagine being apart from them.)

Because your feelings for other people will spill over to your taste/smell child, who will appropriate these feelings as her own, even when she's still just a baby, you can play an active role in helping her overcome separation and stranger anxieties. For example, if you're introducing a new babysitter, you will want to communicate to your child your own affection for this person, being as warm and friendly as you can. The more comfortable you are around the babysitter, the more comfortable your child is likely to be. And of course the reverse is true as well.

Jacqui, a mother with whom I worked, was trying to figure out what to do about visits from her mother-in-law, because the woman always seemed to upset her five-month-old daughter, Georgia. "Georgia just doesn't seem to like her. She's such a happy, smiley baby, but when Eve picks her up, Georgia always cries. She's fine with my father-in-law, but not with Eve."

I had already identified Georgia as taste/smell, based on her heightened sensitivity to all kinds of sensory stimuli. And when Jacqui and I talked about how she herself felt about Eve, the picture began to become clear. Her mother-in-law was "pushy," Jacqui said, and she didn't enjoy spending time with her. I explained that it was natural that Georgia didn't either, since she was taking her cues from Jacqui. As an experiment, I suggested that Jacqui try to be more positive in her interaction with Eve and in general act in a more welcoming way. A few weeks later, Jacqui called to tell me that things were going better—she could see a clear difference in the way Georgia responded to her grandmother now that Jacqui had made a point of being more warm and affectionate with her.

How the Taste/Smell Baby Discovers the World

How the taste/smell baby makes her first forays into discovering and exploring the world around her is seen most clearly through the lens of her extreme need for routine. Although it's true that most babies do better on a regular eating, sleeping, and playing schedule, the taste/smell baby reacts especially strongly to any change in her daily routine. Many parents with whom I've worked have reported back to me that it's their taste/smell children who have the hardest time with traveling or even the slightest deviation in their daily schedule. If a mealtime is off by half an hour, their taste/smell child is screaming. If bedtime is later by an hour, there will be hell to pay for everyone. Taste/smell children have very sensitive bodies, which means they tend to have strong reactions to changes related to sleeping and eating. For this reason, many parents of taste/smell babies have found it easier to manage their highly sensitive children by doing everything they can to avoid such changes and by preparing for them in advance when avoidance is not possible. These strategies may at first seem like you are being ruled by your baby's needs. However, once you realize how sensitive she is to any changes in her waking, feeding, and nap schedule, you will feel more motivated to make the necessary allowances. This is especially true in her younger years.

For instance, if at home you always put your baby in the same portable play yard while you're doing things around the house, bring it along when you go to your neighbor's house for a coffee break. If you are going to Grammy's house for vacation, bring a travel cot with you and use it at home for a week or so before you go away so that your toddler can get a feel for the new sleeping arrangement. And when you're away, be sure to stick with whatever rituals are part of your nighttime routine at home—reading the same storybooks you always do, covering the child with the same sheet and blanket, perhaps even bringing a night-light from home if you use one there.

How the Taste/Smell Baby Begins to Play and Interact

When it comes to engaging your child in activities, it's a good idea to establish daily playtime routines that your baby can count on; again, a predictable schedule helps this child feel secure and comfortable. Even as an infant, your baby will appreciate the regularity and recurrence of what may seem to you like very small details—such as the warmth of the sun that comes in from a particular window, spilling light over the softly textured cushion of an area rug where she plays every morning with her toys while you sit next to her on the floor.

Like tactile babies, these children often want to be physically close to parents or caregivers when they are playing. And they are not content to be left alone for any amount of time.

These babies seem drawn to nature and enjoy being outside—as long as they are dressed so that they feel physically comfortable. But heaven forbid if they get too hot or too cold—they will not be able to focus on anything else and will cry with displeasure or squirm in agitation, letting you know they are not happy campers.

Taste/smell babies are drawn to toys that squeak, rattle, or have mirrors or interesting textures—anything that appeals to their sensitive ears, eyes, or fingers. However, as you introduce new toys to your taste/smell baby, she will probably react very positively to some and ignore others entirely. The yellow rattle may be a favorite toy that she'll reach for, while she ignores the cloth blocks you're constantly dangling before her. Often the toys that she likes are those that have some kind of emotional value to her. If you gave her the doll, for example, she will love the doll. If the cloth blocks were a gift from a visiting friend whom she doesn't know very well, she might overlook them forever. Of course, she is probably not conscious of who gave her the gift, but something inside of her has registered that fact. I have observed many taste/smell babies clinging to toys and objects that their parents told me were gifts from special people. Often you may not be able to understand your child's preferences, and at this age she certainly can't explain them, but you can be sure that there is some basis for them, even if you are never able to uncover it.

The Everyday Life of the Taste/Smell Baby

Sleeping

Your taste/smell baby may have difficulty going to sleep alone in his crib. No matter what you try—singing songs, rubbing his back, or walking him around on your shoulder—he may still be fussy and wakeful. But if you are stressed out by this and react by getting ever more anxious and agitated, as many a tired parent quite understandably will do, you may set a difficult cycle in motion, because the baby is likely to respond in kind, and no one is going to get much sleep. Hard as it is to do when you are exhausted and feeling as though you have come to the end of your rope, it's important to try to stay relaxed when putting your child down. So take a few deep breaths to calm yourself, use a gentle, singsong voice, and smile even if he's fussing. Chances are the baby will settle into your calmness and drop off to sleep.

If your baby continues to have trouble going to sleep, you might have to create a more rigidly structured bedtime routine that includes, for example, giving him a bottle or nursing him, reading him a story, rubbing his back or holding his hand, and encouraging him to try to fall asleep in his crib. However, even if none of these works, it's not a good idea to just let a taste/smell baby cry himself out, mainly because that doesn't usually happen. Instead, the child just gets more and more upset and the crying escalates.

Some parents bring their baby into their own room, where the child sleeps either in a bassinet (or some other kind of mobile crib) or in the parents' own bed. It's been my experience that most taste/smell babies do enjoy co-sleeping with their parents, but this option must, of course, be comfortable for all involved. If not, the child will pick up on the parents' discomfort. If you do choose that route for your can't-get-enough-of-you taste/smell baby, know that all babies who co-sleep do eventually want their own bed.

In one family, the parents welcomed their newborn into their bed for the first year, and the happy threesome did fine. The baby slept well, barely waking when she was nursed, and everyone in the family got a lot of sleep. But the mother became pregnant again around the time the child reached her first birthday, and the mother and father thought the little girl should start sleeping in a crib in her own room so that when the new baby arrived, she wouldn't feel that the baby was responsible for her being "kicked out" of her parents' room. Rational as this idea was, the parents were having trouble with it, because they felt so guilty about doing anything that might make her unhappy or, after the baby arrived, jealous.

When they came to see me, I assured them that if they could make peace with themselves about helping their daughter transition to greater independence, she would do fine. They just had to get over their guilt. And that's what happened. Over the course of several weeks, the parents gradually moved the little girl into her own room. They stayed with her in her room for a while each night and gave her lots of loving encouragement (including a new teddy bear who needed her). But I believe the single most important factor was their attitude: The more upbeat and positive the parents were, the more secure their daughter felt, which enabled her to make the move. Of course, the transition wasn't always smooth. There were some bad nights and some occasional relapses when they allowed their daughter to sleep with them again, especially at first, as transitions are always a process. But within little more than a month, she had negotiated this milestone quite successfully and felt safe and secure on her own.

Feeding

As you might expect, feeding a taste/smell baby is first of all about creating a soothing environment that will help him feel safe and secure. Since the baby will pick up on your emotional state, that means that you yourself need to be relaxed. Do everything possible for your own comfort and ease. Maybe you have a chair that is particularly comfortable, which you can put near a window that looks out on a scene that you like, or you can wrap yourself and the baby in a soft, pretty blanket, or you can play music (so long as it's not loud or jangly) that always puts you in a good mood, or you can light a candle that creates a gentle glow during middle-of-the-night feedings. If your baby seems fussy at feeding times and you don't know why, ask yourself: "Am I more anxious than usual? Is there new or added stress in the family? Have I taken enough time out for myself so that I can approach my baby in a calm state?" The key to understanding what is happening with him may lie within you.

Having rituals that you replicate each time you feed your baby will help him fall into a comfortable routine. Repetition and regularity are all-important for this baby. This means that he will tend to want to be fed in the same place, with the same blanket, in the same position, and so on, each time.

Changes are always potentially problematic, particularly any changes that might affect the taste or smell of the baby's food. One mom who had to go back to work three months after her baby was born began pumping and freezing her breast milk so that she didn't have to switch to formula. But the baby rejected the thawed breast milk because it tasted different. So after nursing in the morning, the woman pumped enough for two daytime feedings, then dashed home in time to nurse by 4:00 P.M. Of course, most women would not be able to accommodate such a schedule. Now I advise mothers of taste/smell babies who are planning to go back to work to start pumping, freezing, and introducing thawed breast milk to their baby from the start so that their child gets used to the taste.

Anytime your baby begins to resist nursing, you might want to check in with yourself to see if you've changed your diet in any way or eaten any foods that might be affecting the taste of your breast milk: One mother recalled that her daughter wouldn't nurse after she ate certain foods, such as broccoli or anything with curry powder in it.

This hypersensitivity to taste will affect babies on formula too. If, for example, you're using formula and you switch to a different brand, your baby might refuse to eat. The bottle and the nipple you use can also cause problems. Glass bottles are usually preferred to plastic and, since rubber is generally revolting to these kids, silicone nipples will probably be better accepted than latex ones.

Once he starts on solid food at six or nine months, your taste/smell baby will still be fussy about what he eats. Because he continues to be hypersensitive to taste and smell, he'll probably prefer bland foods to those with a lot of flavor, and you may need to heat food in a particular type of container—usually one that is made of glass rather than metal or plastic. When he gets a bit older, he may show a preference for a particular spoon or bowl or cup, because his sensitive palate can detect subtle changes in the way food tastes, depending on the material in which it is served.

And again, since taste/smell babies will pick up on any strong emotion or mood in the room, it's best to remain as calm as possible during feeding times. This can be a challenge, since these kids don't like to be rushed, and both bottle-feeding and nursing can take quite a while. But try to be patient with your taste/smell baby. He has his own sense of pacing, and if you can just accept his rhythms, life will be much more pleasant.

Dressing and Diapering
What matters most to this baby about clothing is that it be easy to put on—nothing too tight going over the head, for example—and comfortable. So long as you yourself are not rushed and don't show any signs of frustration with the occasional problems that arise, getting your baby dressed should go smoothly.

As with feeding, you should try to be consistent in everything that involves dressing and diapering, and this includes how you launder the clothes. For example, switching to a different laundry detergent or using dryer sheets that smell of lavender could irritate a taste/smell child. In general it's best to use gentle, hypoallergenic, unscented soaps to wash baby clothes and cloth diapers. And unless there is a problem with the diaper ointment or baby lotion you are using, you should stick to it. Your child will quickly grow accustomed to the scent (or lack thereof) of any product, and will always prefer what she's accustomed to over anything new and different.

Taste/Smell Toddler Basics, from Ages One to Three

How the Taste/Smell Toddler Communicates and Manages Emotions

These toddlers will be highly emotional little people, feeding off the energy and feelings of people around them, both children and adults alike. Surprising their parents and teachers with an early ability to cue into the feelings of their peers, they'll be the two-year-olds who cry when their friend gets a boo-boo, or the three-year-olds who run over to hug the child who fell off the slide. They show signs of empathy earlier than children in any of the other sense groups.

Because the taste/smell child is so tuned in to everyone else's feelings, she can be especially upset by any anger, tension, stress, or other intense emotion in the air. For this reason, she may seem moody or changeable, as she reacts to the emotions of others around her. Also, she doesn't understand that emotions come and go and that often they have nothing to do with her. So your taste/smell toddler needs to know that if you are angry with her, you will not be angry for the rest of your life; that if you are disappointed in her behavior, you do not stop loving her; and that if you are having a fight with your partner or someone on the phone, it's not because of anything she did. These concepts may be self-evident to you, but your highly sensitive taste/smell child needs to hear this information again and again and again.

One technique to help familiarize your toddler with the nature and range of feelings is to play a game with Mr. Potato Head in which you keep changing the face parts to show different expressions—mad, happy, sad, curious, and so on—and ask her to identify those expressions, teaching her the words for the different emotions. This will help her begin to get comfortable with the idea that the same person can feel many emotions. At the conceptual level, what you're doing is showing her that we are not defined by our emotions. We can be sad today and happy tomorrow, depending on what is happening. This will give her a better ability to deal with your changing emotions as well as her own, which can sometimes be overwhelming to her.

The taste/smell child needs a lot of reassurance and may be very clingy at this age. Throughout the day he'll make constant demands on your attention, always wanting to be carried or snuggled or told that you love him. One three-year-old I know keeps asking his mother if she loves him more than his brother. This is a common enough question among toddlers, but the taste/smell child needs to be reassured of his special place in his mother's heart more often than most kids do.

Taste/smell children take their emotions very seriously and can also be very articulate about expressing them. However, even though they are able to express their feelings, they still need help, like most kids at this age, managing them, especially when it comes to being sad or fearful about separating from their parent or caregiver. In one case, Nathan, a three-year-old boy, was resisting going to nursery school. One day his mother, who was trying to help him get over his fears, noticed that the sign for the school had an image of Pooh Bear on it. So she bought Nathan a Pooh Bear and told him that he was going to have to take Pooh to school so that the bear could say hello to his friend every day. If Pooh couldn't see his friend, she said, he would get lonely and scared, just the way Nathan did when he went to school by himself, but if Nathan and Pooh stayed together at school, they would both be okay, because they would have each other to talk to and cuddle with. For the taste/smell child, it's easy to shift into imaginary mode and give animals or toys human qualities, so these fantasy scenarios can be very effective ways for you to help your child manage his intense feelings.

In general, the taste/smell child is very aware of what's expected of her and doesn't want to misbehave, so it's usually only when she has been pushed beyond her limits that she erupts in a tantrum. But when the taste/smell child does have a tantrum, she tends to break down quite dramatically, with lots of tears and screaming. If you sense that she is on the verge of a tantrum, you may be able to defuse it by talking to her about what she is feeling, because this is a child who may actually be able to tell you. Once you understand the problem, even if there's nothing you can do about it, simply listening and acknowledging her feelings may be enough to soothe her. If she's crying but hasn't gone on to the tantrum stage, a kiss and a cuddle can also help. The warm and loving environment of Mom or Dad's arms may be all she needs to calm her down. Another technique is to do some fantasy play. Talk to her about how her crying is making her teddy bear sad and ask her if she can make a happy face or give him a kiss to make him feel better. Or you can also try shifting her attention by talking about someone she loves—engaging her in a conversation about what she and her best friend did on their last playdate, talking about what she is going to do when the family visits her favorite uncle for Thanksgiving next week, or recalling how much fun she had with her grandmother last summer at the beach.

If none of these strategies is effective and your child has worked herself up into a full-blown tantrum, you may want to try crying yourself—really! The point is that when you show your own feelings, your taste/smell child will more than likely shift her attention to you and stop her own tantrum.

How the Taste/Smell Toddler Explores the World

The taste/smell child is an eager, curious, and playful learner who is drawn to the natural world and his native intelligence and intuition about plants, animals, and nature. Rather than compiling facts for facts' sake, the taste/smell child absorbs what is around her in a sensory way. On a nature walk, she will take in the calls of the birds, the ripple of the stream, the smell of the leaves that have fallen to the ground. She will make observations that seem unusual, showing the breadth of her perception. Sometimes these observations will seem to come out of the blue, but this highly imaginative child often makes connections and associations that are invisible to the rest of us.

How the Taste/Smell Toddler Plays and Interacts

Children whose dominant sense is taste/smell will start to demonstrate their strong imaginations at this stage. They love to create elaborate fantasies with their toys. Their dolls come alive to act out dramatic stories about families, their stuffed animals populate a loud and busy barnyard, and their action figures fight epic battles across the living room floor.

These children often become very attached to certain possessions, including toys. This is especially so once their world begins expanding, leaving them without the constant familiar presence of Mom and Dad and exposing them to new people and places. For them, anything that is new can be scary. Like Linus in the *Peanuts* comic strip, they may want to carry a favorite toy or blanket with them everywhere they go. The blanket, teddy bear, or doll acts as both a security object, which soothes and comforts them, especially during their parents' absence, and a transitional object, to which they can attribute human characteristics, thereby learning to relate to people other than their parents. You may hear your child talking to his teddy or singing to his blankie, and you should not do anything to discourage this behavior, since it will help him separate from you. This kind of fantasy play also gives him an outlet for his emotions. If he is feeling sad, then you can bet Teddy is feeling sad too, and you'll hear him comforting Teddy—which is his way of comforting himself. You can learn a lot about what your child is feeling by listening to his interactions with Teddy.

Of course, children in all of the sense groups often develop such attachments to objects, and for similar reasons, but the hypersensitive taste/smell child may be particularly dependent on his because of the role it plays in helping him deal with his fears. Never is this more true than when he is faced with having to separate from the people he feels closest to.

One little taste/smell boy began carrying around his toy Thomas the Tank Engine everywhere he went after he started going to day care. His mother thinks he became so devoted to it because he associated it with the many happy hours he'd spent watching the

Thomas the Tank Engine television show with his two older brothers, to whom he was very attached. It was as if by keeping it with him when he was in a scary new environment, he felt he could bring his older brothers with him too.

Whatever object your child ends up attaching to, you should be sure to have a replacement on hand, since it will be quite a catastrophe if this beloved item is lost for good. Better yet, keep switching the objects so that each of them becomes steeped in the familiar smells of the child's environment. Otherwise, if the original item is lost and a new one put in its place, a taste/smell child might notice the difference and reject the replacement, even though it seems to you to be identical to the original.

Taste/smell children are often more fearful of new experiences and more intensely unhappy about separating from Mom than other children. So they may be slower to adapt and make friends when first exposed to new environments such as day care and nursery school. Also, because they have extremely vivid imaginations and are able to use them to help them cope successfully when they are thrust into situations that might otherwise overwhelm them, they can enjoy solitary play for much longer periods of time than other children do. However, once they are comfortable enough to come out of their private worlds, they will make their first tentative steps toward socializing with other children. Usually they make only one or two friends at this stage, but they may connect very intensely to these friends, talking about them constantly at home and wanting to spend time with them on weekend playdates. Even in these early days they tend to form close bonds and to be thrilled with special one-on-one relationships. But if anyone they feel close to hurts their feelings, they may feel the pain of it for years to come.

The Everyday Life of the Taste/Smell Toddler

Sleeping

Though they may have been clingy as babies, as toddlers taste/smell children begin to show more independence and are likely to want their own bed as a way to consolidate their new sense of autonomy. Bedtime rituals will continue to be important, however. This child may want you to sing the same lullaby to him each night or read him the same bedtime stories while he snuggles close, finding a sense of safety and security in his strong connection to you. Though you may think it would be a good idea to start introducing some new books, during this period your child is likely to insist on the old standbys; the familiar words and sounds provide a soothing, comforting background patter to which he can fall asleep. Even as a toddler, he will identify strongly with the emotional content of the stories you read to him. Those dog-eared books that he asks you to repeat endlessly are likely to be his favorites in part because of the satisfying emotional journey the characters make during the stories, and the relationships among the different characters.

Consistency and regularity are as important to these kids as rituals. Just as your child may like to eat from the same plate each day and hear the same stories each night, he'll want to go to sleep in his own bed under his special blanket with his cherished teddy bear next to him on the pillow. If anything in his environment changes, he may have a very strong and seemingly irrational reaction, accompanied by much crying and fussing. No matter how well you think you know your child, the reason for his preferences may be a mystery to you. But never underestimate their importance to him.

Feeding

As taste/smell toddlers move beyond simple baby foods, they show very strong opinions about what they eat. They tend to like foods that are bland in taste, are smooth in texture, and have little or no color. This is the child who demands to eat buttered spaghetti, no sauce, every day without fail. (One mom with whom I worked referred to her daughter as a "beige food eater.") Once the taste/smell child has discovered a few foods she likes—be it grilled cheese sandwiches, mashed potatoes, or Mom's tapioca pudding—she'll want those same foods again and again, and she'll want them prepared the same way each time. This means you buy a new kind of cheese or a different flavor of yogurt at your own peril.

These children may also show a strong preference for specific brands. There might be a single brand of milk they will happily drink. If you happen to switch to another brand, look out—it tastes different to this child, and when it comes to these kids and food, different is not good. The taste/smell child also prefers that the foods on his plate be kept separate, and may become upset if they touch each other. So if the tomato sauce from the spaghetti gets in the beans, he may refuse to eat them. He may also be what's called an around-the-clock eater, eating one thing at a time, in sequence. In general, parents need to be very patient about the taste/smell child's food preferences. They may seem silly to you, and you may fear that you are spoiling the child by giving in to him, but this is about allowing the child to feel that he has some control over an area of utmost importance to him—the question of what he eats. In the same way that the visual child needs to control his visual environment and the auditory child needs to control his aural environment, the taste/smell child should have some freedom to choose his own foods.

I worked with one mother of a taste/smell child of two and a half. She was finding it hard to understand a number of her son's behaviors, especially those relating to food. For instance, she would make up a batch of macaroni and cheese and the first day the boy would happily eat it all, but the following day, when she fed him exactly the same food, he would spit it out. The last time this had happened the little boy's reaction was so strong that he had actually gagged and then tossed the bowl to the floor. The mother felt that since he had enjoyed the food the day before, he was just being naughty, and she was furious with him. However, I explained to her that the fact that the food was a day old would have made it taste slightly different from the day before. Perhaps it had picked up some odors from being stored in the refrigerator, or maybe reheating it had altered its flavor. This child could obviously taste the subtle difference and that's probably why he refused the food.

Many taste/smell children have a problem eating leftovers, so it's better to give them fresh food every day if possible. If that's just not doable, then whenever you cook up a batch of food that is intended to last for a while, you should freeze individual portions of it (food tastes fresher if it's stored in the freezer instead of the refrigerator) and then be careful to reheat it in the same way each time. Microwaving it to defrost and heat it is often a good way of preserving its original taste. While it may seem like more work at first, taking this kind of care is infinitely preferable to doing battle with your child, whose food predilections are not evidence of his being difficult but simply the product of his extreme sensitivity to taste.

Dressing

Helping a taste/smell toddler get dressed will be all about one-on-one time with Mom or Dad. If you're in the room, giving encouragement and positive feedback, the process will be enjoyable.

And your toddler's choice of clothes will probably be related to the strong emotional connection she feels to you. Perhaps she wants to wear a pink shirt like Mom's or jeans like Dad's. Or she may choose something on the basis of the person who gave it to her. You will be surprised how well she can recall who gave what to her, and how much this means to her.

Toilet Training

Taste/smell children move into toilet training easily, especially if introduced to the process in a calm, gradual, gentle way. However, if their parents show any impatience with their progress or any annoyance when accidents occur, they will be very hurt and upset by the negative response. It's important that they understand that mistakes happen and that their parents are not upset with them and don't love them any less. You should also be aware that your taste/smell child is so eager to please you that she may try to accommodate your wish for her to be toilet-trained even when it is still beyond her physical capabilities. So ask yourself: Is she truly ready to be toilet-trained, or is she merely responding to what she senses you want?

Even once the toilet-training process is well under way, a taste/smell child may still wet the bed at night if she has had a difficult day. It's one of the many ways her extreme sensitivity may be expressed. This means it's a good idea to keep using diapers at bedtime until you feel confident that she's gotten beyond the accident stage. The diapers will make her feel less pressured about making it through the night, and they'll also reassure her that you aren't expecting more of her than she can live up to. And of course they'll also protect her from waking up in a wet, smelly bed. Since these kids are by definition averse to bad smells, anything you can do to protect your child from them during the toilet-training process will make it more pleasant.

During this challenging time, it's especially important to stick to the bedtime rituals that are so comforting to your child. Of course, do everything you can to help her avoid accidents, such as making sure she goes to the bathroom and doesn't drink any liquids before bed.

Although it can sometimes feel like she's taking two steps forward and one step back during toilet training, be sure to give your child lots of encouragement and praise, and don't try to rush her. Any impatience she senses will be so upsetting to her that it will only backfire.

Taste/Smell Preschooler Basics, from Ages Three to Five

The Taste/Smell Preschooler's Emotional Life

By the time they are preschool age, taste/smell children will often show signs of being highly intuitive. They may seem to know what you are thinking before you say it, anticipate your requests before you make them, and respond to your mood before you even become aware of them.

Often described as being "oversensitive," these kids also tend to be more emotionally mature than other children their age, showing a strong ability to be compassionate and empathetic, a capability that most children are just beginning to develop at this age. Even at this young age, this child will try to play the role of caretaker to the people he loves. When Mom has a headache, this child will instinctively moderate the noise he's making, quieting himself down in hopes of soothing her. If his babysitter arrives for the afternoon feeling sad about a breakup with her boyfriend, he will pick up on her unhappiness and try to comfort her.

Taste/smell children are motivated by a desire to make sure everyone is happy, and they'll lavish compliments on their loved ones, trying to connect with them and make them feel good: "Mom, you're the best mom in the world." "Dad, I love when you take me to school." "Tyler, you're my favorite big brother." This behavior might be mistaken for manipulation, but it's not. Rather, it comes from a genuine desire to create an atmosphere of harmony and happiness for those they love.

However, the flip side of their feeling that it is up to them to make everyone happy is that if they think they have done something wrong or disappointed someone they care about, they can become terribly distressed. Their sense of self-worth is very much tied to how they think others see them.

Pamela, the mother of three young kids, sought me out for help with her middle child, five-year-old Lawrence, a taste/smell boy who had become very difficult to manage. Recently Lawrence had been acting out badly, becoming hysterical over what Pamela thought were minor issues. Shortly after Pamela first came to see me, she reported that Lawrence had come home after school and gone berserk when he couldn't find his homework notebook. Lawrence, always very organized and careful about his things, had never lost or misplaced his homework before, so he was beside himself with worry about what his teacher was "going to do to him." Although I understood that Pamela felt Lawrence was overreacting, and that part of her wanted him to toughen up, I discouraged her from taking that approach and urged her to find a way to help him out of his jam and let him know that she sympathized.

Not only did Pamela tell Lawrence that she would buy a note-book to replace the one he lost, she also wrote a note that Lawrence could take to the teacher to excuse his missing homework. She knew that Lawrence wouldn't have gotten in trouble, but since he was so sure he would, and nothing she said could convince him otherwise, she responded to the fear he was feeling. Getting singled out in class for bad behavior is absolute humiliation for a taste/smell child. No matter what, the taste/smell child doesn't want to be in trouble, doesn't want to stand out in any way. "I am very disappointed in you" is the worst thing you can say to a taste/smell child.

The taste/smell child's eagerness to fit in means that she will often adjust her own behavior to match that of the people around her. She does this by observing how others behave, and acting accordingly. If she's playing with a friend who makes a lot of noise and runs around, she may play more boisterously; when she is with a more demure playmate, she will be more likely to play quietly. If she's sharing a bedroom with a neat-as-a-pin cousin while on vacation, this child will adopt neatness as her own style for the duration of the visit. On the other hand, when she's hanging out with her messy older brother, she may mimic his sloppy manner. These children show a kind of protean ability to adapt to the sensibilities and behaviors of the people in their immediate environment. Much of this mimicry of behavior or mood is motivated by the taste/smell child's desire to make everyone feel good about himself. For example, if the taste/smell child sees another child acting boisterously in a room where no one else is behaving that way, she may worry that that child will feel lonely and start acting boisterously herself.

Because taste/smell children respond so sensitively to people, mirroring both their emotions and their actions, the parents and siblings of a taste/smell child might all be convinced that the child is very much like them—no matter how different they are from one another.

As taste/smell children continue to grow more emotionally aware, they also show an uncanny ability to pick up on the feelings and moods of others. They will sense, through nonverbal means, when their older sister has had an argument with her boyfriend, when there is tension between Mom and Dad about money, when Grandma is happy about some good news from her doctor, or when Uncle Jim is sad about his youngest son leaving for college. Because taste/smell kids are so intuitive by nature, their parents sometimes even describe them as seeming a bit "psychic."

The taste/smell child is quick to have his feelings hurt. He feels the sting of criticism very deeply and often is sure that no one understands him. When he's upset by the way someone has treated him, the taste/smell child will tend to retreat into himself, withdrawing to the interior world he relies on for self-protection. Once there, he may be very reluctant to leave that safe place. So if you want to redirect his behavior, you'll find that positive cues will be much more effective than any kind of negative reinforcement or discipline.

At the age of four or five, these children are not only sensing emotions and responding empathically but also trying to manage and/or control their sensory environment. Just as auditory children and visual children try to assert aural and visual control over their respective environments, taste/smell children try to keep their immediate surroundings quiet, serene, and not too stimulating. Loud noises or crowds, strong smells, and too much visual stimulation will unnerve and unsettle these kids. They will either tell everyone to be quiet or need to leave the room.

The Taste/Smell Preschooler's Learning Style

The taste/smell child has vivid recall of events: He remembers going to this park because the last time he went, he was with his dad and it rained; he remembers that book because you read it to him after he slipped in the tub. In other words, he will be able to remember a lot of detail about events and situations if he can also recall how he felt at the time and whom he was with. This facility for association will help him later when he goes to school and begins to read and is expected to remember story plots, characterizations, and other narrative details. A good talker and a good listener too, the taste/smell child typically has a long attention span—if he is engaged in the subject. If not, he will simply drift away. So if you are reading aloud to your child, ask him questions about the characters—the more vivid these personalities become, the more real and memorable the story.

As the taste/smell child begins to grow intellectually, she will often seem a bit dreamy, seeming to prefer the realms of the imagination to the ordinary day-to-day facts and events. The taste/smell child uses her imagination very actively to create positive feelings in herself, especially if there is something that is making her feel bad at the moment.

The taste/smell child continues to be innately curious about the natural world, paying close attention to animals and insects, to the clouds floating in the sky, and to the subtlest of signs indicating shifts in the weather. This is the child whose sense of smell allows her to catch the hint of rain in the air before anyone else knows it's coming, who cries if she thinks her new kitten is missing its mother, who loves stroking the fuzzy leaves of the African violet in the pot on the sill. As they get older and their fine motor skills are better developed, taste/smell children tend to enjoy expressing themselves through art, often choosing nature as their subject.

The taste/smell child has the capacity to learn about his world through many different modes. He is experiential, visual, auditory, tactile, and intuitive, all rolled into one. Because of his highly developed senses, he is capable of digesting knowledge he reads in books, retaining information he hears from his teachers, and memorizing material he sees printed on a chalkboard or displayed on flash cards—as long as he's in an environment where he feels comfortable and secure. If something is troubling him, either at home or at school, he is often unable to compartmentalize enough to allow him to put his feelings aside and focus on any kind of learning challenge.

Not surprisingly, the relationship this child develops with his teacher is often the single most important factor in determining how well he learns and how he feels about school. If he likes his teacher and feels comfortable in her presence, he's likely to love going to school and will thrive in the classroom. Once he's gotten to know her and has overcome his natural fearfulness about new experiences, he'll saunter right in to begin his day, making a bee-line for his favorite activity or his best chum. If, however, he doesn't like his teacher, parents can expect him to resist going to school. He may claim that he doesn't feel well—which in fact he probably doesn't, at least in an emotional sense. He may beg to stay home for a quiet day of reading and cuddling, or may cling to his mother's coat when she drags him to school against his wishes. It's important to try to get your child off to a good start with a new teacher; if something has happened to disrupt that relationship, even if you feel sure that it's just your child being overly sensitive to some imagined slight, you should intervene with the teacher to discuss the child's fears and anxieties and see what can be done to make him feel more comfortable.

This child will work well on small-group projects, such as making a large mural or collaborating to write a story or a play, particularly if he's put with other children he knows well. Or he may gravitate toward one best buddy whom he always wants to partner with, because that's the person he trusts. He will also work very comfortably alone on independent projects, because he's adept at buckling down to concentrate on his work, retreating into his own fertile mind and shutting out the noise and distractions around him. If he's doing an art project, he'll enjoy drawing people, creating portraits that show his subjects feeling the entire spectrum of emotions, because people and their relationships to each other are what most interest him. His vivid imagination may lead him down very individual paths, and this is the age at which his originality may start to visibly flower.

Taste/smell children who are encouraged to explore their own interests often grow into adults with unusual talents and accomplishments. Their ability to see beyond the obvious informs their life choices. Parents who can accept and even celebrate the unusual, nonconforming aspects of their taste/smell child—as they should for any child, of course—will help foster the lasting sense of self-worth that will enable the child to grow into the highly original person he is destined to become.

The Taste/Smell Preschooler's Social Life

Comfortable in a world of his own creation, this child will act out elaborate, magical fantasies with very little need for props or toys. He may pretend to live in a land where animals speak strange languages or people can fly on the crest of the wind. Because he has such a powerful imagination, he can sustain these fantasies for extended periods of time, happily engaging in long periods of solitary play as he returns again and again to his favorite fantasy settings. This is the child who streaks across the backyard in elaborate pantomimes of sword battles or holds court in the living room, giving directions to his invisible companions as they construct an imaginary castle that reaches toward the sky.

Since taste/smell children can play so contentedly on their own, in their own imaginary universe, they sometimes need a bit of a push to come out of themselves and make friends. If they are shy and need encouragement, parents can help their taste/smell children to build bonds with other kids by relying on the fantasy and role playing that they are so good at. For example, you can ask your daughter to pretend that she's going to a birthday party, and tell her to act out how she'll behave once she's there. What should she do if she's feeling too shy to talk to anyone? You can help her to understand that other children feel shy too, and suggest ways to approach someone who seems to be standing on the sidelines and would probably enjoy having someone to play with. Or how should she respond if someone is mean to her? Because this is the type of child who often internalizes slights, give her some guidance on how to stand up for herself and speak out when her feelings are hurt. One way of doing this may be to remind her of the way she sometimes stands up for others. By this age, the taste/smell child's highly developed sense of empathy can often lead her to pick up on any kind of injustice done to another child. If, for example, a child tells a lie about another child, or says something cruel, she may go to the defense of the victim. As a parent, you need to tell her she can be strong for herself as well as for others.

By the time they are preschoolers, these children are coming into their own and developing their highly distinct, individual personalities. Perhaps because of their independent streak, as well as their desire for deep emotional ties, these children continue to prefer to spend time with just one or two friends, as opposed to a crowd of acquaintances.

Taste/smell children will demonstrate some of these same tendencies toward individuality and independence in sports and the other activities they choose to pursue. They are drawn to sports such as swimming, tennis, or running, which give them the chance to play independently or one-on-one. They tend to shy away from more competitive, team-oriented sports, and may prefer single-sex sports.

The Everyday Life of the Taste/Smell Preschooler

Sleeping

Taste/smell children need regular sleeping habits and a lot of sleep. They take in so much emotional and sensory information that they can get quite pooped by the end of the day. And now that they are at the preschool stage, their days are filled with more activities than ever before, which can make them especially tired.

Keeping to a regular sleep schedule continues to be important during these years. So if you've been helping your child get to sleep for the past few years with a regular wind-down routine—perhaps a bath, reading time, a quick snuggle, and then lights out—she will probably want this to continue. She may also need to have a little chat before turning in each night. Perhaps she'd like to revisit the highlights of her day. Or maybe you have worked out a funny formula for how the two of you say "I love you" to each other that is as tightly scripted as a Broadway play. My advice is to stick to it. This is a comforting, meaningful way for a taste/smell child to close out the day. Routine, especially regular sleep, is so necessary for this emotional child, who has a very difficult time holding herself together when tired.

The taste/smell child will also likely have a favorite stuffed animal that she'll want next to her in bed each night, and a favorite set of sheets with fairytale princesses or cartoon figures printed on them. These much-loved things help to create and sustain a familiar environment, which will help her relax.

For the taste/smell child, falling asleep and staying asleep also depend on your setting the right emotional tone. If you send this child to bed in a fit of anger, or if you and your partner have had an argument that she has overheard, she will never be able to settle down enough to sleep.

Often taste/smell children need to go to bed with a full tummy—not because they are hungry but because the sensation of fullness calms them and makes them feel complete. One mom said that even at seven years old, her daughter still had to stick to her old routine of drinking a sippy cup of milk before bed. Another mom shared that her son always tells her, "I can't go to bed without my dessert!" It doesn't matter what it is—fruit, milk with honey, ice cream, or a cookie will do. It's that the sensation of sweetness is something that shifts his body and mind into sleep mode. And Lawrence, from the example earlier, can't go to sleep unless his older brother is in the room with him.

A taste/smell preschooler will still cling to certain toys and objects. She may have a favorite doll that sits in her rocking chair, a single beloved stuffed monkey who sleeps at her side during the night, and a page-worn book that she reads to herself again and again before bedtime. These are important sleep aids. Take them away at your own risk.

Feeding

Though they may start to become slightly less fussy about their food at this stage, taste/smell kids continue to be picky and to have strong likes and dislikes. This is the age when you may suddenly start seeing some surprising displays of stubbornness. These kids really know how to dig in their heels if thwarted in areas that are important to them.

As was true at earlier stages, the taste/smell preschooler is not likely to be an adventurous eater, and he will expect to see the familiar, tried-and-true favorites on his plate. Bland is always better than hot or spicy, because too much flavor overstimulates his sensitive taste buds. The taste/smell preschooler is still capable of rejecting a perfectly good-looking plate of pasta or vegetables or even dessert with a complaint about its smell. He's a plain-vanilla eater, one who can show a remarkable—and to some observers remarkably tedious—ability to eat the same few dishes over and over again. In fact, once he's settled on the foods he likes, he may insist on eating only those things for weeks or months at a time, only to lose interest in them one day and decide he likes something else. Leftovers will continue to be a tough sell to this child, so even though he'll want to eat the same meal many times, Mom may still wind up having to make a fresh version each time. To complicate matters further, your picky eater is now becoming very self-conscious and will not want to be singled out for his pickiness; always concerned about fitting in, he'll be upset if anyone points out that he's eating chicken fingers and ketchup while everyone else has fried chicken and mashed potatoes.

Certain rituals may continue to be important to him at this age. Even if he has graduated from toddler plates and utensils to the "grown-up" versions, for example, he may have a particular drinking glass or a favorite plate that he'll adopt as his own. He's also likely to feel possessive about "his" seat at the family dining table, insisting on sitting at the same place every night and refusing to switch seats with a sibling or a guest.

Although taste/smell children are sensitive about how they appear to others and tend to be rather docile and cooperative most of the time, they can also be quite insistent about getting their own way. One family I worked with was struggling with the willfulness of their preschooler, five-year-old Amy. Amy's parents, Neil and Carla, came to me feeling frustrated with their daughter, who at five seemed at once remarkably mature for her age and also capable of "acting like a baby" a lot of the time, they said.

"She can be incredibly patient and almost weirdly grown-up sometimes," Neil said, "and yet she'll fall apart if we put the wrong food on her plate, or if Carla makes a playdate with the wrong kid from the neighborhood. Lately she's refusing to eat any meat at all. I mean, can a five-year-old just decide to become a vegetarian?"

Spending time with the family, I began to understand the situation from Amy's perspective as well as that of her parents. Amy was clearly a taste/smell child: Her finicky eating habits and keen imagination were two of the indicators. I also observed that Amy took sensitive, protective care of her younger brother, Pete, at one point reaching her hand out to keep him from hitting his head on a sharp corner, a remarkably intuitive and almost motherly gesture that seemed striking in a five-year-old child.

Neil and Carla were concerned about Amy's lack of interest in playing with other children. "She can sit for an hour in her room, having conversations with her doll collection. I just don't think this is normal for a little kid," Carla said. Carla told me she'd been inviting a series of children over for playdates, but often Amy would balk at the idea and want to stay in her room when they came over. Carla was very worried about whether Amy would ever develop any social skills or be able to make any friends.

Mealtimes were especially difficult for Neil, who would often lose his temper and yell when his daughter refused to eat her dinner. "I hate yelling at her, but I do get frustrated," he said. Carla also worried that Amy's stubbornness about food was actually impacting her social life. Amy had begun resisting going on playdates because she was afraid she would have to eat foods she didn't like.

I explained to Amy's parents about how taste/smell children have very strong responses to food and also to people. It might seem to them as if Amy was just being stubborn and bratty by refusing to eat the hamburger on her plate, but in fact there was probably something about its taste and smell that was so repellent to her that she felt unable to eat it. Moreover, Neil's angry outbursts at the dinner table could only be making the situation worse, since the pressure he was putting on her would take away any appetite she might have had for the food, and was probably the reason for her meltdowns too. I suggested that rather than battle over food, the parents sit down with Amy and come up with a short list of foods that she would agree to eat, thus eliminating all the conflict that had been so upsetting to everyone in the family.

I also suggested to Carla that she talk to Amy's preschool teacher about which children Amy seemed to connect with during the school day. (Again, taste/smell children tend to form close bonds with just a few kids, rather than superficial bonds with many.) Building on what the teacher told her about which children Amy gravitated to at school, Carla approached their parents to set up playdates. Now that the children Carla invited to the house were children Amy already knew and liked, these playdates went much more smoothly than the earlier ones. When the invitations were reciprocated, Carla spoke to the parents ahead of time to explain Amy's food peculiarities, and packed her a lunch or snack to take with her so that there wouldn't be any problem about what she ate. Bringing her own food made Amy more willing to go on playdates, much to her mother's relief.

"What an education," Carla told me when we met next. "Once we stopped trying to make her into a different kid, things got a lot better for all of us. Rather than focusing on making sure she'll eat everything, we've found a few things she likes, and we let her have them. And she's had playdates with several of the girls in her class, which seem to have gone well. I realize that it's not up to me to make my child an adventurous eater or a social butterfly. It's my job to help her discover her own path in ways that make sense to her. There's no one 'normal.' "

For parents concerned about nutrition, it's best to take the long view—to look at your child's diet on a weekly basis, rather than meal by meal or day by day, when trying to determine whether she is eating enough from each of the food groups. Although it can be hard to change your child's eating habits, one technique you can try with a taste/smell child this age is to talk to her about what the various foods do for her body. Because children in this group tend to be conscientious, if you tell her that milk is important for strong bones so that she will grow big and tall and not have to worry about breaking anything if she falls, she may start drinking her milk—especially if she knows someone who has broken a bone recently. If she's constipated, tell her that eating fruits and vegetables will help, and maybe she won't have to take that icky medicine anymore.

You may also find that your taste/smell child might try a new food if it is served by her best friend's mother, her beloved grandparent, or a favorite teacher at school. One child I knew would eat fruit only at the neighbor's house. This is yet another way in which the strong emotional connections she feels to certain people can affect the choices she makes.

Dressing

This child will also show a kind of sentimental preference for certain items of clothing. The sentiment could have something to do with her attachment to the person who gave her the clothing or with an experience she had while wearing it. Perhaps her favorite jeans are the ones she wore when the family went to the zoo, her favorite T-shirt the yellow one her godmother sent her from Disney World, and the only barrettes she'll wear the ones that Aunt Tata gave her last Christmas. The sweater you bought for her on a trip to the beach may be particularly cherished because it still smells—at least to her sensitive nose—like salt water, and it reminds her of the fun she had playing in the sand. Rather than being attracted to clothing by how it looks, as a visual child would, or how it feels on her skin, as a tactile child would, taste/smell kids tend to make their choices on the basis of emotional associations.

Mismatches with the Taste/Smell Child

Taste/Smell Child with Taste/Smell Parent

These two sensitive souls usually get along quite well. The relationship with the baby is seamless, as the taste/smell parent loves nothing more than taking care of this wonderful new creature.

There's a danger, however, of doing too much caretaking. If the mother becomes so involved with her child that she forgets to take care of herself physically, she may burn out and become exhausted or ill.

If mismatch issues arise, they usually do so around issues of separation and independence. When the taste/smell mom is finally ready to separate from the child (stop breastfeeding, take the child to drop-off playdates, or encourage her to sleep in her own bed) and the child is not quite ready for such a transition, then both people will become very upset, reacting to the other's extreme hurt feelings. In this way, the two might get stuck in a kind of quagmire of guilt—unable or unwilling to hurt the other and therefore not able to fully move on. In other words, a mother might know it's best for her child to have some more independence, but the child doesn't necessarily understand why this is a good thing, preferring their comfortable bond of intense intimacy. Of course the reverse can happen too, with the child being more than ready for the transition but the parent unable to let go. These developmental milestones can be made easier if the taste/smell parent takes special care to be sensitive to signs that the child is ready to become more independent and gives her clear permission to do so. The child will need to hear this permission again and again before she is able to be comfortable venturing away from her mother's emotional embrace.

Taste/Smell Child with Tactile Parent

This combination of parent and child can be very volatile. Since, as a tactile parent, you tend not to be as sensitive to feelings as your taste/smell child is, you may hurt your child without meaning to. If your manner is abrupt and to the point, as is often the case with tactile types, your hypersensitive child, whose feelings run so close to the surface, may react badly, either by withdrawing into herself or by having emotional meltdowns—or both.

As a person who is eminently practical, you need to be aware of how sentimental your taste/smell child can be. This is often expressed through what may seem to you to be a completely irrational fixation on certain clothes and other possessions, and it usually has something to do with her feelings about the people she loves. So if little Debbie wants to hold on to her ragged blue Smurf when you move in to a brand-new, spanking-clean house, you may want to resist pitching the "filthy little thing"— it means a lot to her because her favorite uncle gave it to her for her birthday last year. You may feel like you're spoiling her by giving in to all her little peculiarities, but it's actually hard to spoil this child, because at heart she is so eager to please those she loves that she misbehaves only when she's pushed beyond her limits.

Steamrolling through the day, as you like to do, is not going to work with this kid. She'll be very particular about food, she depends on routines that can become almost like rituals, and she likes to take her time and allow her imagination to run free. If you push her, she'll feel bullied and misunderstood, and may balk in ways that will be very upsetting to you both.

It's a good thing, however, that tactile parents like to express their love in physical ways, as the taste/smell child will feel very reassured if she gets lots of cuddling. So physical affection is a great way for tactile parents to connect with this child, especially if they're not comfortable expressing their feelings in words. Again, don't withhold affection for fear of spoiling her; the taste/smell child craves affection and thrives on it. The more you can give her, the happier and more self-confident she'll be.

Taste/Smell Child with Auditory Parent

The biggest source of tension between an auditory parent and a taste/smell child will be in the arena of emotion, and it will play out in many different ways. First is the fact that as babies, taste/smell children need a lot of one-on-one time with their parents or caregivers. Though not as physically needy as a tactile baby might be, they want to feel a constant sense of connection to their parents. Auditory parents, who often tend to be rather solitary people, may begin to feel a bit overwhelmed by this need.

Then there's the clash between reason and emotion. Auditory people tend to be very rational and analytical; taste/smell children are highly sensitive and emotional. The auditory parent may have little patience for a child who wears his heart on his sleeve and has his head in the clouds. But it's crucial that parents of these children try to accept their children as they are rather than always trying to change them and make them more "sensible." If you can be flexible about giving in to your child on some of the relatively minor issues that are hugely important to him—the food he eats, the possessions he's attached to, the clothes he wears—then he'll feel heard and understood, and it will be easier for you to tackle the bigger issues.

Auditory parents and taste/smell children will also have a different sense of time. People who are auditory tend to be very organized, managing their time in an efficient and structured way. While taste/smell children need routine, they don't like to have a tight schedule imposed on them and they also don't respond well to being rushed. This difference can be the cause of considerable friction when it comes to day-to-day life. Although it's not going to be possible for the auditory parent to accommodate all of the child's whims in this area, she will need to try to be as patient as possible while helping her imaginative taste/smell child learn to move through the day in a more timely manner.

Taste/Smell Child with Visual Parent

The visual parent and the taste/smell child both feel strongly about appearances. But the choices they make are based on very different considerations. The visual parent chooses clothes and everything else in her environment according to her own aesthetic, whatever that is. The taste/smell child makes her choices— if she's allowed to make them, that is—for emotional reasons, not because of how things look. For example, if you are visual, you will be astounded that your daughter wants to wear an old T-shirt from Disney World that is covered with stains. You think of this souvenir as "that ratty old T-shirt from Disney World" and want to get rid of it. But the taste/smell child loves this shirt and doesn't want to part with this living memory of the family trip to Orlando two years prior.

Aside from having these emotional connections to things, the other most important factor governing the taste/smell child's preferences is that they help her to fit in. She is self-conscious and doesn't want to be set apart from the crowd in any way. Though some visual people like to impress others with their car, clothes, jewelry, or house, anything that is flashy or conspicuous may actually embarrass the taste/smell child, who mainly wants to blend in, not stand out. In general, tension will arise between these two when the visual parent does not take into account how necessary it is for the taste/smell child to feel comfortable with her peers or in new situations.

Taste/smell children make their way in the world by both reaching out to others and retreating within themselves when necessary. Sensitive to taste and smell as well as all the other senses, and quick to pick up on all the emotional currents in the atmosphere around them, they tune in to life so intensely that they must often tune out as a way of getting a respite. Their vivid imaginations endow them with rich inner lives that sustain them during these periods of withdrawal. As babies, they connect with their parents and other caregivers by mirroring their emotions, and they depend on familiar routines that they'll want re-created time and again. As toddlers, they come early to a capacity for empathy, which is reflected in the connections they make to others and the kinds of play they enjoy. As preschoolers, they begin to expand their inner circle by forming close relationships with teachers and friends, all while relying on their lively imaginations and ever-sharpening intuition to help them steer a course through their days.

Understanding the taste/smell child means accepting her preferences and predilections, even when their meaning is a total mystery to you. It also means recognizing that the emotions you see in your child are often a reflection of your own. By becoming more attuned to your own feelings, you can sometimes use these to guess how your child is feeling or what she is trying to work through. When you can help your child to understand her intense emotions, you can set her up to win—for life.

EIGHT

Managing Your Child Under Stress

The birth of a new sibling; a death, illness, or divorce in the family; a move to a new home or a new school; a parent's remarriage, which brings a stepparent into the picture and perhaps some stepsiblings as well—all of these can put stress on young children and can result in regressive behavior, acting out, tantrums, and more. Of course they cause stress to adults too, but children are only just beginning to learn to deal with transitions and the emotions that accompany them, and they have few coping mechanisms to blunt the impact of these dramatic life changes. So imagine your stress load multiplied several times over and you can get some feeling for what your child is going through. However, if you help your child discover good coping strategies that tap into his dominant sense mode, you may be able to avoid or minimize a lot of the problems that occur in situations like these.

In this chapter I will focus mainly on toddlers and preschoolers, since they are the ones more likely to have really strong responses to the kinds of major change described in what follows.

Siblings

The addition of a new baby brother or sister is one of the more common upheavals in a young child's life. As we parents know, each new addition to the family brings unique joys, and also profound changes to family dynamics and household routines. When a new baby sister or brother is born or adopted, siblings can react with a range of emotions and reactions: excitement at the thought of a new playmate and companion, curiosity at the baby's every move, anxiety and confusion about their own place in the family, and jealousy at all the attention paid to the new baby or sibling by Mom and Dad.

Being Prepared

Long before the baby arrives, the anticipation of a new sibling is on the horizon, and with it plenty of change in the life of a young child. Mom's belly is growing ever larger, new clothes and toys and furniture are showing up at home, both parents are spending time talking about and preparing for the new member of the family, and there's a general feeling of expectation in the air. But it's important to keep in mind that every child will react differently to the arrival of a new sibling. Using your knowledge of your child's dominant sense, you can look for ways to include your child in the process of welcoming and forming a connection with the new baby both before and after the baby is born.

Not too long ago, I met a family whose five-year-old twins, Anna and Will, had vastly different reactions to the birth of their baby brother, reactions that were shaped by their dominant sense modes. Anna's dominant sense was taste/smell and Will's was visual. Before the baby was born, Anna was very excited about the prospect of having a little brother. As a taste/smell child, she had imagined vivid scenarios in which she would be playing the part of big sister and doing all sorts of things to take care of her new sibling. She was going to wash him, feed him, and look after him all on her own, and she was busily practicing her caretaking activities on her doll.

Will, however, wasn't so sure that he wanted a little brother. As a visual child, he was greatly bothered by the fact that his mother was getting bigger and looking so different; the fact that she wasn't able to do all the things she had done before worried him. He made such comments as "Is Mom going to be able to play soccer again?" "I don't think this baby is good for Mom; it makes her tummy hurt—look, it's so big!" and "She can't even see her shoes!"

After James was born, Anna was at first very eager to care for her new brother, often spending time near him, touching him, talking to him as if he could understand her, and even sniffing at him, taking in that sweet new-baby smell. Will kept his distance from the baby and often showed regressed behavior, including asking for a bottle, sucking his thumb, and in general acting more clingy around his mother. But as time went on and the baby began to grow, change, and develop, Anna's and Will's reactions to the baby changed considerably, and the two siblings were soon at loggerheads with each other.

By the time Josie, their mother, came to see me, almost five months had passed since James was born, and she was overwhelmed by the unpleasant squabbles between Anna and Will. After an introductory session in my office I made a home visit during which I determined the dominant senses of each of the children, including the baby, who, like Will, was visual. Once I knew their sense modes, I was able to understand how each child was experiencing the situation and could help the mother figure out ways to change the family dynamic.

Anna, the taste/smell child, was very emotional and very imaginative. Having developed an elaborate fantasy of what her relationship to the new baby was going to be like, she found that once he was born the reality was quite different, and very disappointing to her. Newborns are fragile and therefore moms are pretty protective, so Anna was not allowed to dress, feed, or bathe her baby brother, as she had imagined doing. Worse still from Anna's point of view, as James got older, he was showing a definite preference for Will, who in an initial effort to scare the baby had actually hit upon the very thing that made him laugh. Now James and Will were happily enjoying playing peekaboo while Anna looked on with envy. Will pranced around, showing off his ability to get James to smile. In fact, Will seemed to go out of his way to play with James, teasing Anna.

Anna felt very hurt and left out. Not only would her mother not allow her to do any of the things she had fantasized about doing with the baby, but even when she was allowed to hold him under her mother's close supervision, James would cry. As a result, her mother discouraged Anna from interacting with James, and Anna became very difficult and uncooperative.

We started with Josie. I explained the senses and how they worked. We talked about how emotionally sensitive taste/smell children are. They have a strong desire to be liked and appreciated. It was clear to me that Anna was feeling not only as if James didn't like her but also as if she was being excluded from all the fun that her two brothers were having. I suggested that Anna be given special "big sister" responsibilities to make her feel better about herself and help her feel that she was an important part of the family.

Josie was dubious about letting Anna play any role in looking after James because she wasn't sure that she trusted her. I explained that she should employ Anna in an "assistant" capacity and of course not give her any real caretaking responsibilities. For example, Anna could get the diapers, check the temperature of the bathwater, or be given the task of making sure that the diaper bag was always packed and ready to go. It could also be her job to choose which toys they took on any outings or what music they played for the baby. The goal was to help Anna feel she mattered and that she was special and had a special bond with all of them. Praise, responsibility, and little jobs help to create those good feelings.

So Josie talked to Anna about how important she was as a big sister and what a help she could be if she would take over some of Josie's tasks. Anna was eager to show how much she could do, and soon Josie had plenty of opportunities to tell her what a great helper she was. One day she showed Anna how to make funny faces at the baby to entertain him. Anna was reserved at first, but when James laughed and she saw how much he liked what she was doing, she kept at it and started to have a great time with him. Next she played peekaboo, as she had seen her brother Will do, and was delighted by the instant smiles she saw on James's face. By the end of an hour she was ecstatic, feeling that the baby now liked her and that she had learned a few reliable tricks that would help her relate to him in the future.

The change in the home after these minor adjustments were made affected every member of the family. Mom now had an assistant—two, in fact. Will stopped teasing Anna, as she was now able to play with James as well as he could. And Anna returned to being her usual happy self.

When you're expecting a baby or have a newly arrived one on the scene, think about what this is like from your child's perspective and about some sense-specific strategies you might be able to use to make the situation more comfortable and pleasant for him.

- A tactile kid may be desperately curious to know what is going on inside Mom's tummy and may become very "grabby" and clingy toward Mom. Letting this child touch your belly, especially when the baby is moving inside, can help make the baby real to him and also help him make sense of this experience. Giving him a baby doll on which to practice "big brother skills" can provide him a tangible, physical outlet for processing both his excitement and his fears. A great way to stay connected to your tactile child during this stressful time, in addition to doling out lots of hugs and cuddles, is to grab a ball and head to the park. This one-on-one playtime can help your tactile child feel grounded and loved.
- An auditory child may feel threatened or confused by the amount of time that Mom and Dad spend talking about the baby and even to the baby while it is still in utero. Encouraging this child to sing songs to the baby can help her feel included in the changes that are afoot. You might also try reading a book about a family with a new baby, for your auditory child loves both the sound of your voice and the cozy experience of being read to.
- A visual child will take particular notice not only of Mom's growing belly but also of changes to her wardrobe and other aspects of her appearance, and may be alarmed or upset by how different she looks. Showing this child photographs of Mom before, during, and after she was pregnant with her might help calm her and soothe her worries about Mom's physical transformation. To connect with your visual child, you might sit down at her arts and crafts table and spend an hour drawing pictures together. You may

be surprised by the feelings and fears she shares with you on the page, even if she doesn't know how to talk about them.

• A taste/smell child may become very protective of Mom, sensing the physical and emotional tumult that often comes with being pregnant. Because she identifies with you so closely, your taste/smell child will be very curious to know how it feels to have a baby inside you, and will be attuned to every nuance and change in your body. She may also be concerned about the baby, wanting to know what the baby is feeling. This child may need extra reassurance that everyone involved—she, Mom, and the baby—will be safe and cared for as the pregnancy progresses, and this will require special one-on-one time with you.

Blended Families

Of course, new siblings are not just born into families. Sometimes they arrive with a new stepmom or stepdad. Many children will have to confront the challenge not just of a new stepparent but also of new stepsiblings when they become part of a blended family—a real double whammy. The addition of stepsiblings to a young child's life can be a very threatening experience, and a lot of parents approach this hurdle with trepidation. Using what you know about your child's dominant sense can help you offer much-needed comfort, reassurance, love, and security during this time of great change, and can also help facilitate the beginnings of a healthy sibling relationship.

It's important that all the children involved in this transition be allowed to be themselves. Each child's individuality should be appreciated and affirmed, even as your new family starts on its blending process. In one family I worked with, Tamara, a five-year-old

visual child, seemed to retreat into her desire for order and sym-
metry as soon as her new stepfather and Kate, his three-year-old
daughter, moved in with her and her mother. The mother noticed
that whenever Tamara seemed tense or unsure, she reacted by becoming very bossy toward her stepsister and extremely possessive
about all her belongings. Though she had always been quite particular about arranging all her things just so, she became even more
so than usual, organizing all her toys and dolls on her shelves and
dresser in an elaborate display. If Kate so much as touched anything, Tamara became very upset. Once Kate went into Tamara's
jewelry box, which resulted in a huge fight between the girls.

Rather than telling her she had to be a "good girl" and forcing
her to share everything—her toys, her space—it was important
for Tamara's mom (and her new stepfather) to respect and understand Tamara's need for some private space. Since in this case it
wasn't possible for Tamara to keep her own room, which would
have been ideal, I suggested that they put up some kind of boundaries around Tamara's space, making it clear to her new stepsister
that that area and everything in it belonged to Tamara. The same
applied to clothing. A visual child, whose clothing is very important to her, will probably react very badly to anyone else's trying
to wear any of her clothes. The sight of her stepsister wearing her
mittens one day really set Tamara off. It may seem trivial to us parents (unless we're visual too), but to a visual child, the ability to
be able to express her personal taste and to have a sense of ownership of her space can matter a great deal.

Of course, regardless of your child's dominant sense, you will
want to do everything you can to help her preserve her sense of autonomy and individuality at a time when she is likely to feel threatened by all the changes in her world. Making sure to give your
child short periods of undivided attention every day is an impor-

tant aspect of managing this particular transition. This isn't always easy—you've got a new spouse and new stepchildren who are vying for your attention as well—but it can make a critical difference in helping to ease the child's stress and fear as she deals with the natural confusion she will feel about where she fits in this new family. You can make the most of this one-on-one time by choosing activities that correspond to your child's dominant sense.

• A tactile child might act a bit aggressively toward a new stepsibling, or shower a new sibling with too much physical affection. This is the tactile child's way of trying to make a connection. Regardless of whether he is acting more aggressively than usual or if he is simply overabundant in his display of affection, he is telling you that he needs help making this connection. Correct overaffectionate behavior by being more gentle with him and encouraging him to be gentle as well. Correct aggressive behavior by redirecting him to a more positive play or other activity. He will also need more hugs and cuddles as well as lots of time spent with you, and he'll enjoy being asked to help you with little tasks because it will help him feel needed at a time when he is fearful of being overlooked. By tuning in to the basic needs of your tactile child, you can help him feel grounded during this time of change. In due course, he will more than likely welcome having a new stepsibling to play with. But you might get a head start on the bonding process if you can get them involved in physical activities they both enjoy. Whether it's a game of catch or tag in the park, a walk through the woods, or a swim in the local pool, let your tactile child be the guide, and hope that the stepsibling will be just as enthusiastic.

• An auditory child may respond to the arrival of a new stepparent or stepsibling by retreating and becoming a bit more solitary. While you want to give him his space and allow him time to become accustomed to the new family arrangement, you also may want to encourage him to participate in family activities or pastimes you know he enjoys. If he loves the routine of watching a nature program on television every night after dinner, sit down next to him and then invite everyone else to join in too. And talk to him a lot. Reassure him in words that you still love him the same as always, that although it may feel as though everything has changed at home, soon everything will feel normal again. As much as possible you should try to stick to your regular routines with him. This is the best way to help your auditory child, with his love of structure and order, to absorb the change with a minimum of fuss. It's also important to listen to your auditory child, even if he seems to be saying the same thing over and over. It is his way of processing his feelings. If at times he seems to be verbally hostile, try to talk to him about what is bothering him. More so than other young children, the auditory child is open to a rational problem-solving approach and will appreciate your hearing him out and trying to help him.

You should also be sensitive to his need to be able to control the sound level of his environment. If his new sibling is noisy, he may want to retreat to the quiet and seclusion of his own room, if he has one, or to block out the noise by playing his iPod. Keep in mind that this is a time when you should be particularly careful to speak to him in a kind, calm voice—and to let your new partner know how important it is too. Harsh verbal reprimands from a new parent could be devastating. And listen, listen, listen!

• A visual child who likes to exert visual control over her environment will need to do so more than usual because of the addition of a stepfamily to her life. As was the case with Tamara in the above example, a visual child may act a bit bossy or demanding until she feels safe and secure in her knowledge that you still care about her and that she and her belongings will not be treated any differently.

If you keep a careful eye on her, a visual child's facial expressions will be a dead giveaway as to how she is feeling. When you can see that she's upset, making a special point of allowing her to have some control over her own space and perhaps even to have input into the rest of the home, especially if you have moved in to a new place, is a good way to comfort the visual child at this time. Take her shopping for a new bedspread, let her help decorate a new sibling's room, ask her to choose the napkins and placemats for dinner, or even allow her to pick the color everyone must wear to dinner—that is, if the other siblings don't freak out. If you make it a game—"Lisa says, 'Today is a blue day, so everyone has to wear something blue!'"—this may not backfire, and could even result in some good laughs.

During the first few months, you should try to avoid reprimanding the visual child in front of her new siblings. As concerned as she is about appearances, this could humiliate her and make her resent their presence.

• A taste/smell child may be particularly unsettled by the changes in her family because she is so tuned in to the feelings of those around her, and feelings usually run high during transitions such as this. Since she will often take her cues from you, be aware that any ambivalence or anxiety you feel, even if it's only from concern about how she will react, will be communicated to her. No matter how upbeat and positive your words are, she will be able to sense your uncertainty.

A taste/smell child should not be rushed into a relationship with her new stepsibling. She'll need time to process her emotions, and often she will do that through the kind of imaginative play that is solitary. However, as much as she will need time on her own, she'll also want one-on-one time with you. It's very important that you spend time with your sensitive taste/smell child now, even though there will be many demands on you. She will need to be reassured that she is still special to you. Lots of memorable outings with you, even if they're brief, are a good way to let her know you love her. And make sure she is not tired or hungry when you leave on such outings, so that you make such an event a win-win for all. It's also important that you let her know in advance what you are planning, even if it's just a quick trip to the local library to check out some more picture books by her favorite authors. Don't spring surprises on this little girl.

Relocation

All children, to one degree or another, are creatures of routine. Afraid of the unknown, they rely on the regularity of their daily schedule as well as the comfort of the familiar to ground them and make them feel safe. Any big change in a child's environment can bring about stress and uncertainty, and a move to a new house, a new neighborhood, and possibly even a new city certainly ranks as a big change. Small children in particular, who are unable to understand what it means to make such a move, may become fearful that their parents may suddenly disappear or change, just as their familiar surroundings (and perhaps their friends and other family) have disappeared.

Even the preparations for a move to a new house can easily unsettle a child. Pulling clothes out of closets and drawers, taking all the books off the shelves, packing up everything in the house and then watching as the movers carry everything away, then reversing the whole process at the other end are all potentially alarming to children. When they can't find some of their belongings it may seem to them that the whole world is chaotic; when their parents are frazzled and distressed, as most of us are when we are getting ready to move or just settling down after the move, children will feel off-kilter too. Even older children who understand the concept of a move will find the sights and sounds of this controlled chaos very unsettling and disruptive.

And of course, once you've actually settled into the new place, the stress may be even worse for a while. Anyone who has packed up and moved to a new house or a new city knows full well that they have left not only a home but also an entire world that's familiar. For the child this means his favorite park, his school or day care and the teachers and children he's become attached to there, the local pool, the neighborhood recreation center, and so on. Children are also leaving neighborhood friends and perhaps extended family. And all this happens at the same time as you too are experiencing all these changes and losses. Under such stressful circumstances, it's not surprising that even parents who have learned the basics of adapting their communication style to their child's sense mode may forget to put what they know to use.

Rebecca and her husband, Dave, had an experience like this with their son, Trevor, when they made a cross-country move. Trevor was a high-energy, tactile five-year-old, and his parents were both auditory, as we had determined when I had worked with them when Trevor was three years old. At that time, they had come to see me because Trevor's constant movement and general noisiness were driving his parents crazy. Not only that, he had been co-sleeping with his parents since he was a baby, and they didn't have the heart to move him into his own bed, but everyone was sleep- (and privacy-) deprived and disgruntled. When I explained that there were other ways of providing Trevor with the physical affection that a tactile child needs without allowing him to sleep in their bed or in their room, they began to have a brief period of wrestling and rough-housing with him before bed, and then a longer period of story time and cuddle time when he was in bed. During this transitional period they waited for him to fall asleep before they left. After a few weeks they were able to leave Trevor before he fell asleep. Gradually Trevor not only became acclimated to sleeping in his own bed but felt a huge sense of accomplishment about it. And then came the move.

"The move really threw us all for a loop. It was like we all went back to our old selves," Rebecca told me. Trevor began stubbornly acting out, throwing fits on the floor when it was time for bed, kicking furniture when he was angry—even throwing his food once or twice at the dinner table. For their part, Trevor's parents too had lost ground: Absorbed by all the tasks of the move, they reverted to giving Trevor attention, direction, guidance, and even affection by speaking to—or yelling at—him. They had forgotten how important physical messages are for a tactile child.

"I finally caught myself one afternoon, while unpacking in the new house, trying to calm Trevor down by talking to him from across the room," Rebecca said. "My child simply needs a different kind of communication from me. I already knew this, but I had to learn it all over again. I reminded myself that I needed to reassure him with lots of hugs and cuddle time. Also, because I remembered how much tactile children like to have a job, we asked Trevor to help us unpack, even though this slowed us down." The changes they made in their behavior helped Trevor change his, and within days he had started to calm down.

Whatever the type of move you are making—from one apartment to another in the same building, from one city to another, or even from one country to another—don't be surprised to see your child's behavior regress for a time as she works through the uncertainty of the transition. Her dominant sense may become even more hypersensitive and reactive during the period when she feels that her physical surroundings are in flux. Be prepared for your tactile child to cling to you as she did when she was younger, or for your visual child to demand to wear the same sweater and skirt every day for a week. Your taste/smell child may refuse to eat anything that comes out of your new refrigerator, and your auditory child might cry at every new or scary sound she hears.

Understanding the impact of your child's dominant sense can help you find practical coping strategies—and the patience you'll need before those strategies start to be effective.

Here is some basic moving advice for children in each of the four dominant sense modes:

• A tactile child will need to feel physically comfortable in his new room. Make sure to transfer some if not all of his intimate belongings to the new space—his comforter cover, throw rug, sheets and pillow, stuffed animals, et cetera. You may want to have everything be new, especially if you're a visual person and you were just waiting until the move to throw out all that tired-looking, worn-out stuff. But your child will want the reassurance of the familiar. He'll want his bed, his clothes, and his toys to feel the same. His bed will be especially important because that's where he receives his most important cuddles of the day.

A tactile child might actually enjoy and benefit from helping you pack and unpack some of his things—this is a practical, physical way for him to be involved in the move and stay connected to you in the process. So instead of doing everything yourself, put him to work. Carrying small boxes, stacking empty boxes up against the wall (where they can be played with and made into cars and pretend houses), throwing the stuff you want to get rid of into a large garbage bag—he'll love thinking he has a job to do. It will make him feel important, and it might even help you—if only by keeping him busy and happy. Finally, find out where he can be his physical self. The first chance you get after the move, show him where the local park is, where he can go swimming or play football or ride his bike. And as soon as you can, introduce him to a play buddy, preferably someone as active as he is.

• Before you move your auditory child into his new room, consider any sound-related changes you could make to help him adjust to it. The more familiar it is to him, the better. If there's a hardwood floor where before he had carpeting, what about putting a carpet down in the new space? Does the new room face a busy street while before his room was in the back of the house where no sound came through the windows? If so, can you muffle the sound with heavy drapes or double-paned windows, or use white noise to drown some of it out?

One of the best ways to help an auditory child with a move is by talking him through it in advance—preparing him verbally by telling him the sequence of events that is going to occur, from packing up all your furniture and other belongings to putting them on the truck and unpacking them at the new place. Allowing him to ask questions and verbalize any worries and concerns will help reassure him.

If you have music playing while you unpack, let your auditory child pick the CD. You might also want a tape of the old home sounds for bedtime. Be very aware that with so many other stresses in his life, it's important for you to sound as calm as possible when you speak to him. Agitated, upset voices are very distressing to an auditory child. It might even be beneficial if your child is not present on moving day, if possible, because when things go wrong, as they usually do, there can be lots of yelling. If your child is old enough, once you're moved in let him make telephone calls to family and friends; hearing familiar voices will be reassuring. And again, remember to listen, listen, listen and give your child plenty of auditory space (think iPod) to retreat into.

• If your child is visual, you may want to arrange the furniture in her new room so that it's similar to the way it was placed in her former room. If her wall had been covered by fanciful illustrations, she will want to see those again. If she shows an interest in decorating her new room, let her choose the color of the paint. It might be a good idea to have her keep a picture of her former house or backyard next to her bed. If you've moved to a new city and left friends and family behind, you might want to put pictures of the people she'll be missing on her wall. The visual child will look to her surroundings to soothe her. The more carefully you arrange her belongings and the tidier you keep her room, the calmer she will feel as she adjusts to her new home.

• A taste/smell child may be attached to the overall "feel" of her bedroom, as well as to its familiar smell (which may not even be apparent to you). This child may balk at even the most detailed re-creation of her original bedroom in a new space if to her sensitive "feelers" it seems somehow foreign to her. And be sure to paint her room before the move if at all possible; a taste/smell child will be very sensitive to paint smells, so you'll need to allow the room to air out before asking her to sleep in it. If possible, allowing her to spend some time in her new room before you've actually moved to the new place will help her become familiar with its details and quirks so that she will acclimate to it more easily once she's living there. And when you do make the move, be sure to bring as many of her possessions with you as possible, from toys to clothes to bedding and furniture. The more things she has from the old space, the more comfortable she'll feel in the new one.

One way to use this child's vivid imagination to smooth the path to her new life would be to set aside a quiet time to spend together every day, beginning a few weeks before the move, to give her an opportunity to talk about the move and what she expects it will be like to live in the new place. You might encourage her to make up stories about life after the move, so that she can fantasize about both the good and the bad and have an opportunity to express her fears in a way that is natural for her. Even if you've been careful to make all of these preparations to help ease the way for her, don't be surprised if she wants to sleep in your room for the first couple of nights. In general, just try to do everything to make her comfortable. Make her favorite meals, be sure to bring a good supply of her favorite foods if you have any doubt about whether they are available in the new neighborhood or city, and give her lots of extra attention and encouragement.

School

Starting school brings big changes to a child's life, and both children and parents can expect to feel a complicated bundle of emotions as the day gets close. Parents and child alike will approach those first days of school with a hearty mixture of fear, anxiety, curiosity, and excitement. Going to school (whether preschool or kindergarten) actually involves two challenging tasks for young children: acclimating to the new place, with its new rhythms and routines and the new teachers and students he will meet there;

and separating from home and parents. With so much to deal with at once, it's little wonder that starting school is the kind of stressful transition that can bring out plenty of regressive behavior in kids.

The very notion of school will seem mysterious to children who have never been in a school, and leaving home and everything that is familiar each day is a challenge for most children, whatever their dominant sense. If your child has attended day care or spent time at a babysitter's house, you have probably already contended with some separation challenges. It is typical for kids to dig in their heels and resist this separation at first, and often their resistance takes the form of tantrums and other difficult, regressive behaviors. But with or without prior experiences of being separated from their parents on a regular basis, when children first go to school (as opposed to day care or a babysitter) it's such a big change from what they are used to that they may again revert to tantrums. The tantrums may not be as extreme as they were at an earlier age and the child may be better at getting control of himself after a brief explosion, but don't be surprised to see some tantrums erupting even if you thought they were a thing of the past.

If your child does become very upset when taken to his new school, the first, best thing you can do for yourself is to take a deep breath and look around you. You're likely to see a classroom full of parents struggling to untangle themselves from crying, unruly children. It's normal. Patience is key here: Your child will adjust to his new routine and will master this transition. In the meantime, it can help to remember that he is not deliberately misbehaving; rather, he's trying to cope with a vital but unsettling change in his daily life. You should also use what you know about his dominant sense mode to help you come up with stress-reduction strategies that are very specific to his way of dealing with the world. Cynthia, the mother of a visual child, helped her daughter cope with separating for school by giving her a colorful bracelet to wear. She made a special presentation of this "big girl" gift and explained to her daughter that it was a symbol of their special bond. "I told her that whenever she felt sad or scared to be without me, she could look at the bracelet and remember how much I love her, and all the fun things we'd do when she got home from school."

Making friends and learning to manage relationships with other children becomes an important part of a child's life when she starts school. Most children have had practice with this at playdates, but extended, daily exposure to their peers is a big step forward. No child rises to this new challenge perfectly. All children, at some point or another, experience problems with peer relationships at school. Often when a child is overwhelmed by a challenge, she will reach into her past for some behavior that helped her to cope—and this frequently has a connection to her dominant sense.

Leila was an outgoing four-year-old who had recently started daily preschool. An auditory child, Leila had strong verbal skills and was a quick learner. After her initial fearfulness dissipated, Leila swiftly grew to love her new school and was full of stories to tell when her mother picked her up in the afternoon. Ann Marie thought Leila was making smooth, trouble-free progress—until Leila's teacher took Ann Marie aside one day when she came to pick up Leila and informed Ann Marie that her daughter had been disrupting class by fighting with some of the other children.

"It was yelling, calling kids mean names, talking like a bully," Ann Marie told me when we met to discuss the situation. "I was mortified."

This is a common reaction for parents, but I assured Ann Marie that she had nothing to be embarrassed about, for herself or her daughter. All parents will confront some kind of misbehavior when their child is adjusting to a new situation, such as school.

Although Leila seemed to be enjoying school, clearly something was going on that was upsetting her, and she was acting out by becoming verbally aggressive. It made perfect sense that Leila would meet a challenging situation this way. As an auditory child, with such a knack for language, she'd be much more likely to use her voice and her verbal skills to assert herself than to get in physical fights, the way a tactile child might. The important thing was to focus on figuring out the source of Leila's stress and how to come up with a solution.

The more I learned about her home life, the more I understood Leila's behavior. Leila was an only child and had been used to being the sole focus of attention at home. When she chatted away to her parents at the dinner table, showed off a new song she had learned, or recited a nursery rhyme, there was no one interrupting her or competing with her for time at center stage. Now at school, she was just one of many children seeking attention from teachers and peers. Leila didn't have much practice with this situation, and she seemed to be reacting by overasserting herself as she tried to compete with her peers for talking time. When she encountered resistance, she fought back with name-calling. Leila was also unaccustomed to the level of noise generated by her classmates, and I suspected that this was setting her on edge.

Ann Marie and I brainstormed about how to help Leila adjust to being part of a group, particularly when it came to learning verbal and conversational cues and norms. We came up with several strategies that they could use at home and at school. Ann Marie was already speaking firmly to her daughter about why she must not engage in name-calling. Now she felt she needed to show her daughter how conversation actually worked. At home, Ann Marie and her husband started to play "listening games" with their daughter. During dinner or at bedtime, the couple would take turns telling little stories or funny jokes, pulling some of the focus away from their daughter and encouraging her to listen and wait for her own turn to speak. Ann Marie also invited some of her daughter's schoolmates over and created a tea-party game for them, where the girls would practice "big-girl talk"—taking turns speaking, then listening when it was someone else's turn.

Ann Marie alerted Leila's teacher to her daughter's heightened sensitivity to noise. The teacher suggested moving Leila to a quieter worktable, away from the center of the room, where she was slightly buffered from the full impact of the noisy classroom.

The combination of home and school adjustments began to make a difference, Ann Marie reported to me when we spoke a month later. "It didn't happen overnight, but I can see her making progress. Her teacher sees it too."

Here is some basic advice for helping kids make a smooth entry to school:

• A tactile child, with his hands-on, practical nature, will be anxious to know what he'll do when he's at school. Making a list of activities he's likely to participate in and then giving him a chance to practice some of these activities at home will help boost his confidence about this new experience. Set aside some time every day to "play school," and go through the motions of arriving at school and sitting down in a circle. If the playground at your child's new school has a climbing wall or any other special equipment that you think will be enticing to him, drop by and let him try it out—your tactile child will be thrilled that "his" school has such a fun thing to do, and as his first day approaches, he'll be excited about the chance to do it again. Also, once he begins school, make sure to let him run around in the playground or ball field after school lets out. Not only will this allow him to let off physical steam but it also will help him become comfortable with his new environment.

• An auditory child will benefit greatly from talking through the school day before it happens. He'll be full of questions: "Where is my school? How do we get there? What will I eat? Can I bring my teddy? Who will help me with my boots? When do you come to get me?" Taking the time to talk through the details with your auditory child can help calm his anxieties. Playing music on the way to school or letting him listen to music on his iPod will also help calm him. And reassure your child that his teacher will know how to call you if he gets upset and needs to talk to you.

• Talking to a visual child about what she'll encounter at school is not nearly as effective as sitting down to look at a picture book that illustrates a typical school day. Offering your visual child images of children enjoying school will give her a picture in her own mind of the new world she's about to experience. Another good way to get a visual child excited about this new experience is to take her shopping for a new outfit or discuss what she is going to wear to school on the first day. The combination of focusing on something she enjoys—shopping or getting to choose her own outfits—and spending time with you will be very grounding. Your child may also like for you to wear something that matches—if you wear a red scarf, she can wear a red hair ribbon. Or if you have a little boy and he has a friend who is going to the same school, perhaps you can confer with the friend's parent about getting them the same lunch boxes. These "same-same" techniques do wonders for giving a morale boost to your visual child.

• Although all children can benefit from visiting school ahead of the first day, this is particularly true for taste/smell children. In particular, your taste/smell child can benefit from meeting her teacher ahead of time. This child seeks comfort and security in personal bonds, and having a head start on her relationship with her new teacher can make a big difference. It's also a good idea to introduce her to at least one child before the first day so that she has one person to connect with and look forward to seeing. Encourage your taste/smell child to create a classroom of her own at home, using her dolls and toys as classmates. This kind of imaginative play gives a taste/smell child the chance to explore her feelings about the new relationships she's soon to develop. A taste/smell child also may be particularly concerned with how Mom will feel when she's at school. She may worry about her mother being lonely or sad at her absence. You can comfort and reassure a taste/smell child by showing her the things you'll be doing while she's gone, helping her to create an imaginary picture of you, busy and safe, during her school hours.

Divorce

Divorce is an increasingly common event in the lives of children, one that can bring about a great deal of stress. However, despite its upsetting nature, there is a lot you can do to help a child weather this stressful change in his life. Being supportive, engaged, and aware of the individual needs of your child, and of the ways in which the child's dominant sense mode will affect how those needs are expressed, will be very important during this critical transition.

Of course, there are certain responses that tend to be common to all children in this situation, no matter what their sense mode. When parents separate, the very basis of a child's normal world—his primary family unit—is fundamentally changed. There is a world of guilt, fear, anger, and sadness in the air, and it is natural for the child to feel anxious and insecure during this time. Moreover, children often come to believe that this upheaval is somehow their fault. But if parents are careful to put the comfort and security of their child before any feelings of acrimony or hurt they may be feeling toward each other, they can make a bad situation much better. In other words, if parents refrain from criticizing each other in front of the child and if they make it easy for the child to see and be with both parents in as friendly an atmosphere as possible, then the storm of divorce can be weathered very well.

Difficult as divorce is for children (and adults) of any age, children under the age of four have the additional challenge of being unable to understand what a divorce or separation means. All they really register is that Mom or Dad is now gone. They are likely to be very upset over the absence of the missing parent and distressed by having to go back and forth between their parents' separate homes according to whatever the terms of the custody agreement are. Often young children will become very clingy toward one parent and reluctant to go to the other parent's house, even if both parents are making an honest effort to encourage the visits. Young children may also start having difficulty eating and sleeping, particularly in the home that is less familiar to them. This is one of those times when you can really make good use of what you know about sense modes.

Bree and her husband, Paul, divorced when their daughter, Carly, was three. "Our divorce was more amicable than some, less than others," Bree told me. At first the couple didn't communicate much beyond what was involved in dropping off and picking up their daughter. "We knew she'd need some time to get used to this new life, but we started to worry when she seemed to be getting worse, not better," Bree said. Carly, a visual child, was having trouble sleeping in both homes and was throwing tantrums when her father came to pick her up, screaming at both parents as she clung to her mother and wailed. It was a heartbreaking ritual for Bree and Paul, who realized that their daughter wasn't going to adjust to her new life without more help from them. "We realized that we needed to give her more continuity," Bree told me. "We couldn't get back together, but we could work on smoothing out some of the differences between our homes and giving her a stronger sense of routine."

The couple, keeping in mind their daughter's visual sensitivity, started working on ways to ease their daughter's anxiety about going back and forth between the two houses. They bought duplicates of some of her favorite toys and clothing—her most cherished dolls, her bright purple bedroom slippers—so that Carly could enjoy them in both places. They passed her picture books back and forth, so that Carly could look at her favorite story no matter where she was staying, and Bree made her a special bookmark with photos of all three of them so that she could mark her page and pick up right where she'd left off the night before. Paul decorated his daughter's room in the same color scheme as her room at her mother's house, to help his daughter feel comfortable and at home. As time passed, Carly began to adjust to her new situation: Her sleeping improved, and she slowly stopped clinging to her mother when her father came to pick her up for a visit.

"We realized that we couldn't just hope for her to start feeling safe and secure," Bree said. "We had to show her she was secure, had to demonstrate it in concrete ways that would be meaningful to her, that she would understand."

If parents provide a simple, straightforward explanation about their divorce, older children, ages four and five, will be able to comprehend that their parents are separating and will be living apart. In this conversation and all other divorce-related discussions you have with your child, your body language and facial expressions are important, because whatever your child's dominant sense is, he will be searching for signals that will reveal your true feelings. A visual child will latch onto tense looks between parents or the frown that comes on your face when you discuss your ex-spouse; an auditory child will find meaning in a clipped tone of voice. A tactile child will be very sensitive to body language. A taste/smell child will have an almost uncanny read on the dynamics between his parents and will be vigilant in searching out signs of emotional distress in Mom and Dad. How you present yourself to your child during the process and aftermath of a divorce will have a major impact on the kind of stress and anxiety he experiences.

Often young children at four or five years of age are seeking an explanation of their parents' behavior, and they can easily misunderstand what they perceive. Children this age are particularly prone to blaming themselves for a divorce. They may also have fears of being abandoned or "left behind" somehow. Under these circumstances, children may find protection in old behaviors or in behaviors that are exaggerated versions of those characteristic of their dominant sense. These children need an abundance of reassurance: that they are not to blame, that they are still loved, that they will not be left or abandoned. Simple, sensory-rich methods of communication can help you make sure that these messages get through to your children when they need them most.

Frances became very concerned about her four-and-a-half-year-old taste/smell daughter, Polly, who had become withdrawn in the wake of her parents' recent divorce. She played for hours alone in her room. Her appetite waned, and she had dark circles under her eyes from fitful nights of sleep.

"I was so worried. She seemed to go so deeply into herself," Frances said, shaking her head. "I tried talking to her, but she would just wait patiently until I was through, saying nothing, and then go back to her room. Her father and I sat down together with her, many times, to tell her how much we loved her and how she wasn't to blame for anything, but nothing seemed to help."

One afternoon, sitting in her kitchen sick with worry, Frances came to a stark realization. "I kind of looked outside myself and realized that I was sitting there waiting for my daughter to relate to this experience on my terms, on my turf. To me, words are what matter. That's always been the way to communicate with me. Meanwhile, I had never considered that I might try to reach her on her turf."

Frances got up and walked quietly into her daughter's room, where she found Polly playing with her stuffed animals on the floor. She sat down and asked Polly if she could play too. The response was instant: "Polly handed me a silly stuffed frog, and I almost cried right there," Frances said. Beginning with the frog, Frances let Polly lead her into her very vivid imaginary world, and soon the two were dealing with emotional territory that hit close to home. Their pretend play almost always involved families—children or animals lost and in trouble, mothers and fathers angry or estranged. By engaging with Polly in a fantasy world where she felt safe to express her feelings, Frances was able to get her daughter to voice the fear and guilt she was having over her parents' divorce. And in the course of participating in her daughter's fantasy life, she was also able to show her how some of the scenarios she was imagining could have other outcomes. Children who are lost get found because their parents love them and never stop looking for them; mothers and fathers who seem angry can make up and be friends again even if they're not going to live together again.

"Polly is a quiet child, and I don't always know what she's feeling or whether my words are getting through to her," said Frances. "But now I have a method I know I can use to reach her. When we act out stories about families and children, it's a chance for me to get a glimpse of what she's feeling, and also to show her that she's safe and loved."

Divorce is so unsettling for parents that most of us just assume that it will be completely traumatic for a child. In fact, I've observed numerous instances when kids I've worked with have described feeling better after their parents' divorce because it put a stop to all the fighting and unhappiness in the household. Of course, it's nearly impossible to predict the ultimate impact of a divorce on a child, because so many complex factors affect the outcome. But what I can say with confidence, from both my personal and professional experience, is that we make the situation much easier on our children if we keep our explanations simple and straightforward and deliver them in a nonjudgmental tone that is age-appropriate. And by putting our own emotions aside we give our children freedom to express their feelings rather than simply mirror their parents'.

Following are some suggestions on how to smooth your child's adjustment to the changes that accompany divorce. (See also the suggestions above about how to cope with moving, since some of the same issues may crop up if the divorce involves moving to a new home or having the child shuttle back and forth between two homes.)

• Tactile children are very social, and they'll miss having two parents around; as far as they're concerned, the more people in the house the merrier. And if there's not joint custody, the parent who is the main caretaker may find herself spread pretty thin when all the tactile child's needs for physical closeness—for hugging, wrestling, sleeping with, and cuddling—have to be met by her. Tactile kids tend to get very clingy and needy during times of stress, so it may again be a good idea to help ground them with physical affection and activities that you do together, whether it's a sport or a chore around the house. If your partner was the one who was particularly physical with the child (i.e., who wrestled or gave piggyback rides), try to keep that up. And be sure to make time for playing. It's not always easy when we are sad and stressed to remember to play, but the tactile child depends on physical outlets to express his feelings, and playing with him is one of the best things you can do to help him feel safe and loved.

• Although the arguing that tends to go on before and during a divorce is stressful for all kids, it's particularly so for auditory kids (and for taste/smell kids as well). Hard as it may be to exercise self-restraint, if you and your ex are the kind of people who do a lot of shouting and screaming during arguments, make every effort to ensure that your child doesn't hear you going at each other before, during, or after the divorce. And keep in mind that a hostile silence can also be upsetting. Children pick up on the vibes in the air. So don't fight in front of your child, don't bad-mouth your ex-partner within earshot of your child (auditory children are all ears, so to speak), and do try to make pleasant chitchat when you and your ex-partner come in contact with each other while picking up or delivering the child to each other's homes. Watch out for phone calls with family and friends, as the auditory child will be listening. These kids can pick up hostility in your tone of voice very quickly, so don't think that you can get away with saying bad things about your ex-partner in some kind of coded language. No matter how discreet you think you are, the message and the feelings will get through. Be prepared to talk your child through all the changes that are happening in an age-appropriate way, explaining why Mommy and Daddy can't live together anymore, when the child will be with each parent, how these arrangements are going to work, and so on. Try for as much continuity as possible. If your ex-partner was the one who read your child the bedtime stories, perhaps you can make arrangements for him to continue this routine on the phone until everyone settles down into their new lives.

• Visual children have a real interest in appearances, and that goes not just for their clothes or their rooms but also for more fundamental concerns about how the world views them. The visual child may become very upset about how it will look to others if his parents don't show up together for events such as school performances or parents' night. So if you and your ex-partner used to make a joint appearance, if at all possible you should continue this during the transitional time when your child is still trying to get used to this big change. Put on your happy family face for your child's sake—and I mean that literally. Watch your facial expressions when you are with your ex. Glaring looks, curled lips, and hostile gestures are exactly the opposite of what will be helpful to this child.

Storybooks about divorce may be reassuring to your visual child. Talking about the pictures in these books can reassure your child that what happened in his family is normal. He needs reassurance that everything is okay, so try not to appear sad or worried. And don't be spiteful. Allow your child to keep all the gifts and mementos he's received from your ex and don't take away

photos of the absent parent, including photos of all of you together. Even if they are upsetting to you, they will be reassuring
to him.

• The taste/smell child is likely to be deeply affected by the divorce and all the sad, hurt, angry feelings that go with it. Your
child will feel responsible for everyone else's feelings and will
want to try to fix everything. You might find your taste/smell
child speaking more often to an imaginary friend during this
time. That's her way of working out some of the emotions she is
feeling in a safe environment of her own making, and you should
not do anything to discourage it. Pets can play big roles in a child's
imaginative life too. You may hear your child talking to her dog or
singing him a song about what's going on. This kind of fantasy
play is not only harmless but can be very helpful and reassuring.
Although there may be times after a divorce when a move makes
it necessary to give up the family pet, you should try to avoid that
if at all possible. Taste/smell children form particularly close
bonds with animals and will rely on the comfort of a much-loved
pet to get them through hard times.

Parents need to work on their own hostility in order to help
their taste/smell child. Though it may be tempting to tell your
taste/smell child a bit about your feelings, especially since she
may ask you about them and genuinely wish to know, remember
that she is a child and is not equipped to deal with adult issues and
adult emotions. Reassure her that you are okay. And if she worries
about the parent she is not with, wondering if her dad is lonely or
scared, just say very simply that both of you are feeling a bit lonely
now but you'll both be fine. If she expresses concern about leaving you when it's time to visit her other parent, tell her you will
miss her a little but it'll be so much fun to see her when she gets

back that it'll make your time together even more special. Be sure that she feels free to enjoy her other parent.

Death, Illness, and Other Losses

One of the saddest and most difficult tasks a parent may face is helping a young child cope with the death of someone he loves, a serious illness of someone close to him, or another significant loss. Seeking professional help through a therapist or counselor is always an option worth considering at times like these, since you too may be feeling overwhelmed by grief. But even if you don't choose to try therapy, there are many things you can do to help guide your child, gently and lovingly, through the sadness, confusion, and stress that so often accompany these difficult events.

Young children age five and under do not yet have a grasp of the concept of permanence; therefore, they will not understand death the way older children and adults will. But even the youngest infants will sense and respond to the sadness of those around them. Being aware of how your child takes in the messages from his environment and manages his emotions gives you the opportunity to find the best way to soothe and reassure him.

If your baby seems distressed, it's important to provide her with extra affection and comfort—and tapping into her dominant sense is the best way to send these loving messages to her. Give your visual baby extra face time. Sing quiet songs to your auditory baby. Hold your tactile and taste/smell children in your arms and give them lots of cuddles. Parents I know who've gone through a loss like this often say that they find unexpected comfort in attending to their children's needs using these simple, sense-based techniques.

Toddlers and preschoolers will understand that something very sad is happening and may notice that a loved one is missing from their environment. Though they cannot truly grasp the permanence of death or the meaning of a serious illness in the family, they are aware enough to need extra reassurance at times like this, because they can easily pick up on the fear and grief of those around them and start to fear for their own safety and well-being. Children may express this fear indirectly, often in inappropriate ways, venting through their dominant sense the feelings they cannot put into words. For example, a tactile child may throw his toys against the wall. What may look to you like anger or just plain obnoxious behavior is probably fear—but fear he doesn't know how to express, even to himself. Unable to express her feelings of powerlessness, a taste/smell child might revolt at the breakfast table, demanding a certain food only to reject it violently. She might also retreat into a quiet, solitary state, sequestering herself in her room to play intricate imaginary games with her animals. Though you may resent the fact that this puts yet another burden on your shoulders, it's important to allow your child to express her feelings and release them in safe, constructive ways.

Again, all children, no matter what their dominant sense, will benefit from sticking to their routine as much as possible during these times. Familiarity is security for young children, and the simplest of daily habits can send a powerful message to your children that they are safe, even amid the upheaval in your family. Adhering to your child's rituals and routines will help soothe his stress and give him a powerful sense of security when he most needs it.

Here are some basic ways to comfort children within each of the sense mode groups during times of death, illness, and other losses:

• Tactile toddlers in particular will seek out extra cuddles and hugs, needing to be held frequently to reassure them. But don't go overboard. If parents cuddle the tactile child more often than normal and are doing it for their own comfort rather than in response to signals from the child, or if they suddenly want to sleep with the child and it's not the child's choice, the child may feel burdened. Because the tactile child likes to have a job, he may want to "take care" of you if he sees you feeling sad, especially if you have lost your partner. But tempting as it may be to share some of the burden, remember that he is only a child and needs you more than ever to be the strong adult in his life.

If you and your tactile child have a routine of playing catch in the backyard before dinner, make sure to get him outside with his glove and ball at your regular time. During times of sadness, routines can be saviors, as they help get everybody through the day. But don't make the child a prisoner in his home. Let him go to school, visit friends, go to the zoo with relatives, and so forth. This will be good for him and allow you to recharge, so when you do spend time with your child you will have the energy.

• As ever, the best way of communicating with an auditory child is through sound—words, music, tone of voice. If your auditory child is accustomed to singing songs in the morning with Mom and Dad as you all get ready for work and school, don't shush her. She shouldn't be expected to behave like a sober little adult, even in a house of mourning. If she wants to hear (and tell) funny family stories or listen to her favorite music, go for it, even if you're not in the mood. If you have a sick person living with you, use the radio and TV to mask any unpleasant sounds coming from the sickroom. If you feel the urge to have a good cry, try to do it when your child is out of the house or distracted by something in another room.

Auditory kids tend to need lots of explanations; if you don't think you are up to it, ask someone whom you trust to answer the difficult questions plainly and simply until you are more able. And remember, tone of voice is just as important as your words, if not more so.

• The visual child will pick up on the pain her parents are feeling through the look on their faces. Your efforts to comfort her and to get her to express what she is feeling should also relate to her visual sensitivity. Your visual child might open up while looking at family photographs or while you make a collage or drawing together. Maybe she has a stack of picture books she likes to look at at bedtime, with Mom or Dad sitting on the bed beside her. If so, she may reveal something of her feelings in what she says about the characters in the books.

Some people clean out their homes in the wake of a death or illness, but for a visual child, who looks to the environment around her for a sense of continuity, throwing away familiar items could be upsetting. Even the most seemingly irrational of responses should be accepted. One mother came to me very upset because her daughter insisted on putting her now-deceased dad's socks in the wash, sorting them into pairs afterward. The mother thought this was a sign of some deep psychological disorder. In fact, it was a very healthy response—the child's way of keeping her father with her. Sorting his socks had always been her job, and continuing to do it made her feel better.

- Your taste/smell child may have a series of nighttime rituals that comfort him: a glass of juice followed by a cuddle on the couch with Dad, who then tucks him in and tells him a made-up story as he falls asleep. It's important to continue these rituals, because taste/smell children are especially nightmare-prone when they are under stress. Don't be surprised if your child becomes more clingy at this time and doesn't want you to go anywhere without him. He may also be resistant to letting anyone besides family members in the house. He is grappling with fears that make him feel helpless and powerless, so try to give him as much reassurance as you can.

When someone he loves dies, the taste/smell child is mostly concerned about where the dead person has gone. Talk positively about how Granny is looking down from a happy place smiling; depending on your own beliefs, try to be as reassuring as possible about what has happened to Granny and why you are sure she is "okay."

Helping your young child learn to cope under stress is one of the most important gifts you can give him. By guiding him with kindness, attention, and reassurance through difficult events in his life, you teach him that grief and sadness can be dealt with and overcome, that even when life is full of change and uncertainty, he can rely on you for help, comfort, and support. Your child's dominant sense will provide you with meaningful ways to communicate these important messages—and lifelong lessons—in the moments when he needs them most.

A Final Note

Good communication between parent and child is both the cornerstone of a good relationship and the best way to create a foundation on which to build your child's life. When you as a parent understand your child, and your child in turn understands you, not only can you forge a strong, trusting bond, but you can help your child learn to trust himself and give him the self-confidence he needs to be happy and healthy throughout the rest of his life.

As you've seen in the pages of this book, identifying your child's dominant sense mode and using this awareness to respond more sensitively to her needs is a powerful tool for bridging any communication gap. Once you understand how your child views, interprets, and experiences the world, the choices you have to make every day about how to parent will become much clearer.

The information you get about your child by filling in the checklist in Chapter 2 will start you down the road to a more meaningful and mutually comprehensible dialogue. And the understanding between you will only grow deeper as your relationship evolves with every passing day. The result will be a parent-child relationship that allows what is unique and special about your child to blossom, because it will encourage the essence of your child's personality to shine.

Of course, you may encounter occasional misunderstandings and upsets along that road. But instead of falling into frustration, you will be able to rely on the insight you have gained into your child's dominant sense (as well as your own!) to navigate these conflicts. All that is required of you is a willingness to look at the world from your child's point of view. Once you do that, you'll see that any problem, from sleep and feeding issues to temper tantrums and toilet training, can be alleviated by using the sense-based techniques described in this book to customize your response to the unique needs of your child.

I know from my own parenting experience that putting these techniques into practice means you'll soon be on your way to win-win solutions that will make both you and your child happier. And when daily life flows more smoothly, it will be much easier for you and your child to see the beauty in each other. In the end, isn't that the aim of all parents?—to love our children for who they are, and to develop relationships with them that are warm, supportive, and mutually beneficial.

Acknowledgments

Thank you to Tom Dunstan for being so wonderful and inspiring!

I thank all of the families who have taken part in my research studies. Your dedication to your children is inspiring. Thank you for your honesty, your commitment, and your willingness to view the world in a new way. It is quite a leap to entrust your behavior and your children's behavior to another. I am humbled by your bravery at trying something new, and divulging the personal. Without you, this book would not have happened.

To Billie Fitzpatrick, my right-hand woman and writing partner, thank you not only for helping create this book but also for being my friend. Your patience, tolerance, and steadfastness were so very admirable, and your wit and charm through thick and thin were much appreciated.

Beth Rashbaum, thank you. Without your standards and your belief that they could be reached, this book would not be what it is today. Thank you for your patience, your vision, your unwavering belief, your hard work, and the sharing of your expertise. I am very fortunate to have you as my editor.

Irwyn Applebaum, thank you for believing in my potential and seeing what could be.

Nita Taublib—for your advice and expertise, and for giving me such warm advice on direction and career—thank you.

Judi Duran, thanks for always having "faith," remaining true to your convictions, and being a loyal friend.

I thank Max Dunstan, my father, for guiding me through the research process and encouraging me to proceed.

Thank you to my research team, especially Prue Ives, who was the most fantastic research assistant ever(!) and a trusted friend.

I also thank Carla and Peter Weir for helping me set up the research premises; Bob Stein, who helped seal the deal and offered great advice; and Linda La Gasse and Barry Lester for being the first people who believed in the potential of my research and my ability to pursue it.

To my LA team—here's to the start of many great things to come!

Thank you to Jessica Thomas, an able and loyal advocate.

To Ms. W—there are no words to express my gratitude for what you have done for Tom and me. Thank you.

Thanks to Philip Beazley (my rock) and Greg Johnston for being my voice, and to those who were able to see the truth. Tom and I are eternally grateful.

And lastly, to my friends and family who had many a dinner and get-together without me, thank you for your tolerance and patience.

Index

tactile preschooler, 101–2
tactile toddler, 57–58, 90–91
taste/smell child, 19, 43, 205–6, 266
taste/smell preschooler, 239–43
taste/smell toddler, 226–27
visual baby, 171–72
visual preschooler, 197–98, 202
visual toddler, 187

gender and sexual identity, 181–82, 191,
    199

hide-and-seek, 169
hypersensitivity to stimuli, ix, xix–xx,
    18–19, 153, 205, 206–9, 213,
    217–18, 223, 227, 245, 263. *See also*
    taste/smell sense mode

intuition
    parental, viii, xxiv, 55, 107
    taste/smell child, 18, 20, 43, 209, 222,
    229, 232, 234, 240, 248

Lamont, Alexandra, 111
language skills, xxv, 68, 69. *See also* baby
    language; communication
    auditory child, 68, 110, 113, 129–31,
    132, 133, 148, 269
    tactile child, 69, 77–81, 83, 85
    visual child, 68–69, 168, 177, 178–80,
    191
learning style
    auditory child, 145–49, 192
    tactile child, 96–99, 192

taste/smell child, 233–35
visual child, 162–63, 180, 192–93

mismatch between parent and child, xxvi,
    21, 25, 44, 47, 56–59
    auditory child with tactile parent, 58,
    127–28, 141–45, 154–55
    auditory child with taste/smell parent,
    157–58
    auditory child with visual parent,
    155–57
    tactile child with auditory parent,
    97–98, 105–6
    tactile child with taste/smell parent,
    107–8
    tactile child with visual parent, 57,
    77–78, 86–88, 106–7
    taste/smell child with auditory parent,
    246–47
    taste/smell child with tactile parent,
    244–46
    taste/smell child with visual parent,
    247–48
    visual child with auditory parent,
    194–96, 201–2
    visual child with tactile parent, 200–201
    visual child with taste/smell parent,
    202–3
Miss Spider's Tea Party, 174–75
Mr. Potato Head game, 220
music, ix, xxii
    auditory child, xxiii, 16, 38, 109–10,
    114, 115, 119, 121, 123–25, 126,
    131, 132, 133, 135, 136, 138, 140,
    144, 145, 146, 147, 149–50, 151,
    152, 153, 193, 194, 264, 271,
    283–84

stroller
    tactile baby and, 76
    visual baby and, 165–66
swaddling, 72

tactile sense mode, 63–108
    affection and, 9, 16, 77, 78, 94, 103,
        104, 142, 245–46, 257, 262, 278
    author's son as, 15, 20, 74–75
    baby, from birth to age one, 34,
        66–76
    basic facts, 36, 63–65
    checklist for identifying, 34–36
    cognitive skills, 83, 94
    communicating effectively with, xxiii,
        68–69, 77, 79–80, 82–83, 86, 91,
        105, 262
    dance and, 85–86
    death, illness, and other losses, 283
    difficulty self-calming and falling
        asleep, 16
    divorce, 275, 278
    dressing and diapering, 75–76, 91–92,
        102–3
    emotional needs and management,
        66–68, 78–79, 94–96
    food and feeding, 90–91, 101–2
    grabbing and touching, 68–69
    how the tactile baby discovers the
        world, 68–69
    how the tactile toddler explores the
        world, 81–84
    insensitivity and, 20–21
    learning style, 96–99
    mealtimes and, 57–58, 101–2
    music and, 85–86

    need for physical contact, 15, 66–68,
        70–71, 76, 77–78, 89
    outings, 76
    parental, 47, 53–54
    parent and tactile child, 103–5
    parent on telephone and, 128
    physical aggression and, 9–10, 15–16,
        36, 64, 86, 104, 105, 108, 257, 269
    physical mess, chaos, and, 35, 44, 57,
        106
    play and interaction, 70–71, 84–89
    preschooler, ages three to five, 35–36,
        94–103
    reading and books, 74, 85, 98
    relocation and, 261–64
    routine and, 283
    school, starting, 270–71
    self-esteem building, 64–65, 84
    separation anxiety, xvii–xviii, 76
    siblings and, 86–88, 254, 257
    sleep, 71–73, 89–90, 101
    social skills, 70–71, 84–89, 99–100
    swaddling for babies, 72
    tactile child with auditory parent,
        105–6
    tactile child with tactile parent, 103–5
    tactile child with taste/smell parent,
        107–8
    tactile child with visual parent, 57,
        77–78, 86–88, 106–7
    tactile parent with auditory child, 58,
        127–28, 141–45, 154–55
    tactile parent with taste/smell child,
        244–46
    tactile parent with visual child,
        200–201
    temper tantrum, 15, 79–81, 128

ABOUT THE AUTHOR

PRISCILLA J. DUNSTAN is an internationally recognized parenting expert who has traveled around the world observing parents and children for her research. As the creator of a revolutionary infant-cry classification system, part of which is featured in the *Dunstan Baby Language* DVDs, she appeared on *The Oprah Winfrey Show*, the *Today* show, and several other popular U.S. television programs. Her sound advice has also appeared in articles that have run in *Parenting, Baby Talk,* and *Women's World*. A native Australian, Dunstan established her renowned parenting and family clinic, the Priscilla Dunstan Research Center, in Sydney. She has since relocated and now lives in Los Angeles, where she educates parents, health professionals, and academics from her new counseling center. She is the mother of a ten-year-old son.

ABOUT THE TYPE

Johanna was designed by Eric Gill in 1930, based on type originally cut by Granjon, and released by the Monotype Corporation in 1937. He created the typeface for the printing firm of Hague & Gill, which he formed to give his idle son-in-law an occupation, and named the design for his daughter. Only the Caslon foundry cut it for hand composition. It is, as Gill himself described it, "a book face free from all fancy business," with small, straight serifs and a spare elegance that makes it notably attractive and distinguished.

Check Out Receipt

Farmington Library

Date: 4/4/2015 Time: 4:01:07 PM

Fines/Fees Owed: $0.00

Items checked out this session: 5

Barcode: 30036009866193
Title: Gandhi my father
Due Date: 04/11/2015 23:59:59

Barcode: 30036009325992
Title: Hey Ram
Due Date: 04/11/2015 23:59:59

Barcode: 30036009287564
Title: Terminator 3 rise of the machines
Due Date: 04/11/2015 23:59:59

Barcode: 30036010468039
Title: Star wars : trilogy bonus material
Due Date: 04/11/2015 23:59:59

Barcode: 30036010617478
Title: Child sense : from birth to age 5, how to u
the 5 senses to make sleeping, eating, dressing
and other everyday activities easier while
strengthening your bond with your child
Due Date: 04/25/2015 23:59:59

** Library Hours **

Monday-Thursday 9:00 - 9:00
Friday-Saturday 10:00 - 6:00
Sunday 1:00 - 5:00

** Renewals **

Online: http://www.farmlib.org/renew
Phone: 248-553-0300

The library is using a collection agency
to recovery lost materials.